Evangelicals and MAGA

The Politics of Grievance
A Half Century in the Making

Evangelicals and MAGA

The Politics of Grievance
A Half Century in the Making

Ron Duncan Hart

Cabbagetown

To protect their privacy
No one mentioned in this book is shown in these photographs,
except the author who is shown leaving a house in the photo
on the left column, bottom row.

Cover Design by
Gloria Abella Ballen

[Government rulings on civil rights] *Deplete the morale, tear down the morale completely. You are killing the backbone, the very livelihood of our society. Tearing down at the seams...The very thing that put this country together, that made it the greatest country on earth, and they are tearing it down at the very backbone. Like damn termites. It is going to go boom!*

Claude Workman, 1970
Cabbagetown

CONTENTS

Dedicated to the

Memory of David Bidney
Who Understood
the Intersectionality of Religion and Culture

Author's Note

WHEN I HEARD THE "UNITE THE RIGHT" MARCHERS in Charlottesville in 2017 shouting, "Jews will not replace us", I felt a haunting sense of *déja vu*; I had heard it before in Atlanta a half century earlier. After that 2017 rally I began to read about the growing influence of the political right in the United States, and I recognized much of the rhetoric that I had heard previously in Georgia. I found ample literature on the political right at the macro level, but I did not find ethnographic information on the motivations of the people who were moving American politics to the right.

In Atlanta I had made a study of a White, evangelical, working-class neighborhood where people thought America was falling apart morally and economically. They wanted to pressure the government toward what they believed were the Christian foundations of the country. At the time, I thought I was observing a local cultural phenomenon protesting civil rights and the end of the Jim Crow era, not anticipating how quickly globalism would push these people and their grievances to the forefront of national politics. Later, I would recognize that community was a matrix of the Christian nationalism movement, and I had documented their grievances.

After completing the study in Atlanta, I had moved on to do research in Latin America and direct projects with the Ford Foundation and UNICEF and then back in university life as department chair and dean of academic affairs at Inter-American University. Although I had kept research records from Cabbagetown hoping to return to them, I had not done so until the confinement of COVID.

As I perused my library in those months of isolation, I came across a manuscript that I had written about the Atlanta study. I took it out to read and re-discovered the sermons decrying the moral collapse of America, and I saw the calls to make America great again from people who were angry that the country was in decay because of racial integration, immigration, and women's rights among other issues. The material was rich in detail about the religious experiences and motivations of people who were calling for a Christian America, which I recognized as similar to what I was hearing from the contemporary religious right. Given its relevance, I began to analyze the material again which led to the writing of this book.

I came to Atlanta in 1967 as a faculty member at Georgia State University with a plan to conduct research on issues of poverty and religious life in a Black neighborhood.[1] After arriving, I volunteered at the Southern Christian Leadership Conference offices, met Dr. Martin Luther King, Jr., and attended services at the Ebenezer Baptist Church where he was pastor. When I had the opportunity to mention my idea for research to him, he challenged it, saying that it would be more valuable to study the roots of racism.

12

In the meantime at the University, I was approached by the small group of Black students on campus to serve as their faculty sponsor for a Black social club they wanted to establish. I spoke with Tim Singleton, the Dean of Men, about forming the group and their interests in greater visibility. He was supportive and through his office the University invited Dr. King to speak on campus for the first time. When Dr. King came to talk, the auditorium was packed with faculty and students. Little could I have imagined that within months he would be assassinated.

In those early months I had gotten to know people in Sweet Auburn, a Black neighborhood near the university. I could see the barriers between "White" and "Black" in Atlanta, both adjusting to the new world of civil rights and legal equality. Although segregation had been outlawed by the federal government, the mindsets of people were changing more slowly. As I understood the chasm between the White and Black communities, I came to comprehend Dr. King's qualms about the appropriateness of the research I had planned before arriving to the reality of Southern life.

On Thursday evening of April 4, 1968, I began to hear the sound of sirens, non-stop sirens penetrating the quiet of the night. Knowing that something must be wrong, I turned on the television to learn that Dr. King had just been assassinated in Memphis. I canceled my classes the next day at the University and watched in horror over the next few days as riots spread across the country in major cities. On Tuesday morning of April 9th I was at the Ebenezer Baptist Church for the funeral of Dr. King with thousands of others. After the ceremony I marched behind the simple mule-drawn funeral wagon with the throng of mourners across town to Morehouse College for the public service.

Dr. King's dream of White and Black people living together without regard for skin color seemed to fade after his assassination. Although he had encouraged the involvement of "White" allies in the civil rights movement from leaders like Rabbi Abraham Joshua Heschel to common volunteers like me, in the sadness and anger after his assassination I felt a retrenchment in that openness.

In addition to attending the Black Ebenezer Baptist Church, I also had attended the White Friendship Baptist Church in Cabbagetown located nearby only a few minutes walk across the railroad tracks. I quickly saw the racial divide. Although they were neighboring Baptist churches, they were polar opposites culturally and religiously, and they had no interaction with each other.

13

Whereas the Ebenezer Baptist Church identified with civil rights, progressive Baptist causes, and being Democrats, the Friendship Baptist Church belonged to the Southern Baptist Convention with its history of support for slavery, racism, and segregation. Friendship Baptist was part of the fundamentalist wing of the Southern Baptists that believed in the inerrancy of the Bible and absolute truths in Christianity. Members tended to be Republican.

Although the Black people of Sweet Auburn celebrated the Supreme Court ruling on school integration and successes of the civil rights movement, led by their hometown son, the White people of Cabbagetown were upset by civil rights and protested that their children were forced to go to school with Black children. When the Fair Housing Act of 1968 prohibited discrimination in housing, that brought the fear in Cabbagetown of having to live next door to Black people, who were alien and unknown, the Other. The two neighborhoods represented opposite faces of the American reality.

Both neighborhoods are historic districts, located next to each other, just east of downtown Atlanta. In 1976 Sweet Auburn was designated a National Historic Landmark and the same year Cabbagetown was named to the National Register of Historic Places. Dr. King had grown up in the Sweet Auburn neighborhood, and his father was the senior pastor of the Ebenezer Baptist Church, the most important church. The neighborhood was once known as one of the richest Black areas in America. In contrast, Cabbagetown was the old mill village associated with the Fulton Bag and Cotton Mill, a White working-class community. The most famous person from Cabbagetown in the twentieth century was probably Fiddlin' John Carson, a country music singer who wrote songs about antisemitism and the Ku Klux Klan among other themes.

In those months after Dr. King's assassination I re-evaluated my planned research and changed the focus from Sweet Auburn to Cabbagetown. I wanted to study a defined neighborhood with a familial and institutional infrastructure and cultural history in which I could observe the interconnectedness of values and behavioral practices in the interactions between its long time members. Cabbagetown was such a neighborhood.

In that process I met Naomi Jones[2], a VISTA volunteer in Cabbagetown, who offered to introduce me to people. On a cloudy afternoon in September 1968 I went with her to visit the Neighborhood House, a community center on Savannah Street where we met with the director, Leonor Williams. I offered to volunteer at the center, and she asked me to be a playground supervisor for boys after school hours. Naomi gave me a walking tour of the nearby streets, and we went by the Salvation Army and Little's grocery store among other stops.

The playground I began to supervise included basketball courts that were frequented by young White men from the community, ranging from high school boys to men in their thirties, and I began to make friends. I got to know adults who came to the center, and on the warm autumn afternoons I would walk along the street near the center and meet people sitting on the front porches of their houses where a simple hello could turn into a conversation.

I would go to Cabbagetown in the late afternoon after my classes at the University, and there would always be someone sitting on the front porch of their house, ready to talk. I soon learned the local talking points from mundane comments about the weather to questions about their family members, and that would soon lead to family stories. By the second or third time I stopped by to talk, I would begin to hear comments about politics, government, Black people, local gossip about conflicts, preachers, and neighbors. People wanted to tell their stories, and I wanted to listen.

In the 1950s, 60s, and 70s the men and women of Cabbagetown were living socially and legally transformative decades. From the banning of segregation in schools in 1954 to the approval of abortion in 1973 the federal government had changed the American legal landscape. Evangelical preachers in Cabbagetown were denouncing those legal decisions and arguing that the government itself had been taken over by unchristian forces. The older people of Cabbagetown, who had lived their entire lives with White privilege in the Jim Crow South, were protesting their lost of that status.

Cabbagetown in the 1970s was a White working-class neighborhood at the end of America's great period of growth as an industrial power. When the rise of globalism led to the stagnation and dismantling of broad sectors of the American industrial base, the Southern cotton mill industry became anachronistic, and the century of working-class growth imploded. The simultaneous loss of White legal privileges and job losses from globalism produced a double cultural and economic crisis. As people demanded redress, evangelical preachers became their spokesmen, arguing that the problem was religious, not economic. They argued that a return to the nation's supposed Christian roots was the path to revitalization for White America as they knew it.

I was getting to know the people of Cabbagetown as that double crisis was unfolding. As I visited families, I heard their grievances about how their lives were being affected by the political and cultural direction of the country. The combination of losing Bible reading and prayer in the schools, racial integration, and the closing of the manufacturing sector produced a vision of society in collapse. Some preachers were predicting an impending Apocalypse, arguing that Christians had to prepare to fight for their lives and their religion if the Jews and foreigners took over the country and outlawed Christianity itself.

I observed how a sense of disenfranchisement and Christian entitlement led to outrage, as White Evangelicals adopted the ideology of Christian nationalism in backlash to those changes. Although those evangelical preachers probably intended their denunciation of moral decline in family and government to improve society, the repercussions of their blaming Blacks, Jews, and foreigners for the ills they denounced could turn malevolent.

I heard White men talking of attacking their Black neighbors. In each case they stopped before crossing the line into violence or mayhem, but in recent decades I have been shocked as believers in this ideology have turned violent, as we have seen in the Charleston Church murders in 2015, the Unite the Right riots in Charlottesville in 2017, the Tree of Life terrorist attack in 2018, the anti-immigrant El Paso mass shooting in 2019, and the attack on the United Stated capitol on January 6, 2021. These events have

15

given evidence that the "Christian" messages of rejection of government and hatred of the foreign Other was not innocuous rhetoric but could fuel violent action.

When I mentioned to my faculty colleagues at Georgia State University that I was starting research in Cabbagetown, they warned me that it was unsafe, a slum, a place of crime, a dangerous place. Yes, there was crime, and there was the threat of violence, but I found a village of mill workers where religion was more important than violence and protesting about integration was more common than actual criminal action. They were mostly White, Protestant people with roots in the Appalachian Piedmont whose families had come to Atlanta seeking work. They found the Fulton Cotton Mill, which provided people with employment and housing for a century.[4]

What I saw on that first cloudy day in September 1968 was a quilt work of shotgun houses and cottages within walking distance of the mill. One house was often within reach of the next, and the front porch always had an easy view of the street where there might be people walking by, playing, or stopping to offer gossip. These houses tended to be small and dark, cluttered with people and the things of people. When someone was outside on the front porch, they could observe their neighbors with their conflicts and pleasures and maybe play a harmonica. Someone sitting on a front porch offered a possibility of stopping to talk.

I felt the sensory environment, the gravel under my feet, the screams of children, and sweating in the sultry heat. Then, as the evening encroached, I was cooled by the breeze. I heard the heat of young arguments, and the cries of defeat. I saw the fascination of porch sitters with a simple four-man softball game. I saw a life rich in texture, but that could be cruel in daily demands. No one was far from the open life of the street. Even the houses provided little privacy. The three-room shotgun house had a living room, bedroom, and kitchen one after the other. It was said that its name referred to the fact that you could shoot through the front door, and the bullet would go straight through the house and exit the back without hitting anything.

The old fireplaces located in the wall between the front room and the middle room had been blocked up and replaced by gas floor heaters. The two important rooms were the multi-purpose front room where people could watch television, receive visitors and use as a bedroom for children and other family members living there and the backroom kitchen which was also a social space. The middle room was the bedroom for the parents. The bathroom, which was a later addition just off the kitchen, was enclosed from what had been the back porch, and it was the only private space in the house. In these small spaces close personal contact was constant, both affective and abrasive. The interior doors were always open, and front and back doors were open in warm weather and rarely locked during the daytime. Family members could come and go freely from house to house without knocking before entering.

People talked to me only rarely about poverty. Women talked more about their religious lives while men talked about their work at the mill, their grievances toward the federal government, and their fear of Black people. Both women and men were concerned about the perceived threats to their Whiteness and their Christian way of life. They told me they could not understand why prayer and Bible reading had been outlawed in schools, and they thought they were targets of an anti-White, anti-Christian conspiracy.

Evangelicals and MAGA is an American story with the lives of four generations of people whose lives were intertwined around their marriages, education, work, religion, and attitudes, with the messiness of choices made and expectations broken - all with a Southern accent. When I came to Cabbagetown, the mill was still a constant presence from the non-ending thump of the looms to the clashing of steel upon steel of boxcars ready to load along the railway line. The towering twin smokestacks cast a shadow from the setting sun, as smoke drifted across the village. I saw cotton lint. I listened to the shuffling of work boots on sidewalks as men who had spent their day working in the mill came home in the afternoon to eat cornbread and beans, socialize, and maybe have a half pint of whiskey before falling into bed...only to start again the next morning when the whistle blew for their shift.

In the heat of a summer sundown mill workers sat in rocking chairs on their porches, and the neighborhood murmured with the heaviness and tiredness that saturated life itself, as the close of day enveloped houses and streets. The mill worker families who welcomed me into their homes and told me about their lives were mostly people working from paycheck to paycheck, concerned about the basic needs in life from paying rent to putting food on the table. I found hospitality sitting on the front porch or around white

17

enamel kitchen tables in the kitchen. People generously talked about their lives, their heritage, and their grievances.

One of the first people I met on the basketball courts of the Neighborhood House was Johnny Smith.[5] He was older, married, and more mature that most of the kids, and he loved to play basketball. I talked with him more than with the younger kids, and he was curious about who I was and what I did for a living. Knowing that I was interested in getting to know about Cabbagetown with its history and people, he invited me to walk with him to his parents' house. He said that I should get to know them. They were one of the oldest families in the neighborhood and had always worked at the Mill.

That is how I met Cecil and Effie Smith, who shared their life stories and knowledge of Cabbagetown with me, and through them I met their other children, relatives, and neighbors. They welcomed me into their home with the openness that I found to be common among Cabbagetown families. In succeeding weeks I would stop to talk when one of them was sitting outside on the front porch, and I got to know them well.

When Johnny mentioned to them that I was interested in knowing about the history of Cabbagetown, that opened the door to their story telling. They knew that I was at Georgia State University, and after some weeks I asked permission to bring a tape recorder, and I explained that this was part of my work to record their stories. I found the Smiths, like other people in Cabbagetown, ready to talk, and they were proud of their community. Talking about the neighborhood, Johnny Smith told me,

> So, they's some people that calls Cabbagetown a slum, nothing but heatherns and half-breeds, but it's not no bad place to live. And I don't regret growing up down here. And it's just as good as any place in Atlanta. I don't care what who says about it. The people that talk about Cabbagetown, they hadn't lived there, and they don't know. They don't make no better people. Now, you take out in Buckhead and East Point and places like that, they might have better places to live, and they might have better clothes, and their children might have a better education than some from Cabbagetown, but they're not a bit better.

Cabbagetown residents shared a belief that their neighborhood was a good place to live although outsiders disparaged it for its poverty. In their cultural push back, they turned poverty into superiority with the belief that the poor in this life would be rewarded over the rich in the after-life because the poor would be favored in heaven. Their shared Christian identity built group cohesion, but that sense of superiority led to preju-dice and intolerance against those not considered Christian.

I was in Cabbagetown regularly from late 1968 until early 1972. People got to know about my life, as I got to know about theirs. People in the community assumed that everyone was Christian, either religiously or culturally, because everyone they knew was. It did not occur to most people to question my religious background, although occasionally someone would ask which church I attended. I would answer truthfully that it was the Baptist church in Cabbagetown, which I did attend as a part of my research. I thought they would not understand why I also attended a synagogue on the north side of Atlanta or why I was doing intensive readings on Zen Buddhism.

Although my background was on the equality of peoples and respect for cultural differences, in Cabbagetown I entered a world of absolutes, right or wrong, Black or White, good or evil. You were one or the other - no nuances. As an anthropologist I wanted to respect the cultural values of others, but how was I to relate to a White racist carrying a gun prepared to shoot a Black man whom he thought looked threatening? I was surrounded by people who believed in an anthropomorphic God sitting on a throne in Heaven with streets paved with gold, and they thought they were doing the God's will to save America for Christianity.

The genuineness and sincerity of the people showed me how the cul-tural environment in which people live can bend their best intentions and their will toward the social and historical influences around them. I was a part participant in the world I write about, observing and documenting life events, conversations, and everyday life. That meant long afternoons listen-ing to a man talk about his work at the mill or play country music songs on the harmonica and later repeating the process with his wife as she talked about her religious beliefs and her church and told me stories about people in the neighborhood.

People spent much of their leisure time visiting with friends and family members. Sharing food was common. Music and singing were popular both in public and in family groups, and it was an important medium of enter-tainment and exploration of important themes in life. Leisure time was used differently by men and women. A valued way of passing leisure time for women was going to church services, as well as reading the Bible, prayer, or other acts of devotion. In contrast, men would sit on the front porch after work to socialize and drink if they had whiskey.

From experiencing family interactions, hearing and recording sermons, and conducting hours of interviews, I have distilled that information down to these thoughts and stories that people told me and these events that I observed. My guiding focus through thirty-two months of research was to accurately record my observations of people in Cabbagetown, combining my anthropological analysis with their understanding of the world. As I have come back to this material decades later, I have the background of years of studying and writing about religion and culture in different settings. I live in a time when the evangelical, fundamentalist, Christian nationalism that I observed in Cabbagetown is not a regional, Southern ideology, but a mainstream political phenomenon across social classes that can decide presidential elections.

During the research in Cabbagetown I questioned how empirical data could register the spiritual essence of a religious experience, a state of feeling, the understanding of God and the Devil, or the fear of a threatening government. Our capacity as humans to experience, imagine, and create the supra-natural architecture of spirituality and aesthetics goes beyond what we can directly record with social science methodology. At that point narrative becomes the primary link between a person's cognitive process and our knowledge of it. Knowing I could not empirically document the psychic content of spirit possession, I could observe it and record a person's description of the experience. I could not register the neurological process of a belief, but I could record a person's verbal expression of that belief.

I wanted to analyze the cultural constructs that formed the behavioral grammar of people in this context. Culture to me was not a fixed phenomenon but a flowing one. It was not a noun but a verb. As people acted out culture, they were culturing. What were the spoken representations of meaningful sets of experiences and of the metaphysics of those experiences? Culturing is like speaking. In the grammar of behavior, we generate meaningful behavioral units, and we have cultural rules for what we can do and cannot do.

The layers of a culturing system are the building blocks of behavior. We formulate actions with the existing forms of behavior that we know or with new ones that we create. In this study we will look at how the behavioral paradigms in Cabbagetown family and gender relationships, communal norms, and ideological constructs contributed to people's belief that Christianity was superior to all else. Since belief is based on assumed causal relationships, rather than empirically demonstrated causes, the assumption of Christian superiority among Cabbagetown people led them to the conclusion that Christianity and its values were the only possible political path forward for the country.

Cabbagetown is and was a tightly defined neighborhood, bound by railroad tracks on the north, a Confederate era cemetery on the west, Memorial Drive on the south, and a Black neighborhood of Reynoldstown to the east. In the graves of the Oakland cemetery along the west side of the mill village lay Atlanta's notables who had shaped the history of that city, a mélange of Confederate soldiers, industry pioneers, writers, and clergymen. I have walked through that cemetery many times, and it was a way to visit Atlanta's past. I have passed the graves of the known and the unknown from the golf hero Bobby Jones to author Margaret Mitchell with her *Gone with the Wind* legacy hovering around that place as a memory that would not fade away.

In the Jewish section of the cemetery, the most compelling mausoleum was the large granite resting place of Jacob Elsas, the Jewish founder of the Fulton Cotton Mill. As I have stood before it, I have contemplated the impact that this man had on the city of Atlanta and on the hundreds of thousands of workers who had passed through his factory over the century of its existence. Only a few steps away I could see the towering smokestacks and brick walls of the mill in the background. Even in death his creation had persevered long beyond what he might have originally imagined.

In Cabbagetown the jagged architecture of Atlanta's skyline, whose gold capitol dome gleams on sunny days, shapes the horizon to the west. When conquered by the dreariness of foggy days, the skyscrapers blur into toy blocks in a haze. The Peachtree Center and the Martin Luther King, Jr. National Historical Park, both national and international destinations, are only a short distance from this historic neighborhood.

In the shadow of the glass office towers and hotels of downtown Atlanta, 1970s Cabbagetown appeared anachronistic, a neighborhood more from the past century, than from its presence in that cosmopolitan urban center. In the pages to follow, we will see the lives of people who stood at the end of the world as they knew it, calling to Make America Great Again as a Christian nation. Their religious view of the future proved far more prescient than I imagined at the time.

PROLOGUE
CABBAGETOWN A MAGA MATRIX

RELIGION HAS LONG BEEN AN IMPORTANT FACTOR in American political life, and the most recent example is the politics of grievance and Christian nationalism in the MAGA movement. From the grievances and calls for a Christian government a half century ago in Cabbagetown to contemporary politics, the core principles have remained the same although the current rhetoric is more sophisticated and often buried in the opacity of euphemisms. Xenophobia becomes the immigration crisis, and Jews, LGBTQ people, and non-WASP groups are the "progressive left". In this book we will look at the social and religious matrix of these grievances before they were absorbed into the MAGA movement.

Some version of Make America Great Again has been a part of history in the South since the Civil War when the region had to rebuild. The Ku Klux Klan played a part in that re-building, enforcing "Christian" and racial principles to restore the greatness of Southern society. Then, in the early decades of the 1900s, the KKK was resurrected to control Blacks and oppose the immigration of Jews, Catholics, and Asians and preserve the White, Anglo-Saxon Protestant character of the country. In the 1930s and 40s people, such as Huey Long, emphasized the need to Make America Great by preserving the Christian character of the country. Gerald L.K. Smith had a major following with his "America First" and the "Christian National Crusade" movements. Supporters of the fascist governments of Germany and Italy, such as Father Coughlin, Charles Lindbergh, and Philip Johnson, used the concept of Christian nationalism to oppose the pluralism of democracy and the fear of communism.

The Christian nationalism that I observed among Evangelical people in Cabbagetown gives us an insight into how it was fused with the politics of grievance with its deep roots in the American South. When Margaret Mitchell wrote about the Old South of *Gone with the Wind*,[6] she described a society of White privilege and a glorified but tragically lost past. For White people the humiliating defeat of the Confederacy and the loss of Southern honor, combined with the bungled attempt at Reconstruction after the war, left a Southern heritage of victimhood and distrust of the federal government and Northerners associated with it. Making the South great again and restoring it to a place of social and economic respect in American life was a dream for many Southerners.

In Mitchell's writing about the post-war period of Reconstruction, her attitude toward "carpetbaggers" portrayed a distrust of non-Southerners, and many of those who came to invest and rebuild Atlanta were Jews and immigrants. Those carpetbaggers included Jews like Jacob Elsas and Isaac May, who founded the Fulton Cotton Mill and made a major contribution to building the industrial base of Atlanta. An undercurrent of xenophobia and antisemitism did develop in the South, and it was still a factor in the Cabbagetown I observed.

Not only can we see fear of foreigners in Mitchell's portrayals of Northern entrepreneurs, but racism also appears when she describes freed slaves as people of "small intelligence". She portrayed freed Black people as threatening and dangerous, living in shantytowns and incapable of building useful lives for themselves. She portrayed the Ku Klux Klan as necessary force re-establishing the power of White people and protecting White women from the freed Blacks. New South increasingly became a fusion of evangelicalism, Jim Crowism, and distrust of anything non-Southern.

Although White worker poverty existed,[7] in the late 1800s and early 1900s the situation of poor Whites was masked by slavery and Jim Crow laws, and they were privileged in comparison to Black people. White Southerners expected the legal system to keep Blacks in their place, and if not, vigilante rule could.[8] Since the start of the mill in 1880s, the United States has transformed itself from a predominately White, Protestant patriarchal society into one that is racially and religiously pluralistic with increased (although not yet equal) rights for women and ethnic minorities. The move toward pluralism was disturbing for many people in the Cabbagetown of the 1970s and the rise of Christian nationalism to oppose it was a nativistic call for a return to what they had known. Living in the Jim Crow world of White privilege with the promise of a golden life in Heaven was comfortable, even given the rigors of poverty, and for many the new world of racial equality and religious pluralism was out of their comfort zone and even frightening

Evangelical Hegemony

As early as 1831 Alexis de Tocqueville had come to America to study democracy, and he became a keen observer of America life, noting the importance of religion in shaping social life.

In the United States the sovereign authority is religious...there is no country in the whole world in which the Christian religion retains a greater influence over the souls of men than in America.[9]

He went on to say, "Christianity, therefore, reigns without any obstacle, by universal consent." He could have been writing about the Cabbagetown that I observed 140 years later. He also said that "The influence of slavery, united to the English character, explains the manners and the social condition of the Southern States."[10] De Tocqueville was observing a period of triumphant American Protestantism. The revivalist movement was sweeping America, and it had special impact in the South. Most people were Protestant, and they were in a position of superiority, defeating and displacing American Indian tribes and having complete control over enslaved Black people. As early as 1690 Christianity, racism, and nationalism had fused in this country into the belief that the United States was a White Protestant nation with a God-given birthright to create an all-Christian land.[11] There were very few Catholics or Jews to challenge that position in 1690 or even in the 1830s when de Tocqueville was writing.

By the 1840s evangelical denominations (Baptists and Methodists) dominated Southern life and culture, and by 1855 they were 70 percent of all Protestants in the region.[12] As the primary religious groups in the South, they controlled the debate over slavery, which they considered as a fact of life. In the 1840s both Baptists and Methodists broke with their northern counterparts over the issue of owning slaves, which was immoral to the Northern ministers but not so to the Southerners. Although the Southern Methodists would eventually re-unite with their Northern counterparts in 1968, Southern Baptists never have.

Jacob Elsas and the Mill

Jacob Elsas arrived in Atlanta in 1868, three years after the end of the Civil War, and began a dry goods business with a couple of partners. He soon saw the need for commercial bags for grains and other products and meeting Isaac May in 1872 they set up Elsas, May & Company to make those bags. A few years later in 1881, they built their own factory on the site where it still is located today.[13] Shortly afterwards May passed away, and Elsas became the sole owner of the Fulton Bag and Cotton Mill. Between 1881 and the 1920s, Elsas and his descendants built housing for workers next to the mill, and that was the origin of Cabbagetown.[14] An 1881 photograph shows the mill with a cluster of mill houses already next to it. The mill owned the houses and eventually provided neighborhood security, medical and dental services, a nursery, library, and electricity.[15]

By 1890 the mill employed 500 workers, but that number doubled to 1,000 by 1900 and more that 2,000 in World War I (1917-1918). This rapid expansion of the mill led to increasingly crowded and unsanitary conditions in the mill village, which still did not have indoor plumbing or sewage. As the population of Cabbagetown grew during the expansion of the mill, pellagra, tuberculosis, and infantile paralysis[16] were reported. It had become a ghetto, and the crowded living conditions in the village combined with inadequate disposal of garbage and sewage was causing health issues. The Atlanta Sanitary Department condemned the village as a major health hazard.

In writing about working in a Southern cotton mill, Gene-Gabriel Moore[17] described it as oppression of workers by mill owners, who used fear as a means of control. Although that might have occurred, I did not document expressions of fear among the mill workers I interviewed. Jacob Elsas was considered a benign patron and progressive employer in the context of the late 1800s and early 1900s. By today's standards the family had a mixed record. On the one hand, Jacob Elsas hired Black workers when other factory owners would not, but his descendants continued hiring child laborers even after the practice was being denounced. Even under the best circumstances, working in a cotton mill meant long hours in a hot and sometimes unhealthy environment with few amenities.

Antisemitism in Atlanta

In 1913 Rabbi David Marx of the large Jewish congregation, The Temple, expressed his fear of the increased antisemitism in Atlanta,[18] and it soon became public. The Jewish owners and managers of factories and businesses were the immediate target, and they were accused of harsh working conditions. Leo Frank and Oscar Elsas were young factory managers in Rabbi Marx' congregation who were introducing scientific management theory in the factories they administered. Both would face severe repercussions. Frank was charged in a fallacious murder accusation, and Elsas endured a year-long strike at the mill that would have destroyed most businesses.

Although both events were disastrous, the accusation against Frank would be most tragic. Mary Phagan, a thirteen-year-old worker in the pencil factory he managed, was raped and killed, and Frank and a Black janitor became suspects. The latter accused Frank, and he quickly became a scapegoat for the antisemitic sentiments against Jewish factory owners. Popular rhetoric accused him of being a Jewish pervert and galvanized local sentiment against him as a rich northern Jew.[19]

Cabbagetown was a center of anti-Frank sentiment perhaps because Mary Phagan was a young girl working in a factory run by Jews, much like they were. The country music fiddler and singer, John Carson, who worked at Fulton Mill and lived in Cabbagetown, wrote and sang the "Ballad of Little Mary Phagan" which accused Frank with antisemitic innuendos of cruelly murdering the girl.[20] His song became popular in Atlanta, and it incited the growing public anger against Frank and must have contributed to Frank's eventual conviction and lynching. Carson went on to be recorded by a New York record label, and he became a fixture in Georgia for decades. Because of the popularity of his recordings, he was sought after by important politicians for their campaign rallies.

After a month-long trial of protested legality, Frank was convicted of the murder in August 1913 and sentenced to death, only to be taken from the jail and lynched. Mary Phagan's minister was the person who best explained why the Jew was blamed. He said that at first he thought Frank was guilty but changed his mind after the trial because he realized that the death of a Yankee Jew was a more honorable atonement for the memory of Phagan than the death of the Black janitor would have been.[21]

Labor Unrest and the History of Protest in Cabbagetown

In October 1913, two months after the guilty verdict against Leo Frank, a group of workers went on strike against Fulton Mill and its Jewish owners. Over the next several months union employees of the mill began protesting company policies, denouncing unsafe working conditions and the use of child labor, which was still common in factories across the South. According to historian Robert McMath, the antisemitism unleashed by the accusations against Frank was transferred to the Elsas family contributing to the labor unrest at the mill. McMath says:[22]

...the strike coincided with an outbreak of mass hysteria in Georgia surrounding the trial, conviction and lynching of Leo Frank...Cabbagetown was a center of anti-Frank sentiment, and some of that animus was transferred to members of the Elsas family because they too were Jewish and perhaps, because workers connected the labor practices of [the mill] with the system of industrial efficiency which Frank had been installing at the pencil factory.

27

Labor unrest continued to grow, and in May 1914 Oscar Elsas, the president of the mill, fired 100 workers for their union activities. That in turn led to several hundred other workers going on strike.[23] In response Oscar evicted the families of striking workers from the company-owned houses in Cabbagetown. The Fulton County sheriff's office used Black day laborers to enforce the evictions, and photographs of white workers being evicted from their houses by Black men fueled the anger against the mill owners and built support for the strike.[24]

Race, antisemitism, scientific management theory, and labor/capital conflict had become a toxic brew. The remaining workers walked out on May 20, 1914, starting a general strike against the mill that lasted one year until May 15, 1915, attracting national attention.[25] The mill continued to function during the strike by hiring outside workers and would eventually break the strike. The labor strikes against the mill in 1897, 1913, and 1914 among others indicated a willingness of Cabbagetown residents to protest conditions that they found unacceptable.

In 1917, not long after the big strike, Corey White and her husband arrived to work at the mill and live in Cabbagetown. She is the mother, grandmother, or great-grandmother of the large White extended family, and many of the people we will be seeing in later chapters were either members of that family, close friends, or neighbors. They were the largest family network in Cabbagetown.

In 1956 the Elsas family sold part of its interest in the mill to outside investors and began selling the mill houses, terminating their direct involvement in the mill village. Many houses were purchased by the mill workers who lived in them, but some were bought by outside investors, who rented them to mill workers or others who wanted to move into the neighborhood. Based on the demographic survey I did, 75 percent of the residents were still mill worker families in 1970, but that would change in the coming decades. Those mill workers formed the large extended families that gave social structure to the community. Family identity and belonging to a church were key factors shaping people's lives. For almost a century from its inception in 1881 until it finally closed the last operations in 1981 the mill was an important economic presence and employer in Atlanta.

The historian Paul Harvey[26] describes the American South as being economically crippled by poverty, the rigidity of a biblical literalism, and suspicion of outside ideas. Those elements and the social disrespect shown to by other White Atlantans helped consolidate the identity of those who lived in this self-contained and somewhat isolated mini society. Although most said they wanted their children to have a better life, yet quietly, most of their children were tracked into the same lifestyle. Their mill town society was perpetuated by each new generation that dropped out of school and melded into the workforce of the mill.

The Decades That Transformed American Life

After World War II life in Cabbagetown began to change as the federal government initiated mandates on integration, civil rights, religious pluralism, and women's rights that shook the cultural foundations of this community and led to a White backlash fueled by Christian belief. It was White supremacy,[27] not the one of swastikas and neo-Nazis, but one of belief in Christian superiority and evangelical exceptionalism.

Although the first amendment to the U.S. Constitution[28] specifies that there will be no establishment of religion, historically Protestantism was the *de facto* religion of the American South. By the 1950s the segregationist Jim Crow era was ending, and the exclusive status of White Protestantism was being challenged. In Cabbagetown, preachers and ordinary church members told me that their religion and way of life was part of God's plan for America. I observed preachers as they sermonized on the superiority of Christianity, formulating positions that would become those of the religious right, Christian nationalism, and eventually the MAGA movement.

From its origins until the mid-twentieth century Atlanta had been a predominantly White city. In 1940 it was 65.4 percent White and 26.6 percent Black, but by the early 1970s Blacks were outnumbering Whites and beginning to assume power. So, this was a period of change as Atlanta was becoming a predominantly Black city while the legal reforms of the 1950s and 1960s were striking at the core of traditional White Southern life.

The mayor of Atlanta from 1962 to 1970 was Ivan Allen, Jr., and he was the last of the old guard White business political class that had held power in the city since its founding.[29] His predecessor, William Hartsfield, had said that Atlanta was "the city too busy to hate", and Allen adopted the phrase as a slogan for the city, which continues to be used today in some circles. The phrase is distasteful to many because it whitewashes the ongoing fact of racial tensions in Atlanta and more broadly across Georgia.

In 1970 Sam Massell ended the traditional governance of the city, when he became the first Jew to be elected mayor, breaking the line of 120 years of

White Protestant mayors. He was a transitional candidate, followed by the election of the first Black mayor, Maynard Jackson in 1974. Since then, the city has had Black mayors. The old White Atlanta that the people of Cabbagetown had known was becoming the new Black Atlanta, and in this fulcrum of change, defense of traditional Christian segregationist values ran strong in the mill village. As the power base in Atlanta shifted toward the large Black population, White people, who had the means, retreated behind suburban walls of segregation. Cabbagetown was left behind, as a White ghetto, with Black neighborhoods on two sides.

30   The transformative decades between Brown vs Board of Education (1954) and Roe vs Wade (1973) ended the era of segregation and the hegemony of Protestant Christianity while weakening White privilege.

Calendar of the Transformative Decades

1954 - Brown vs Board of Education ended racial segregation in public schools
1962 - Engel v. Vitale ruled that devotional prayer in schools was unconstitutional
1963 - Abington School District v. Schempp ended Bible reading in schools
1964 - Civil Rights Act giving increased rights to women and Black people
1965 - Voting Rights Act outlawed racial discrimination in voting procedures
1965 - Hart-Geller Act opened immigration to Jews, Asians, and others
1968 - Fair Housing Act outlawed racial discrimination in housing codes
1968 - Hays Code that set morality standards in movies was revoked
1972 - Equal Rights Amendment would have given guaranteed rights to women
1973 - Roe v. Wade legalized abortion

From the 1954 Supreme Court decision on segregation to the decision on devotional prayer in schools (Engel v. Vitale 1962) and the ruling on Bible reading in schools (Abington School District v. Schempp 1963) the people of Cabbagetown were angered as elements of their Christian lifestyle were ruled unconstitutional. In 1964 the landmark the Civil Rights Act was signed into law, giving Blacks and women extensive protections. The banning of segregation in public accommodations and employment discrimination based on an "individual's race, color, religion, sex, or national origin" gave a boost to Black people and the Women's Liberation Movement. Both were opposed in Cabbagetown.

The Voting Rights Act of 1965 prohibited racial discrimination in voting. In 1965 the Hart-Geller Immigration Act repealed the exclusionary quotas of the 1924 National Origins Act[30] increasing immigration for Jews and Catholics from Europe and people from Asia and the Southern hemisphere. The Civil Rights Act 1968, known as the Fair Housing Act, essentially ended the housing segregation that had kept Blacks and Whites in separate neighborhoods. In six years from 1962 to 1968 the underpinnings of White superiority in the American South had been outlawed by the federal government.[31]

In 1968 the Hays Code governing morality in Hollywood movies was revoked. It had prohibited even the suggestion of nudity or sexual content in movies, and kisses were limited to three seconds. Suggestive dancing, sexualized attire, or a mention of prostitution were forbidden. But movies had already begun to break traditional standards. The sexualized costumes of James Bond girls (Goldfinger in 1964) and Raquel Welch (One Million Years B.C. in 1966) were outside the moral code of conservative Christians. Rock and roll music was also an issue from the dancing of Little Richard to the pelvic moves of Elvis Presley and the sex and drug culture of the Rolling Stones.[32] Cabbagetown preachers argued that we should have a morality code, not only for movies but for life itself.

Religion, Culture and Politics

When I heard people in Cabbagetown calling for a White Christian America in the early 1970s, it was a harbinger of what was to come. They felt that the Supreme Court had destroyed their traditional way of life, ordering Blacks and Whites to attend school together, then outlawing prayer and Bible reading in public schools. All of which they took as an attack on their religion. Civil rights legislation was making Blacks legally equal to Whites. The final straw was the Equal Rights Amendment and the Roe vs Wade Supreme Court decision which people saw as direct attacks on their family values. Equal rights for women and the right to terminate pregnancies could propel more women into the workforce and minimize their roles as child-rearing mothers, both of which would impact the traditional family structure.

Georgia was even more evangelical in 1970 than it is now, and every community Black or White would have one or more Baptist and Pentecostal Holiness churches. The 1970s were a time of evangelical success in America, called the period of "Evangelical chic". The "born again" country music singer, Johnny Cash, had a program on national television that was highly popular in Cabbagetown and throughout the South. Southern Baptists registered the highest single year total of new members ever recorded, almost half a million in 1972.[3] The Southern Baptist evangelist Billy Graham held a six night crusade in Atlanta in 1973, at the large Fulton County Stadium, that over 200,000 people attended and thousands were "born-again". An Evangelical from Georgia, Jimmy Carter, was elected President in 1976.

In the evangelical heyday of that decade people were calling for Christian leadership in government and restoring White Christian America. To the evangelical people of Cabbagetown making America great was code referring to the following issues:

32

- **Christian Entitlement.** People saw Christianity as being superior to other religions, and the United States should be a Christian nation.
- **Racism.** White people were superior to Black people, and integration would destroy the integrity of America.
- **Anti-Feminism.** They feared that women's liberation would destroy the role of women as the moral center of the family, causing it to disintegrate.
- **Anti-Government.** The federal government was non-Christian and had negated their Christian values.
- **Disenfranchisement.** Government did not represent them, and they protested not having power to change it.
- **Conspiracy Replacement Theory.** Preachers spoke of a xenophobic conspiracy by Communists, Jews, and other non-Christian foreigners to replace them and outlaw the Bible and Christianity itself.

Just as Black preachers had been the primary leaders in the civil rights movement, White preachers were leaders in the opposition to reforms of the transformative decades. They denounced the federal government for the mandates they said were overturning their religious rights.

Preachers in Cabbagetown called the changes a conspiracy inspired by the Devil, Black people, and communists (a loose reference to liberals and foreign non-Christians like Jews).[33] The people who lived in the neighborhood had only experienced Protestant exclusivity and racial superiority until the changes of the transformative decades eroded their traditional lifestyle.

Political and religious leaders in Georgia had created a power base guaranteeing that governmental decisions were coordinated with local religious and racial values, but federal reforms during the transformative decades had eviscerated that White power base of the Old South. In the resulting vacuum, the religious right emerged to challenge federal control. Southerners had argued that the Civil War had been fought over states' rights, not slavery, and that argument was re-energized to combat the new round of federal interference in their lives. Preachers in Cabbagetown told the people that the governmental changes were a conspiracy against Christianity, and that they had to fight to take America back for God.

In my conversations with people, the subject of making America a Christian nation was a regular subject they mentioned, a strand of American thought traceable back to early colonial settlers. The arguments formulated by evangelical preachers about reconstructing America as a Christian nation were similar to the rhetoric of Christian nationalism and the make America great movements that I would see later.

The Evangelical Paradigm

Three religious paradigms were coming together in the belief systems that I observed in Cabbagetown. Almost all people were Evangelicals, meaning that they were proselytizers, spreading the "good word" to convert people to their version of Christianity. They believed that all people should be "born again" as Christians. They supported domestic and foreign missions to spread the gospel and save people's souls.

Most Evangelicals that I observed were also fundamentalists although not all Evangelicals were. Fundamentalists added an element of absolutism in their beliefs about religion, behavior, and politics. Absolute truths began with God versus the Devil, good versus evil. People were Black or White, Christians or sinners, no nuances. Fundamentalists believed in the absolute truth of biblical writings, which they argued should be the guideline for the legal structure of the country.

The third paradigm was the Pentecostal mystical tradition. Although all three groups believed in spiritual power, Pentecostals believed that spiritual power could supersede physical laws. People believed that prayer could remove metal embedded in a person's body from an industrial accident or heal diseases that Western medicine could not heal. They believed that God had all power and could heal anything or intervene directly in human affairs. The Devil also had power. That paradigm of believing in powers above and beyond nature could lead people to accept conspiracy theories beyond natural explanations. A leap of faith could take a person beyond physical reality.

The evangelical paradigm led to a sense of Christian rights and entitlement, a culturing system in which people share the premise that the American way of life and the Christianity associated with it are exceptional and should be given priority in national policy decisions. As we have seen already, key elements include a belief in Christian superiority, separation of the races, anti-feminism, anti-immigration, and conspiracy replacement theory. The people acting out this culturing system included both religiously active Evangelicals and their secular, even anti-clerical family members and neighbors. The anti-clerical, cultural Evangelicals believed in God and shared the same principles and beliefs in evangelical exceptionalism as did their religious counterparts, but with the difference that they did not accept the church system.

Preachers in Cabbagetown were saying that we had to fight to defend Christianity and reclaim it as the law of the land. They argued that the federal government was sabotaging the foundations of American life, and that it had to be replaced by a Christian government. I was observing the anger of White Evangelicals challenging the world of religious pluralism and minority and gender rights that was emerging in the larger society. In later decades, I would see those elements featured in the culture wars of the religious right.

When preachers advocated implementation of Christian principles in government to stop religious and racial pluralism, was this the same as the virtual fascism of the American South during the Jim Crow era? That was a time when law enforcement officers, preachers, and politicians would join together under the hoods of the Ku Klux Klan to enforce Christian values and racism, or was this something totally new? Journalist Jerry Mitchell[34] says that we need a clear memory of the past in Southern history to understand where we are today.

Preachers in Cabbagetown argued for the United States being ruled by Christian leaders according to evangelical values. Was that a call for theocracy? Their referencing Hitler and Stalin as leaders who had gotten things done sounded like a call for autocracy that could be menacing to non-Christians. Hidden in those messages was the call for a strong man who would eliminate existing church/state order to establish fundamentalist Christian values as the governing paradigm.

By 1968 the cycle of civil rights legislation had been completed.[35] Rev. Dr. Martin Luther King, Jr. and Bobby Kennedy were assassinated. Students on college campuses were demonstrating against the Vietnam war. In that turmoil, Richard Nixon was elected President of the country in a turn to the political right. The era of liberal reform was ending. The 1972 Equal Rights Amendment favoring women died of stagnation. The Roe vs Wade decision by the Supreme Court in 1973 marked an end to the transformative decades, but that decision would eventually reversed after a fifty year campaign.

The Origins of Make America Great Again   35

The people of Cabbagetown had experienced within one generation what they perceived as a perfect storm of attacks on their religious practices and status as White people and evangelical Christians. People saw this as an assault on their culture and traditions that fed into the century long memories of defeat in the Civil War. They saw their Southern White, evangelical religious system as God-given and the absolutely true path for humankind, which the legal changes during the transformative decades had not only ignored but destroyed. They were victims. God's plan for humanity was a victim, and their protests gave root to the politics of grievance that would come to re-shape American political life for decades. This early version of MAGA merged racism, religious rage, and the belief in Christian superiority to shape political opinion.

Evangelicals (the people) wanted to Make America Great (the movement) with Christian Nationalism (the ideology). The Southern Baptist Convention, the largest evangelical group in America, was a major advocate for Christian nationalism during that time, as it still is today. In the early 1970s there were 11,000,000 members of more than 30,000 Southern Baptist Churches. Over the next 50 years Southern Baptists added another 5,000,000 members and almost 15,000 churches. Although Southern Baptists are the largest evangelical group today, they are less than a quarter of the overall evangelical population.[36]

The Christian nationalism that I observed in the Baptist and Holiness churches in Cabbagetown was soon to coalesce with thousands of other evangelical churches into a movement across the United States. Rev. Jerry Falwell of the Moral Majority and televangelist Pat Robertson emerged as national spokesmen for this religious political movement with millions of followers.

At the Republican National Convention in 1980 Ronald Reagan said, "For those who've abandoned hope, we'll restore hope, and we'll welcome them into a great national crusade to make America great again."[37] He then made "Let's Make America Great Again" a key slogan in his 1980 campaign. Reagan's positive message of America as a light on the hill for democracy contrasts with Donald Trump's more negative MAGA message of grievance and victimhood. The hidden meaning for Evangelicals was the return to a White Christian America. Even though running against Jimmy Carter, a Baptist Sunday School teacher and incumbent President, Reagan won the religious messaging, forging a political alignment with Southern Evangelicals. He gave them recognition, and they in turn helped elect him President. Evangelical discontent was a political plum for Republicans in the 1970s, and the binding element in the resulting coalition between them was Christian nationalism.

How many of the estimated 100,000 evangelical preachers in America in the 1970s[38] were giving voice to the perceived victimhood of post-Jim Crow Christians and urging them to act against what they called the attack on religious and family values? In the crossroads of evangelical churches in different regions and social classes a religious base was being formed to defend a White Christian America. Cabbagetown was only one version of that much larger religious base.[39]

In this book you will hear preachers and people in Cabbagetown in their protests about the changing world they were experiencing. You will see how they embraced the vision of making America great and Christian again, restoring White people as the backbone of the nation. As the Christian nationalism has been gentrified and gone mainstream over the last half century, many of the goals have been achieved. ERA and abortion rights were stopped. The the Supreme Court decisions on segregation, Bible reading, and prayer in public schools were avoided by a dramatic expansion in the private school universe, which is largely White and Christian.[40]

From those early grievances and protests in the 1970s Evangelicals have become a driving force in national politics, providing an electoral edge for Republicans in the U.S. Congress, helping elect four of the six presidents of the country between 1980 and 2016, and influencing the shape of the Supreme Court of the early twenty-first century.

Endnotes

1   While doing graduate work at Indiana University I had studied the peoples of Africa and African history in the Americas and being in Atlanta seemed to be an opportunity to continue that interest. I was in contact with a graduate student friend, Ulf Hannerz, who was doing research on street corner life among Black men in Washington, D.C. His study was published in 1969 as *Soulside*. I envisioned doing a study in Atlanta that would focus on family life.

2   In keeping with the practice of preserving the identity of key informants in research, I have changed the names of Cabbagetown residents to protect their confidentiality and privacy. I have kept the real names of public personalities and individuals who are quoted publicly. No photographs are used with the purpose of preserving the anonymity of those who shared their lives with me. Founded in 1965, Volunteers in Service to America (VISTA) is an anti-poverty program designed to provide needed resources to nonprofit organizations and public agencies to increase their capacity to lift communities out of poverty.

My methodology was participant observation that included tapes of conversations and field notes of events that I observed and conversations that I heard. You will see long passages of quotations from recorded conversations with the families. Every evening after a visit to Cabbagetown, I went home and immediately typed detailed notes about what I had observed and any untaped comments. I also transcribed the tape recordings.

3   Miller 2014: 10-31. Fahmy 2019.

4   Butler and Porter 1976

5   This is a pseudonym in keeping with the privacy practice.

6   Mitchell 1996 (Reprint)

7   Israel 2017:174

8   Anderson 2016

9   Alexis de Tocqueville 2002:334 and 335

10   Ibid.:47

11   Gorski and Perry 2022:47

12   Carden 1986:16

13   In 2018 and 2019 the Breman Museum, which documents Jewish history in Atlanta, offered tours of Fulton Bag and Cotton Mill Lofts as a "Historic Jewish Atlanta Tour", recognizing the importance of Fulton Mill in the Jewish history of the city.

14   See William & Mary, Center for Archaeological Research. "The Southern Mill Industry."https://www.wm.edu/sites/wmcar/research/danvilledig/history/southern-mill-industry/index.php. Consulted January 25, 2023

15   Cors 2021

16   "Southern Labor Archives: Work n' Progress – Lessons and Stories: Part III: The Southern Textile Industry." In Research Guides. Georgia State University Library. Consulted January 25, 2023

17   Moore 1998

18   Dennison 1994: 181

19   Corrigan and Neal 2010:156 to 161. Frank was accused of being a pervert with bulging satyr eyes and fearfully sensual lips, who took advantage of Mary Phagan as a defenseless Irish poor girl.

20   Goodson, 2007:174

21   MacLean 1991:917

22   McMath 1989:9

23   The classic study of religion and a cotton mill strike was Liston Pope's study of the Loray strike in 1929. See Pope 1965:239-284.

24   Fink 1993:69

25   See Kuhn 2001:16-19ff and Fink, 1993:45ff

26   Harvey 2019:70f

27   The belief in supremacy is not unique to Christendom, because it can occur in a context of belief about any human system from religious to political, economic, and others.

28   "Congress shall make no law respecting an establishment of religion, or prohibiting the free exercise thereof; or abridging the freedom of speech, or of the press; or the right of the people peaceably to assemble, and to petition the Government for a redress of grievances."

29   See Gary Pomerantz 1996 for a comparison of the families of Ivan Allen and Maynard Jackson and how they reflect the changes in Atlanta.

30   This Act had blocked the immigration of Jews fleeing the Holocaust, as in the case of the 900 Jews on the ship M.S. St. Louis which was turned away.

31   Gutiérrez 2021:258. This was a remarkable series of legislative changes made during the presidency of Lyndon B. Johnson.

32   Sheff 1988.

33   The term communist was a trope referring to all that was foreign and was a common euphemism for Jews.

34   Mitchell 2020:385

35   Atlanta was becoming the economic hub of the New South, and capital and talent flowed into the city from other parts of the country. Fulton Cotton Mill was sold to an outside corporation, ending the role of the founding family in the mill after nine decades. The city conducted an active publicity campaign in national media, advertising in the *New Yorker*, the *Wall Street Journal,* and *Fortune* among others to highlight the city as a good place to live and do business. An expanded airport was designed to accommodate the anticipated growth of the city, and the first international flight left the newly named Hartsfield International Airport in July 1971. The Hyatt Regency, a world class hotel, opened at the same time.

36   Hall 2009. Fahmy 2019.
37   Reagan 2004: 22.
38   Randall 2017
39   I did extended research in Cabbagetown until 1979. I started with participant observation from 1968 to 1972 and short term follow up visits in 1977 and 1979. Alexander 2004:1-30. Stein 1989:249. Stein talks about the need for "thick description", detailed information about local and particular expressions of Southern Protestantism. My intention is to provide thick description of religion and society in Cabbagetown.
40   Southern Education Foundation 2024

Important People in this Study

Almost uniformly these Cabbagetown people argued for reclaiming segregation and prayer and Bible reading in the schools. They supported Christian nationalism to make America great.

Corey White. She was the mother and grandmother of the White family network. She told me about coming to Cabbagetown with her husband Charlie in 1917 to work in the mill, shortly after the big strike. She and Charlie had five children: three sons (Sonny, Howie, and Ross) and two daughters (Ruthie and Effie) and dozens of grandchildren. Ross was the only son to stay and live in Cabbagetown, but he had only occasional contact with his sisters, Ruthie and Effie who, along with their children and grandchildren, were the core of the White extended family. Charlie died when Corey was in her late 30s, but her family and her life were in Cabbagetown, and she never moved from there.

Ruthie White Elmore. Corey's older daughter Ruthie married Sam Elmore who worked in the mill, and they had twelve children before he died. Many of her children married and stayed in Cabbagetown and had some forty children of their own, making a large extended family. The sisters Ruthie and Effie lived near each other their entire lives, borrowing and re-borrowing food and life's necessities daily. They supervised each other's children and helped each other survive.

Effie White Smith. Corey's other daughter Effie was the mother of a daughter and two sons: Johnny, Esther, and Billy Joe. She was married with Cecil Smith, who was from Cabbagetown. Her three children and grandchildren formed the other extended family within the White family network.

Cecil Smith. Cecil was the husband of Effie and father of Johnny, Esther, and Billy Joe. His family was from the foothills of the Appalachian Mountains north of Atlanta, but they moved to Cabbagetown when he was young. He worked in the mill his entire life, and he was staunchly anti-clerical, not so much anti-religious as anti-preacher and anti-church.

Johnny Smith. Johnny was the oldest son of Effie and Cecil. As he grew out of childhood, his focus was on playing sports and memorizing sports memorabilia. He loved the neighborhood of Cabbagetown and life there.

Esther Smith Durham. Esther was the middle child of Effie and Cecil, and she followed in the religious footsteps of her mother, becoming a devotedly Christian person. She married Dewayne Durham when she was fourteen years old and dropped out of school, only to be divorced some fifteen years later after having four children. She continued to live in Milltown.

Billy Joe Smith. Billy Joe was the youngest child of Effie and Cecil, and the child who was most distant from the rest of the family. Although he dropped out of school like his brother and sister, he learned skills in the construction industry. He believed in self-reliance and was doubtful of formal education and church attendance. He married the granddaughter of the family that lived across the street from his parents. He became a successful craftsman, and moved out of Milltown, "making it good" in local terms.

Dewayne Durham. He was the divorced husband of Esther Smith, and he continued to be present visiting his children on occasion. He was a regular at Kwitcherbellyakin Bar.

Claude Workman. He worked at the mill and was a neighbor of the White family. At the time of these interviews, he was in his late 30s and a veteran of the Korean War.

Rev. Arthur Davis. Rev. Davis was a Baptist preacher, and he was the most socially active member of the clergy in Milltown. Like the other preachers listed here, he was from Cabbagetown and well-known in the community. He had worked at the mill earlier in his life.

Brother John Adcock. Brother Adcock was the preacher in the largest Holiness congregation, which averaged 75 attendees. He did not have a church building and was renting the gymnasium of Robinson School for Sunday services. He was especially known for faith healing

Brother Hoagy Jones. Brother Hoagy had married into the White extended family and was leading a small Holiness congregation that was basically composed of White family members. He was not a preacher, but he was the only male member of the White family in the congregation which made him the *de facto* leader, and he had a car to take people to services.

CHAPTER ONE
A FAMILY AFTERNOON[1]

ONE AFTERNOON I DROPPED BY TO VISIT the Smith family. The father Cecil was sitting on the porch after getting off work, which meant that he was ready for a visit and conversation. As I walked up to the house, he invited me to take a seat.

He was telling me, "I just don't like to work for nobody that is always watchin you. I don't like for people to tell me what to be doin all the time. I'll work as good or better than the next man, but don't be botherin me. No, siree."

He got up and went in the front door, and I could hear Effie telling him, "Why don't you put that bottle in there by your bed where it's easier to get. We all know you've got it anyway." Although everyone knew he was drinking whiskey, he did so in the bathroom, not allowing anyone to see him.

He came back out to the porch, and he continued, "You know, Ron, kids is really gettin bad about fightin down here. Use to, police wouldn't let things like this go on all the time, but it's different now."

Mary Ann walked up to the porch, said hello, and started in the front door. Little Mama was in the front room, and she said, "Hell, how are you today young lady?"

Mary Ann said, "Fine, Mama sent me over after some flour. She said to put it in this sack."

"I think we can take care of you."

It was near the end of the week, and Mary Ann's visit meant that Aunt Ruthie had run out of flour, so she had sent her granddaughter Mary Ann over to borrow the flour she would need to make biscuits. Effie owed her flour anyway. Mary Ann got the flour and left without saying a word to us.

Little Mama got her Bible and sat down to read it before anybody else came over to visit. She did that in the late afternoon before they ate supper and started watching television. Even though the weather outside was nice, Little Mama had her sweater on and stayed inside where it was warmer.

I said something about Billy Joe, the younger son, and Cecil said, "Good Lord, yeh. Billy Joe'd fight a circle saw, but Johnny, my oldest boy, he has always been kinda...well, didn't seem to have too much temper, but that Billy Joe has a temper, boy, oh boy."

He went on to say, "Oh, Ron, I'm a tellin you, the Lord has been good to us. Johnny got behind in his schoolin, three years behind, and he couldn't catch up. He could do all right, but he just got so far behind. Now, that Esther she is easy to learn in school. Ain't one of them like her.

"Course Billy Joe's easy to catch things. If he sees anybody do anything, he can go right and do it, just like them. He's always been kinda like me, Ron. I ain't braggin, but I could always do a little bit of anything that anybody else could do. I learned plumbin that way. When I started to work down there at the mill, I didn't know one pipe fittin from another, but I hadn't been there a month till I could get out there and run them pipes as good as anybody who'd been there five or six years. You got to take an interest in anything if you want to learn it. S'cuse me, Ron, I've got to get me a little drink."

In a few minutes, he was back and sitting on the porch, and he had his mouth harp now. The mournful sound of the old mouth harp warbled out the tune to "It's Supper time, It's Supper time." When he finished with that one, he blew "The Wreck of Ol' 97." He always liked the ones about trains. He sucked in on his breath and made the wailing sound of the freight train whistle. I sat there listening. Nobody was saying anything, just listening. Clickety-clack. That mournful wail again. Clickety-clack. Clickety-clack.

Cecil was happy now. He been drinking the half pint of whiskey he had, and he was blowing the harp.

"Now, I'm goin to blow you a love song. Tell me who sang it."

He started the tune for "Your cheatin heart will tell on you. You'll cry and cry..." He did not blow more because he never played all of a song.

I answered, "Hank Williams."

"Won't nobody ever be able to sing like him again."

Mama pushed open the screen and stuck her head out.

"Supper's ready.

She looked at Cecil, "I don't guess you want nothin since you've started drinkin, do you?"

"No, Mama, I think I'll come in a little later and eat me a tomater or something."

"Drinkin that stuff all the time and eatin out your insides and not eatin anything, I don't see how you live. I guess the Lord just ain't ready for you to die yet."

"No, I don't reckon He is. He takes care of me and gives me my little drink."

"You oughta be ashamed of yourself talkin like that. Ron, you come on in and eat with us."

I went back to the kitchen, and Effie, Little Mama, and I sat down around the white, enamel table, and Effie said the blessing over the meal. Supper was a pot of beans with pieces of meat and cornbread. Effie and Little Mama talked while I listened.

Cecil came through going to the bathroom where he had his whiskey bottle. On the way back he stopped in the doorway leading into the middle room, he was weaving a little.

"Ron, you aren't very careful about who you eat with."

Effie stood up noisily and said, "Ron, how about some more beans?"

"Oh, I'm a tellin you, Ron..."

"How about some more coffee, you haven't eaten hardly anythin."

"Don't you listen to her, Ron, she won't tell you nothin but lies." Effie caught my eye and shook her head. She sat back down.

"Lots of times, I've been in jail. I've paid enough money to pay for this house three times. Did I ever tell you about the time she had me locked up?" He pointed toward Effie. "That made me mad."

"Don't listen to him, Ron, he's not right when he's drinkin."

"I was under $350.00 bond. One time when she was goin to Brother John's church down on Gaskill. She's a liar and always tellin things on me but only tellin her side of it. She won't ever tell you about her and Brother John. She said I burned up all her clothes."

Effie said, "I didn't do no such thing. What really happened was that one day I was gettin ready to go to church. I dropped my house dress in the corner, and he come in and threw his jacket on top of it. He was drunk and was mad because I was goin to church. It's the truth. Ruthie can vouch that I had to borrow shoes from her until I could get some more."

Cecil retorted, "You're a liar. I come in here and there wa'n't no fire and no coal, and I threw that old dirty, greasy jacket in the stove for some heat. If you hadn't put your dress where I kept my jacket, I never would have gotten it. Then, she called the police out here, and they locked me up. She said that I burned up everything, but it wa'n't nothin but a dress. She's told things so bad on me that I wouldn't even repeat them."

"I called the police to protect him; he would have burned himself up."

"I had to spend so much money."

"You never had to spend over $25.00."

46

"I paid $75.00 that time. She's always callin herself a Christian and goin to church, but she ain't nothin but a hypocrite. I'm just Cecil 365 days a year. I don't go to church, but I'm always the same." He walked out.

Effie hollered at him, "Be a good boy."

"I'm always good. I might not look good, or I might not smell good, but I'm always good."

Effie looked at me and said, "I used to be embarrassed, but I got over that. People don't like to come around here on account of him. When he's drinkin, he just as soon cuss you as look at you. He'll cuss you one minute and outdo himself bein nice the next."

We finished eating and talking a bit, I went to the front porch where Cecil was while Effie and Little Mama did chores in the kitchen.

"Dog eat dog," Cecil said when I sat down on the porch, "Life's like that for shore." He had the silly smile on his face that said that he would not last much longer. He lighted a cigarette and stood there for a minute. The cigarette trembled a little as be pulled on it, and he turned and with shuffling, unsure steps, he made his way to the door.

"Ron, you make yourself at home now. I'm goin to take a little rest."

The sun was going down on Mr. Barnes' awning across the street, and everything below was in shadows. The air seemed to split for a second as two boxcars banged together up at the tracks and then another one. A couple of sparrows pecked around on the ground for any cornbread crumbs left from what Cecil had thrown out for them that afternoon.

From the neighbor's house I heard the radio,

"...nobody makes a truck like Ford makes. The exciting all new Ford F-100, See your Ford dealer today. It's 6:15. Hi there, it's the Sam Polk Show. We've got a WPLO Pick Album of the Week. It's Rod Stucky, 'Just sittin in Atlanta station.'"

Effie came out just as Sandy and Jake, the boy she ran away with, walked by going to her mother Yvonne's house next door. He was holding her by the arm in a protective way.

Effie started telling me about a fight in front of Yvonne's house last night. She said it had started in the apartment building down the street where the renters live. Sandy and Jake were staying there. One of the Cox boys had slapped Betty Manson around because of something she said to him, but her husband, Jack, did not want to start trouble, so he did not take it up.

47

Jake saw what was happening and jumped in and hit the Cox boy. There was a little scrap, but no one got hurt. After it was over Sandy and Jake came up to Yvonne's house, and the Woods and Cox boys came after them. They threw rocks against the house, and they were calling Jake to come out and face them. When he did not come out, they called him a son-of-a-bitch and a coward that did not have any balls. After a while they quit. Effie said that Yvonne had come over and asked her to call the police, and a little bit later a squad car arrived. The boy had been hit in the face with a rock, and Yvonne had almost been hit by a brick. The police said that they could not do anything until someone caught the boys, and they left.

Pretty soon the boys were back, throwing rocks and hollering that Sandy was nothing but a slut, and they had all had their way with her anyway. They threatened to break down the door and take her with them. After a bit they went away. Everyone was on edge that it might start again. Effie said that she had heard that the boy had gotten a gun in case there was any more trouble, but there had not been any sign of the Woods and Cox boys since then.

The radio tuned in "20 to 7. If you were a dropout, where would you go, except maybe to an employment office? Dropouts have a hard time finding jobs. Especially good jobs. So, be smart, school it.

"School it? Well, O.K, if you say so. WPLO Country's Voice. Here's Peggy Little and 'Mama, I Won't Be Wearing a Ring.'"

The sun had already set and the last shadows of the smokestacks from the mill bad been erased from the house by the greyness of the twilight and that in turn was being engulfed by the blackness of the night. It was getting cool outside, too cold to sit on the porch any longer. Effie called out to Cecil, "I put it in there by your bed."

Effie told me to come back to the kitchen where they were. Cecil still had his overalls on and was stretched out on the bed. He was singing some song about a little bird that he made up as he went along. He had his eyes closed, and it seemed like he was asleep, but he continued mumbling the song. Even when he seemed to be totally out, he still seemed to know what was going on, and he would call out if anything seemed to be amiss.

Effie and Little Mama were sitting around the table hulling beans and talking. In a little while someone came in the front door. It sounded like Aunt Lucy's voice, "Effie are you here?" Effie got up and went to see what it was.

Then we heard Effie's loud sing-song prayer voice coming from the front room. She got louder and louder, "Dear Lord, we are your humble servants, and we come to ask you to help us. Take this child..."

It was someone who was sick and had come to ask Effie to pray for them. Little Mama was curious to know who it was, and she got up to look. It was Kathy, and Aunt Lucy had brought her so that Effie would pray over her.

From the front room I heard, "This child is sick, Lord, and she needs to be well. Oooh, Lord, I don't know what is wrong with her, but you do. Oooh Lord, Oooh Lord, do for her what she needs to have done. Oooh Lord, you can, and we can't for we are as nothing in your sight. Oooh Lord, Lord, intervene now and heal this child..."

Little Mama was telling me the story about J.L., who was a cousin of Lucy. He had shot and killed his daddy one day when he was drunk. His daddy, Marvin, was a jackleg bootlegger down on Gideon Street. J.L. had been living over on Berean Street, and Marvin went over there to see him, and they got into an argument over something. Before it was all over, J.L. shot him three times. Marvin ran all the way down to Memorial and fell dead on the sidewalk there, right in front of Kwitcherbellyakin Tavern. The police went up to the house and got J.L. He was just waiting up there, drunk as he could be.

"Have you all finished shelling them beans in there?" Effie's voice startled me from the story about J.L. killing his father.

"Just about got them finished Effie. Why?" asked Little Mama.

"Put some of them in a sack for Lucy. Kathy's been sick, and she's been takin care of her. She'll need some to cook for tomorrow."

Little Mama got up, put the beans in a sack and took it to the front room. Pretty soon, she and Effie came back in. Aunt Lucy had left. Effie said, "You know that little Kathy is the cutest thing. She's been sick for the last couple of days. Today when her daddy came in from work, they started to take her up to the hospital to see what was wrong with her, but she said no that she wanted to come over and have her Aunt Effie to pray for her instead. So, they brought her over here. She didn't look none too good. She's all pale, and her little eyes were sunk way back in her head. I don't know what is wrong with her."

Effie said that she wanted to watch television, and we went to the front room. Little Mama had a pinch of snuff in her lower lip, and they sat down in the two rocking chairs with the spitting can between them. The telephone rang and Effie talked to Aunt Ruthie for a few minutes, then in a moment of silence we heard from the television,

"Hello, I'm Johnny Cash", and the Tennessee Three broke out playing their theme song. Then Cash was singing with his wife, June, and asking her if he were a carpenter and she were a lady would she marry him anyway and have his baby. They seemed like happy people, and they looked at each other as they sang. The telephone rang again. It was Eva, and she was telling Effie to turn on the television to see Johnny Cash and June singing together.

Little Mama leaned over, spit a brown stream into the spitting can and said to Effie, "Your daddy could really pick a guitar, but course you don't remember cause you was so little when he died," and Effie answered that she did not remember anything about that.

What I had intended to be a short visit with Cecil on the porch had become a meal that could not be refused and a longer visit than planned. I thanked Effie for the supper.

As I walked out the door, she said, "You're welcome. Come back when you can."

Endnotes

1   The narratives and quotations in this book are based on my field-notes and recordings. Quoted comments are from recordings or fieldnotes.

PART ONE
THE DISSENTING BASE:
THE PROTESTERS

Men were the most outspoken dissenters and protesters. Along with preachers, they defined the politics of grievance. Many of the men I interviewed had something negative to say about the government policies described earlier.

Those attitudes were regularly combined with the beliefs in evangelical exceptionalism and that America should be a Christian nation although their view of what that meant might not be the same as the church-going people. Although men were part of the evangelical society and accepted the basic principles of God and the Devil, Heaven and Hell, many did not find an acceptable place for themselves in organized churches. They would break down the barriers between Church and State. They would outlaw abortion. They would make America a great Christian nation but not go to church.

Chapter Two
They Don't Give a Damn about the White Man

In Cabbagetown the Make America Great Again ideology was rooted in a fusion of White nationalism and evangelical exceptionalism, resulting in a politics of grievance about racial integration, civil rights, and lack of Christian practice in the schools among others.

Racism was a major factor, and the Baptist preacher, the most important religious leader in Cabbagetown, denounced integration and the mixing of White and Black people in these terms:

> *The problem today is that we are losing the children to the Devil. Negroes[1] and Whites are together, and it ain't right. It's the communists who are behind it...*

In his book *White Too Long* Robert Jones[2] argues that Southern Evangelicals have received most of the attention as the religious right wing in our country, partly because of their history of support for the Jim Crow laws and segregation. White superiority has been linked historically to Christianity in the American South from preachers as Ku Klux Klan members to Christian legislators banning books as unchristian and passing laws to ensure White political control.

Whiteness and Blackness were about more than skin color. Being White included social and legal privileges and economic position. Being Black was the opposite, implying poverty and lack of legal or social rights within the community. Many of the middle-aged and older people of Cabbagetown perceived their Black neighbors through the lens of violence. Black families lived to the north of them across the railroad tracks and in Reynoldstown, the neighborhood on the east side of Cabbagetown. Both were places where White people would not go. Johnny Smith told me, "We used to go out to the Boy's Club on Joyce Street, in the Negro[3] section now, and we'd go down there." As Black families moved in, Johnny and the other boys stopped going.

However, Black people did enter Cabbagetown, and there was contact between the two groups. Older Black and White people were beginning to share the health clinic, and occasionally Black women attended the song fests held in Cabbagetown. Black youths walked through the village on their way to school or other destinations. Younger people had Black classmates, and White kids played basketball and other sports with Black kids. On occasion I saw White and Black 13 or 14-year-old boys hanging out together off the basketball court. Young girls did not have comparable public spaces for hanging out, and I had less opportunity to observe them.

54

One summer day I was in the Neighborhood House, and a woman came running in saying that Black kids were rioting over on Short Street. She said that they had taken over the school yard and would not let any White kids play. They had jumped one White boy and taken four dollars from him. She had instructed her boys to get out the "man eatin dog" (i.e., a German Shepard) and put him on the porch, and she had stayed in the house out of fear to protect her elderly mother. She said that if this kind of trouble were to continue, she would get out her gun, and she commented that her brother had already shot a young Black man who was running through his yard.

Although preachers were the leading spokesmen on race, Claude Workman was one of the articulate community members who could talk about it. He wanted to make America great again, and he argued that White people had made America great and that racial integration and civil rights were breaking it down. I had stopped by to talk with him on occasion when he would be sitting on the porch of his house during warm afternoons. In those conversations I came to know Claude as a man who spoke to me openly about his political opinions.

Claude and Claire Workman lived on Wylie Street, the northern edge of Cabbagetown. Claude was thirty-seven years old, and Claire was twenty-one, and they were living in her old family house. In fact, she had lived in the same house her entire life. They had been married seven years and had three children.

Claude Workman worked at the mill, and he said he believed in God although he was not a churchgoer. He stated that God had created Blacks inferior to Whites, and he saw Christianity as a White, European religion. An image of Jesus as a blue-eyed, light skinned young man regularly hung in Cabbagetown houses. Claude Workman's racism was reminiscent of historian Clifford Kuhn's reference to Protestant fundamentalism and "virulent white racism" as being common among the inhabitants of Cabbagetown in the early 1900s.[4] Claude's beliefs about integration and the moral decay of society aligned with those of the preachers in the neighborhood.

I arrived one Fall evening[5] when the weather was beginning to be cool, and everyone was inside the house. I was in time for the evening news, and Claude was sitting in a platform rocker in front of the television. I sat on the couch. Claire came in and sat in an easy chair next to Claude. He had just finished an eight-hour shift in the mill without a lunch break and had supper as soon as he came home. Some nights, he would have been drinking by this time, but this night we started talking about the news. I asked if I could record our conversation, and he nodded yes. He was a short man, proud of his strength before being "shot up in Korea". Now he was beginning to bald a bit. We talked about his experiences in the War, his work at the mill, his car, and about "Negroes". He was telling me,

55

They haven't ask the White man; they don't give a damn about the White man. It seems that way...They know just what the Negro tells them. They are looking at that. And they's been multitudes and more multitudes of things been done against the Negroes that shouldn't a been done. They have been stomped on, they have been strung to trees, but I'll tell you, just how many could you or I find right now that should be hung to trees? Actually it would be justice to the community to hang them to trees...No, I'm not goin to get out there and be a part of hangin nobody to a tree, but there is plenty of them that I do know should be, White and Black.

When we started talking, he was smoking a Camel, but he soon forgot it, and the cigarette lay neglected. I watched as it slowly burned itself into ash leaving only a black mark on the table where it had been. We sat looking at each other, but he did not rock. He would frequently lean forward to make a point or excitedly bash the arm of the chair. In the ceiling above him there was a black hole where he had shot one night with his 38 Special when he was "out of his head drunk". It was the same gun that he carried around for days and days when the police failed to turn up his wife's alleged rapist.

Claude quickly came to the heart of his own fears about sex and race, and he became flushed as he talked. There was a night, not long before Easter, when he had left for a few minutes to take their children to visit his wife's family. When he arrived back a short time later, he found his wife sitting on the floor in the living room near the telephone, crying and distraught. Her story tumbled out. Not long after he had left, a Black man had pushed his way through the front door and knocked her down and raped her, running away when a car stopped in front of the house. She called the police, but it was a long time before they came, and there was no trace of the suspect. As Workman leaned forward in his chair and looked at me, he was agitated. His wife was a victim. He was a victim.

His preoccupation was with sex and violence, rape, and particularly the threat to his wife and children. Although he was not afraid of fighting or physical pain himself, the idea of his wife being raped was unnerving to him, and he trembled as his control wavered.

But when I lay in there on that bed and turn over, and think that my young'un is not here, and he is five minutes late, and my wife goes to the drive-in, and I don't know whether I'm goin to find her bruised, beaten, raped body layin out yonder. That is too much.

Claire Workman's rape was suspect because there was no evidence of how the man had entered the house, and there was no medical confirmation of a rape. Claire's best friend and confidante told me that she doubted that it had occurred, suggesting instead that Claire was emotionally manipulating her husband to get more attention. Claude's voice trembled as he talked about his wife's reported rape, his perception of the vulnerability of his wife and children, and his fear that he could not protect them. Whatever was in his mind, it produced a dangerous emotional outpouring. White supremacy and male supremacy re-enforced each other, and Claude talked about his responsibility for protecting his wife from the dangers of Black men. It was part of his masculinity, as was the necessity of ensuring the purity of the race.[6]

I saw Claude several times over the next few weeks, and he continued to be emotionally distressed, even longer than Claire in my observation. For days he carried his gun everywhere. Although Claude and his buddies talked for days about "goin huntin for the Negro",[7] eventually nothing happened. I had heard similar talk about Black families that had moved into houses on the edge of Cabbagetown, and when men got drunk, they talked about attacking them and burning their houses. Although it turned out to be drunken brava-do, open threats of violence toward Blacks was common parlance.

Most people that I spoke with in Cabbagetown denied that their rejection of Black people was racist or discriminatory, on the contrary, it was God's will. Preachers and mill workers alike said that Black people were created separately from White people and that God did that with the purpose of keeping them apart. In a conversation with Cecil Smith, he told me,

The Lord isn't pleased with it. Now you take this little ol mixin this race of people. Christ created this world, even to the largest and smallest little insect. He made them exactly like He wanted them to stay, and today these ol people get out there and mix and mingle, and oh, it's awful, and I just believe He ain't goin to let it go on too much longer.

57

The Cabbagetown White people regularly expressed fear of Black people and saw Black men as dangerous. As Black people gained political rights, many in Cabbagetown saw their own way of life threatened. Workman admitted that discrimination existed, but to him it was justified. As we talked that night, he said,

This is just for instance. If a White lady goes over here and finds her a Colored boyfriend, and she takes a notion to marrying him and wants you to accept it, but you can't. No way I'll accept it. No way you will accept it, anyone ever will, never will accept it. No way. The very flower of wonderful womanhood, we can't accept it. Neither could a Colored boy or man accept it if you went over there and got the very flower of their womanhood. They can't accept it either.

Now, I will tell you, they've did a lot of wrong down here, but what can I do to show you I know I'm wrong? What can I do to help you?

The Negro says back, 'See, I don't want money, and I'm better than you anyway. Got any money in your pocket?' And pow! He knocks me down, takes my billfold and everything else.

All of a sudden I say, 'Wait a cotton-pickin minute. I been wrong all this time? Maybe, I was right in staying away from that man over there; maybe I was right by not associating with him. All of a sudden, their government up there says, 'Nah, got to go over there. You've got to associate with them. You've got a house, you got to rent it to him. You can't run your school without our money.'

I know that the Negro has been discriminated...but where does it come from? Does it come from the individual person? Where is the policy? I told you before that nobody, I mean nobody, has never taught me to discriminate against the Negro, except that a man is what he is. You respect a man for his ways. What he does, stands for him kinda like a tree.

As Claude was saying that he could not accept intermarriage between Blacks and Whites and that the discrimination against Black people was because they could not be trusted, I countered that White and Black people were going to have to live together. With a nod he started answering my comment.

Now they always goin to be a Black and White community. They ain't no way the Black man thinks the same way I do. The thing you got to try to iron out is discrimination. Tell you what. I've got a good a friend as I ever seen in my life, black as an ace of spades. I can take you out to my car and take you out to his house right now. What do you feel? Will you feel the same way sitting at his house as sitting at mine? Bring him over here and sit him down right there, and he won't feel the same. I think I ought to have my home to do what I want to. I can accept anything I want to, that is my business. If I don't want to accept him, I don't have to, and he should have the same privilege.

To Workman the problem was not one of racism and discrimination, rather it was that Black people were different, not like Whites. Federal government intervention enforcing integration was an unjustified interference in local culture and values, not unlike the Revenuers in the past intervening in the heritage of making moonshine liquor. The Smith family, the Whites, the Workmans, and others said that they had done favors for Black people, and each one denied being personally prejudiced.

Another afternoon I stopped by Claude and Claire's house to continue the conversation, and Claude assured me that he did not have prejudice toward Black people. He told me,

I can be classified as one of the prejudiced, one of the bigots, which I'm really not. I'll give you one hundred dollars if ever at any time I've done or said

anything to discriminate against anybody because of his color. I've never took anything away from a man because of his color, race, or religion. I'm a liberal kind of guy. I don't intimidate anybody. I got three inner tubes in back of my car, and I've got four tires standing out there in the hall, and I'd just as soon give them to a Black man as give them to anybody. I don't think Black and White. I think human to human.

So, I asked him to tell me what he thought about Black people, and his answer was:

You know as well as I know that the Negro mentally and socially is absolutely nowhere close to the White...Now are you going to reach down and get somebody by the arm and bring them up with you, and he is going to kick your teeth in in the meantime? Physically, they are stronger, some of them. Socially and mentally, they are a thousand years behind...Only thing they can do is pull us back down, and it would be wrong, discriminating against us all. Discrimination is wrong.

Claude did admit that part of the problem for Black people might come from discrimination by White people, but he insisted that it was a minor problem and that the real one was with their own society and culture. He said that Black people should assume responsibility for their own problems and make a concerted effort at self-improvement because he, and White people in general, could not help enough to improve the circumstances for Black people. As he looked at me, he said,

I'll say twenty-five percent of the Colored people's problems is the White people. Seventy-five percent of the Negroes' problems is home life. Now, what is expected of me to remedy this? I could do away with my twenty-five percent of it. I ain't never had it to start with, but...I'm pretty sure I did...I can do away with my twenty-five percent. Who is going to take care of the other seventy-five percent? Me? Am I supposed to get rid of his? What is expected? I'm only so big.

I asked him how he thought the civil rights legislation would affect White people, more specifically how it personally affected him.

I already told you that. Deplete the morale, tear down the morale completely. You are killing the backbone, the very livelihood of our society. Tearing down at the seams, and they said they were going to. The very thing that put this country together, that made it the greatest country on earth, and they are tearing it down at the very backbone. Like damn termites. It is going to go boom!

Workman talked about the victimhood of White people, which he called the "backbone" of America. He thought that American was being destroyed by the government decisions on civil rights and only a strong leader could re-impose White superiority rule. I mentioned that no White leader had emerged for people to rally around like Martin Luther King in the Black community, and he answered,

You know why? They are in the penitentiary. Yes, I'll give you an example. What happened in Tennessee. What is his name? ...Casper? Casper was his name, wasn't it? In a school here in Tennessee it first started before Little Rock. He was makin speeches like. He is over in the Federal Pen. Every White leader that comes up like that, causin any kind of trouble, they got them for inciting riot...The F.B.I. and the federal government stopped him, cut him right there because they knew it was going to be a blood bath. Let the Negro leader go on and do what they please...Tell me mister, can I get up there and say what Stokley Carmichael says without going to the penitentiary?

I pointed out that the F.B.I. and the government were made up of White people mostly, and I asked him, "Why then are the White people arrested, and Negroes allowed to go free?"

There just ain't no way in the Hell you can take discrimination in reverse and come out with a right. In other words, discrimination one way and then they turned in the other. Just plain footed, straight-out discrimination in reverse. That is all there are to it. Discriminating against you. Where there was any discrimination, it was done against the Colored man. Now, they've turned it back on you.

I was trying to sort out what he was saying about the differences between Black and White people, so I asked if it was a difference in kinds of behavior. He answered,

Right. That is your problem right there. That is what I have been trying to say all the time...the pattern of behavior entirely...

Cause they are Black, and they despise you and me. Despise! That is a word that everybody can understand, in a word, they hate. I'll tell you what I'll do, I'll prove to you without a shadow of a doubt that there is more racist prejudice in the Colored man, than there are in the White man. I'll take you where there ain't nothing but White people, and I'll let you walk down that street. And then, I'll take you to where there ain't nothin but Colored people and let, you walk down that street, but I'm taking my 38 Special with me when I go. The last place we go, I know, we are going to have to shoot our way out of it, and they look down on me! Why? I don't hate them, I don't love them either, I just don't trust them because I can't. They give me no reason why I should. Up Alabama Avenue I come walking up there last Spring, and they kick my teeth out of my face, I've got a tooth right there that turns sideways in my gum right now. I can take a pretty good one, but I can't take that many, and there was five. I had just about sixty cents in my pocket. A human being is a human being, if he is a human being, and if he is a human being with common sense, he doesn't have to do that. Man, can you accept something like that as a community? Can you accept it and understand it? Can you think of anything that you have done to them people in order for them to do that way? They do it to each other! That is why I said I would prove to you that there is as much prejudice in Colored people. 61

Like in Workman's story above, the fear of violence was repeated by other people in Cabbagetown in story after story about Black people, who were assumed to be dangerous. As evidence of the danger, people told me stories of Black people being cruel to animals and mugging innocent victims on city streets. These stories were punctuated with the comment that such things never happened when White people lived there.

As we talked, Claude said that the difference between White and Black people was that Black people were genetically inferior and dangerous. He went on to say that he would not interfere in the daily lives of Black people if they would not interfere in his daily life. For him the ideal state would be living separately and equal. He said that he did not wish Black people harm, he did wish them to be segregated. He insisted that racial interaction was not a matter of concern to the entire society, rather it was a strictly personal matter. Claude went on to say,

And if I am capable of getting a job, no matter what area I live in, I think they ought be able to [get a job]. I don't think the fact that I fail a job, I don't think I should be able to say you done it because I'm Black. I didn't get the job because I'm Black...I don't know what the Colored man's views are. I don't know what he is thinking about, but I have a good idea he is thinking like I do. Leave me the hell alone, let me raise my family, let me live where I am able to live, let me be able to buy groceries where I want to. If I want to go to a store to buy me a drink or a steak, I want to be able to do it. If I am capable of a job, I'd like to feel I could get it.

62   Continuing this line of thought, Claude said that education should be maintained separately and equally like every other area of life, and everyone should have the right to high quality education. He thought integration caused the quality of education to decline. He said,

I do say this: because the young'un is Colored, do not deprive him of a decent education. That is wrong. Now, let's say that you've got three schools, a Black one, a Black and White one and a White one. Now you say, 'O.K. you over on the White side you are all White over here. Now some of these people got to go over here, and some over there, and we've got to run some buses in here, otherwise you ain't going to get no money.' That is downright stupid. Let us go at the quality of the teachers and the methods of teaching to make sure that this solid Black school over here got just as good of teacher, and just as good of recognition from the State Board of Education and National whatever it is. That is what I call rights. Make sure when a teacher goes in, he knows what he is doing. Black or White. No difference.

But this one in the middle we have already forgotten about. First thing you know says you got sixty White people there and only forty Colored. 'You are going to have to have ten more Colored attend, or we are going to cut off your funds.' Ol Workman working up here and paying them funds part of them. The thing is their interest is on mixing, not on quality but on mixing...Now, I don't care if you get over there and there is a Black school over yonder, and when you get out of high school, and you have the equivalent of a college education. 'Naw, we ain't gonna have that you are going to have to put some White kids over there. You are going to have to mix them up.' Now, that is downright ridiculous. Now tell me what is the motive? Is it education or mixing of the races?

I asked him why he thought that Black people had been making this push for their rights now when they had not done so for so long.

The reason is they didn't have any leaders. Nobody had motives enough to get out there and try to disrupt the whole community. And, when they did get them, like Martin Luther King, Mr. Wilkins, and a few of the more honest ones, they didn't get no response. The NAACP, I say, really, the only tool that the Negro should authorize. It might take three, four, five, ten years longer, but it would of passed and been a whole lot easier...At times they go a little overboard...But all of a sudden the dam runneth over. People die, towns are destroyed. People are disorganized. And the first thing you know you have bayonets sticking in your bellies...

63

Assuming that the real problem between Black and White people was one of personal adjustment and understanding, Workman went on to say that the way of dealing with the problem would be through organized sessions of personal interaction between Blacks and Whites. He felt that the federal Government effort to force change through legislation would destroy the very fiber of American society. He said these were human problems to be dealt with on the individual level and not on the governmental level.

I asked him, "Well, what do you think the government ought to be doing if it is not deciding things like that?" He answered,

I think they should do anything within human possibles, without shoving something right down somebody's throat. I think that they should do any kind of little programs, any kind of little get-togethers. You know, like preachers and church people and things like that, I think they ought to get together, that's good. Get together, maybe that way you get to know what each other's thinking...Get the White people that live here, the mothers and the daughters, get in there and talk these things over, learn each other, give and also forgive. Suppose I'm mad at somebody across the street. There ain't no way the government's going to settle that. We've got to settle this...If they could promote more understanding between people, between Colored and White. Just a normal discussion, you know what I mean? They've tried it up in the police department in New York; they've got them in there. That is the way to do it, I've seen it on television. In Texas they tried it. That is smart. Somebody is smart.

While the White mill workers were rejecting Black people as inferior and dangerous, White middle-class professionals in Atlanta seemed to think the same about the White mill workers, as expressed by my own colleagues at the university that I mentioned earlier. Kenneth Morland documented a similar attitude toward mill workers among middle class people in Kent.[8] Mill people had traditionally been rejected by middle-class people, and they themselves had rejected Blacks as beneath them, leaving them isolated in their own communities.

Claude Workman said that he is not completely against Whites associating with Blacks, but he was opposed to being forced to associate them without a right of choice. Ambivalence was salient in Workman's view of Black people. They should have rights but not at his expense. The fear of this breakdown of the separation of the races was a key theme in his thinking, his Othering. He was afraid of his own powerlessness and of having to interact with Black people in situations that would be anathema to him. Behind it all lurked the fear of his own displacement within a society that he no longer saw as belonging to him.

To me the racial attitudes of the men from Cabbagetown were a combination of sex, religion, and politics. Although Workman insisted that he accepted some Black people as equal social companions, he talked about them to me using racist terminology. His was most emotional about his sexual concerns in racial interaction, and it unnerved him to think about any White woman being married to a Black man. That thought shaded his concern about school integration since marriages often result from school acquaintanceships.

Claude pointedly said that Black people from the neighborhood next door could walk through Cabbagetown, but he believed that he would not be safe to walk down a street in their neighborhood. He was sure that he would be physically attacked, but he said that he would respond with even greater violence with his 38 Special.

"We live in a ghetto. A White ghetto!"

To Claude Workman, civil rights legislation had pushed him and his neighbors into a ghetto. They were trapped and without power. He said White people had not been allowed a voice on this issue, and he saw the decisions by the federal government guaranteeing Black rights as an injustice to him, his family and other White people. His voice was one of powerlessness compounded by a fear of Black people. In his hostility toward the federal government, race was the primary point of conflict.

He said there was a conspiracy among political leaders that led to integration, and he suggested that the Black working poor were pawns just as much as the White working poor. At times his hostility came out strongly toward the powerful politicians, who had created this situation. "They" lived in a different world surrounded by the accouterments of power and privilege and did not understand the problems their decisions caused for working people.

He said there was discrimination against White people in Cabbagetown because employers, other than the mill, would not hire them, and the middle-class teachers in the school discriminated against students from Cabbagetown. They could not challenge the discrimination because they were White, and no one would believe them. He felt that the Whites of Cabbagetown were disenfranchised and powerless.

Claude Workman was bitter. He hated to lose, but he saw himself as having lost. Power was his only recourse, and he saw himself as having none. He valued his way of life, and he felt that it was being destroyed. Workman's view of the world was that the United States was coming apart at the seams. He said the government should stay out of the lives of people. From the Revenuers in years past to the contemporary interventions favoring Black rights, the "they", the "deep state", was an undecipherable power that interfered with his rights to live as he wanted to live.

Workman's attitudes about the unjustified government intervention in his life made him aggrieved, a victim. Black people had been the winners in this zero-sum game of life determined by the government. Like many others in this White working-class community Workman talked of the government as "they", the "Other", the conspiracy that controlled political decisions. It was a government that did not represent him, and he was calling for a government of White nationalism that would preserve the rights of White people, which he saw as the backbone of the country.

Claude Workman was aggrieved and was reclaiming his White status. He was a part of the protesting evangelical world and ready to fight against the perceived wrongs done to him and his people.

Endnotes

1   A slur term for a Black person was being used.
2   Jones 2020:61
3   A slur term for a Black person was used.
4   Kuhn 1993:45
5   This interview took place in the Fall, 1968.
6   Buck 2001:100
7   A slur term for a Black person was being used.
8   Morland 1958: 178

CHAPTER THREE
BORN TO LOSE:
BEYOND THE CHRISTIAN PALE

"BORN TO LOSE" WAS AN EXPRESSION used by some Men, and the starkness of the phrase was masculinity with a hard edge, the masculinity of disenfranchisement. They had lost on the issues of segregation, Bible reading and prayer in schools, and they feared losing to the women's liberation movement. The sense of disenfranchisement inherent in the "born to lose" attitude was one of the building blocks for White nationalism, or its cousin Christian nationalism, which re-enforced belief in the need to restore America to the greatness that had been, Make America Great Again. This was the same dream that went back to Margaret Mitchell and *Gone with the Wind* of restoring the old glorious America that had been destroyed by the northerners, the Yankees. Now, the northerners of the federal government had done it again in the cultural assault on their way of life.

These men understood strength and a leader who projected strength. I regularly heard that it would take a strongman ruler to re-establish the old order for them. They wanted a man who had the strength they did not have and who could exercise it for them. The born to lose mantra provided the basis for rebellion against governing authority, which they felt no longer represented them. Distrust of the federal government was built into the local heritage, and those born to lose had nothing to lose in opposing its unacceptable governance. Since they were born to lose, they did not have a commitment to the existing order.

Born to Lose and Born Evil

Christian theology says that all people were born evil, based on the first story in Genesis when Adam and Eve disobeyed God by eating of the prohibited fruit. The inherent misogyny in the messages of some preachers was that the original sin was the fault of the woman. It was Eve, who tempted by the Devil, convinced Adam to eat the fruit. This premise

67

spoken by male preachers was that Eve was weak and succumbed first to the enticements of the Devil, putting her at fault for the sinful nature of humanity.

Talking with me about the sinful nature of people, Rev. Arthur Davis, the Baptist preacher, referred me to the book of Genesis, and said that the lost souls today were like those of ancient times. The verses he was mentioning are:

There were giants in the earth in those days; and also after that, when the sons of God came in unto the daughters of men, and they bore children to them, the same became mighty men which were of old, men of renown.

And GOD saw that the wickedness of man was great in the earth, and that every imagination of the thoughts of his heart was only evil continually.

And it repented the LORD that he had made man on the earth, and it grieved him at his heart. Genesis 6:4-6

Humans were "evil continually, and it repented the Lord that he had made man..." Since everyone was born evil, those who did not correct their innate human condition and follow the Christian path would go to Hell after death. The Bible says that it "grieved him at his heart" that God had created humans. They were the "born to lose" people. Some men embraced this belief of being in the Devil's camp and outside of God's chosen circle. They felt that they had nothing to lose, and they were challenging Hell as their destiny, suggesting that they were bad enough to withstand the worst. This was male bravado in defiance of the "hellfire" threats of the preachers.

It was a direct confrontation of the Christian view of a perfect world to come in Heaven. The born to lose expression suggested that hell was already here. It was on earth. The world was broken, and God could not fix it. In a broken world the only relief sometimes was to sit in a bar with a beer to soothe the anger and listen to songs such as Elvis Presley's "Trouble"[1] that could reflect men challenging the system.

The lyrics of that song from 1958 suggest the trouble a person portrays with a "Born to Lose" tattoo, saying,

If you are lookin' for trouble, You came to the right place. Just look right in my face. I was born standing up and talking back...

68

Then, to reconfirm the message later lines said,

I'm evil, evil, evil as can be...
I don't take no orders from no kind of man.

It was an anthem to tough masculinity.

It had been featured in Presley's film "King Creole," and when he re-launched his career in 1968 with a television special, he led off with "Trouble". People in Cabbagetown saw that program and heard this song on the radio. I heard it at Kwitcherbellyakin Tavern on Memorial Drive, the neighborhood tavern. The "born to lose" guys found fellow travelers there. This song articulated what some men in Cabbagetown seemed to feel as they had the phrase rendered in tattoos. It was the spirit of "standin' up" and "talkin' back". This was a person who would not kowtow to anyone. If he were not shown proper respect, he would quit a job, throw a punch, or worse. He would "take no orders" from anyone. He threw a gauntlet of threat around himself "I'm evil", "Don't mess around with me".

The country music song, "Sixteen Tons"[2] was popular, and it narrated the life of a coal miner with "A mind that's weak and a back that's strong", a song with which mill workers could identify. The lyrics tell about the working man who is deep in debt to the company store, and it says,

If you see me comin', better step aside
A lotta men didn't, a lotta men died
One fist of iron, the other of steel
If the right one don't get you
Then the left one will.

The song celebrates masculinity based on threat and toughness. It was another jukebox song projecting a worker's threat to the larger society rendered through the smoothness of a country song.

According to Effie Smith and her church friends, the Born to Lose guys and the drinking class people were the ones giving their community a bad reputation with weapons violations, disturbing the peace, petty theft, and vandalism, and occasionally someone crossing the line into homicide or grand larceny. That gave those guys pariah status. They broke the rules of Christian community living.

Dewayne Durham, Esther Smith's husband, was from that group, and he had "born to lose" tattooed in large letters on his arm for all to see. One summer Esther's four-year-old son, Jimmy, was in Grady Hospital, and I had gone with her and Effie to be with the boy. Later, Dewayne arrived, but he did not say a word to the three of us as he walked in. He went to the hospital bed and picked up Jimmy and carried him to the window to look out. His short-sleeved shirt revealed the muscular arms of a worker, tattooed with life. He had the name "Esther" tattooed on his right arm over the bicep, and down his forearm, a nude female body. On his left forearm longways down the arm was the "Born to lose" tattoo and crossway on his hand was "Hell".

The "Born to Lose" tattoo was a bold confrontation to the exterior forces molding life and destiny, the power structure that shaped life itself even the cosmic "God's will". Some were born to lose. Was it the anger of not being able to change a life of hard work and poverty that could drive a man to lash out even against God? Was the man saying if God created this mess of a world, then to Hell with God? Whether it was the cosmic "God's will", or laws made by the government, men frequently expressed their anger at the system. They were angry with the decisions of the federal government on race and religion, but what could they do?

Impending doom was a favorite theme of preachers, and trust in the future was lacking. They would say that things were so bad that we were doomed to unhappiness, failures, and poverty. Dreams did not survive long in this community because they were consumed by the experience of lost hopes. Some said, "I've never had anything, but I've beaten the system by never wanting anything." Others said, "I never have had anything, never expected anything, and I've never been disappointed."

Since villagers said that people had more of the Devil in them than the divine, they were hesitant to trust anyone other than close family members. That lack of trust toward outsiders contributed to tight circles of closeness with family and friends and "Othering" the unknown. Within extended families, conflict was minimized and whitewashed because of the daily contact and interdependency of the relationships. If a child behaved badly on the playground, he would be corrected when he got home because his brothers, sisters or cousins would tell the parents. If the grocer cheated, he would be set straight in the church, and the entire village would know. When community social sanctions failed to control the behavior of a man, people began to avoid him.

School And Losing

As I talked with Johnny Smith and others about their school experiences, most did not refer it as an accumulation of skills that might improve life options for a person. In contrast, his sister Esther and brother Billy Joe did talk about the possibilities that education could give, and they expressed remorse at having dropped out of school. Those who lacked expectation for a different future had little trust in educators, employers, or the urban society. As the possibility of working in the mill was ending in the 1960s and 1970s, young people turned their attentions to other manual labor jobs, such as stock clerks in retail stores, construction, or truck driving. When the people of Cabbagetown lost the security of traditional mill work, only few had skills to effectively deal with what would come.

The feeling of not having a chance in life was re-enforced in the schools for many Cabbagetown young people because of the discrimination they felt from teachers and other students. They told me that they avoided telling where they lived because they would be categorized as no-good. They expressed feeling alienated in school, and they were afraid of being treated differently because they were from Cabbagetown. Personal dress and grooming defined them as poor, and that became their self-image for many. That in turn contributed to frequent absences, low reading skills, low grades, and high dropout rates.

In an interview with the singer/songwriter Joyce Brookshire, who was from Cabbagetown, she talked about her experience going to school.

Well. We were always called hillbillies, you know, and we went first to Grant Park Elementary, and then to Roosevelt and no, I never did feel quite comfortable at school. There was always that something that, that kinda made you feel like you were second class citizens, specially when they knew you were from Cabbagetown. But you know at the time there, we all banded together, and it was, you know, we got through school OK.[3]

The sociologists Monica McDermott and Annie Ferguson argue that poor Whites can be subject to even greater prejudice than poor Blacks because even with White privilege, they failed in society.[4]

Poor school attendance contributed to failure in school, and it was usually explained by students as a problem of illness, not having clothes or shoes to wear, or personal conflict with a teacher. Lack of reading skills was another problem, leading to poor understanding of written materials, embarrassment, and poor performance. The poor attendance and low reading skills formed a cycle leading to lack of interest, failing grades, and following the community pattern of dropping out of school at sixteen-years-old. The young person from Cabbagetown could develop a negative self-image that people from their community were "no-good", which made them "no-good", a lack of social respect that undermined their sense of rectitude and self-worth.

Both men and women said to me that girls were more intelligent and morally superior to boys. In fact, school records did confirm that girls had better performance in school. As a result, women normally had more education and tended to do the reading and writing for the family. In some cases, they did most of the family interacting with outsiders. These traditional patterns of male-female relationships complicated the concept of self for both men and women.

Since Cabbagetown students were not identified in school records, no specific data was available on their dropout rate. However, school counselors at Roosevelt High School, which Cabbagetown students attended, told me that the overall dropout rate for the school was 50 percent, and they knew that Cabbagetown students had an even higher rate. In the demographic survey I made in the village, I did not register any high school graduates who had grown up in Cabbagetown. Later, I did identify three graduates, not registered in the survey, but they no longer lived in the neighborhood.

In general, behavior was an immediate phenomenon, and people did not build future oriented lifestyles. The belief in destiny meant that the future was already determined, and whatever a person could do had little or no effect on the outcome. The linear chain of experience model of life in which education led to jobs, which led to security and improved standard of living was foreign. When education conflicted with the demands of their immediate life, the young man or woman dropped out of school.

Although each person had a different reason for dropping out, one consistent motive was the pressure or desire to begin adult behaviors. After failing one to three grades in grammar school, as almost all Cabbagetown students had done, they were still in the early years of high school when they reached their sixteenth birthday. Another three to four years of low energy school existence seems a pale choice next to the excitement of a job, income, and adulthood.

Johnny and Billy Joe dropped out so they could begin working, and Esther dropped out to get married and have her own house. Tommy, their fifteen-year-old cousin, planned to drop out as soon as he was sixteen so he could work and buy a car. Dropping out was not a behavior specific to high school, but it also applied to jobs, training programs, and non-formal education. Although much behavior was ranked on the moral scale of good or bad, dropping out of school or quitting a job were areas of morally neutral behaviors.

73

Billy Joe Smith said that he did not like to study books and that prevented his entering training programs that he knew involved book work. On one occasion Billy Joe had an opportunity to study commercial art, but it was time consuming and expensive, so he dropped out. Johnny had the opportunity to enter a vocational training program. It looked good to him, and he was interested, but he did not do it. Troy entered a training program to become a mechanic, and he loved the work. He had to go to another state to complete the program, and he proudly told everyone he was going. However, he made no preparations to leave, and when the time came, he stayed home and went back to roofing.

Some people had difficulty adjusting to leaving the village, even for short periods of time, and that could compromise their access to educational and training possibilities. In one example a community worker arranged a job training program for one of the teen-aged boys who had been arrested repeatedly and had spent considerable time in the Juvenile Home. The job training program was in a nearby state, and the idea was to get him out of the village to help break his cycle of petty crimes. The day before he was to leave by train, he was talking with friends, who later told me, that he had said he did not want to leave. That night he committed another petty crime and was quickly arrested, and he was sent to the Juvenile Home again, losing the opportunity for the job training. After being released from the Juvenile home a few months later, he was back on the streets of Cabbagetown.

In another case, Fannie Dalton's son was drafted into the Army and sent to a distant Army base. He wrote home saying that he was going crazy because he could not tolerate the emotional environment. At the end of three weeks, he went absent without leave from his base and came home to Cabbagetown. Detectives came repeatedly looking for him at his parents' house, but he stayed with his grandparents, and the people of the village cooperated through silence to guarantee that he was not found. Everyone knew where he was, and no one reported him.

People outside the Cabbagetown community were not always trusted whether they were politicians or governmental officials, community organizers, union organizers, teachers, employers, or police. From individual to individual there was a network of family and friends who helped shape their experiences and decisions about life. In this way Johnny, Esther, Billy Joe, and the other young people like them made the decisions that kept them in Cabbagetown.

The Shame of Poverty and Subjective Well-Being

I heard again and again from Johnny Smith to Claude Workman, Joyce Brookshire, Ellie Porter, and others that they were discriminated against in school and for jobs because they were from Cabbagetown. Many felt a sense of shame in their interactions with people outside the village. Jimmy Cross, an eighth grader, cut all classes for three weeks after one teacher asked him too many questions that he felt were personal and identified him as being from Cabbagetown. He said that she was too "nosy", and he could not stand to be around her. To protect himself he simply stopped going to school for three weeks.

Johnny Smith told me about his shame and embarrassment of not having the right clothes or lunch money to go to school. Once a teacher offered to give clothes to him and Esther, and he was so ashamed that he avoided seeing the teacher afterwards. Johnny and Esther both told stories of inability to cope with teachers' criticisms or comments about their social class. Esther remembers her embarrassment from the first grade when a teacher scorned her orthography, and she felt shame because the entire class knew that she had written her letters poorly. Johnny was so bashful in the first grade that he could not talk. He got over that when the teacher came home with him and had a talk with his mother.

This continued throughout his school experience. At one point when he was older, he felt he could not go on a school day trip because he did not have the clothes or the money to do it. He told me,

I had been staying out of school for about a month cause I didn't have any shoes... We were sellin this candy, then for a quarter. Like we did when we were goin to the first, second and third. Trying to get up enough money, the children wanted to go to Indian Springs the last day of school and spend the day. Well, I sold more than anyone in the class, and well, there was me and Billy Joe and Esther going to school, we never was the best dressed kids, coming from a poor family. We always went clean and all. So, we more or less always had hand-me-down clothes, which I wasn't ashamed of it, but this one particular time.

So, about two days before we were goin to leave, one day at recess I went up and told Miss Hall to let someone else go in my place. And she wanted to know why, and I was a little reluctant to tell her. Finally, she kept on, and I told her that I didn't have any good clothes like the other kids wear, and I didn't want to go and me looking like a tramp. And she took me aside and told me, in fact, she got me from class and got Miss Steward, our principal, to come up there and told her about it. She wanted them all to know that she was proud of me.

And then, I told her that I didn't have no money to spend. It took all mother and daddy made to pay bills with. I felt like I ought not to go. And she said, 'You sold more than anyone in class, and you're going.'

Johnny did go on the trip, and he said afterwards,

But I never will forget the only time that I rode on a train. We went down on a train at the end of the spring.

Even education and special training were not enough sometimes. Ellie Porter was one of the few to complete high school, and she did additional training in office machines. Then, she had difficulty getting office jobs, and she believed that being from Cabbagetown was the obstacle. Finally, she was hired for a clerical position in a business firm, but it caused an emotional upheaval in her family. Her less educated husband, who was a mill worker, was upset by the fact that she was working in a position of better social class. According to Ellie, he harassed her to quit. With her sense of shame about being from Cabbagetown and her husband's harassment, she began to feel that her fellow office workers were treating her with condescension. She fought back at perceived insults, which led to her being fired from the job. She ended up working in the mill.

Poverty and Limited Opportunities

The belief in Christian superiority did not save people from the ravages of poverty. Given the immediacy of economic life, all the available members of a family needed to work. Since few families could afford the luxury of nonproductive adolescents, young family members began working early. Being young and lacking skills, they started as unskilled labor, making low wages. Most of the people around them had worked as unskilled laborers all their lives, and many depended on the security of employment that the mill offered and did not develop additional occupational skills.

Use of money was immediate, so that expenses were broken down into the smallest units possible. Rent could be paid weekly with the owner or agent coming to collect. Food could be bought daily sometimes from peddlers who walked through the village selling fruits and vegetables. A part-time preacher sold small appliances and other dry goods on installment plans, and he would come by weekly to collect payments. He knew everyone, and a person could take as long as they needed to pay, even though the ultimate price might be double the usual retail value. Most workers were paid weekly although some were paid daily, and the money was spent accordingly, inevitably bringing crisis in times of shortage.[5] A result of this pattern of immediate use of money was that there was little or no capital accumulation.

Only a rich person was expected to have money in the bank. When extraordinary expenses occurred such as illness or accidents, people would go into debt. In this no-capital economy any surplus money was often spent immediately on special one-off purchases that could not be bought otherwise or on recreational spending sprees with conspicuous entertainment of friends. Johnny Smith told me about one time when he invited two friends to an Atlanta Braves baseball game. He showered them with the luxury of a taxi ride to the ballpark, buying the tickets, beer and hot dogs during the game and a taxi ride home. All of it cost him most of his salary for the week.

Religious women had a sense of well-being anchored in the promise of a future Utopian life in Heaven in contrast to the non-religious people, mostly men, who turned to more immediate pleasures like a half pint of whiskey after work. The belief of religious people in the superiority of their Christian practice gave them an emotional base of security. Hoverd and Sibley[6] have documented that the sense of well-being by religious families in poverty neighborhoods is higher than that of non-religious families.

Problems of Well-Being

There were serious problems in the well-being of people in Cabbagetown, and some that I documented were:

Sexual abuse of children. Although I did not personally know examples of child abuse, I did hear references to it in the community. The Cabbagetown author Eddie Sellars[7] wrote a personal account of child abuse while growing up in the neighborhood living in a three-room shotgun house on Savannah Street. He was born in 1955 and would have been a teenager during my research in the neighborhood. He refers to "sexual child abuse and beatings", which was a subject people did not talk about even though they knew it was happening. He gives personal descriptions of the abuse that he and his siblings experienced as children, and he asks the question, "why with such a large family all around, did no one ever try to stop any of it?"[8] The community repudiated it but did not want to talk about it or address it openly.

Brown Lung. Brown lung (also known as byssinosis) was a problem from working in an environment with cotton dust, but its frequency in Cabbagetown was difficult to measure because its symptoms are like other respiratory diseases such as asthma or bronchitis. Many of the workers in the mill were also smokers, adding to the difficulty of diagnosis. In 1971 OSHA (Occupational Safety and Health Administration) set a level of cotton dust that would be permissible in workplaces.[9] In 1978 OSHA did adopt a Cotton Dust Standard, but that was the same year that the mill closed, so it did not help people in Cabbagetown.

Untreated illness or injury. Treatment for disabilities was curative, not preventive. Professional help was not always sought for illness, and home remedies or prayer were commonly used. If a doctor were consulted, it might not be until the illness was advanced, so even common illnesses could become major ones. There was a high incidence of respiratory illnesses, particularly in the winter months. Manual labor led to incidences of injury, especially among men. Virtually every family had at least one member with some physical disability stemming from an inadequately treated illness or injury. Dental care was a problem, and people could begin losing their teeth in their 20s or 30s. Abscessed and decayed teeth could compound physical problems and lead to further loss of work. I observed a half dozen cases of muteness, deafness, or poor eyesight. These people did not receive training or care and became non-productive or low-productive charges for their families.

Alcoholism. Alcoholism was a man's disease. I observed frequent night drunkenness among adult men. Alcoholism among older men interfered with the ability to work for some and could create economic problems for the family. In the personal story of her mill worker family Sybil Smith[10] also talked about the problem of alcoholism with her uncle. When he was sober, he went to church and sang in the choir, but because of alcoholism he missed work in the mill, lost his job, which meant he lost his house. The tradition of men drinking was preserved in stories about the lives of their ancestors in their Appalachian homelands and in country music.

Impaired maturity. I observed the cases of three adult men who had never assumed adult roles. Two of them continued to live with their families, essentially as adolescents, and did not work or contribute economically to their families. The third was man in his 30s who had never developed secondary sexual characteristics, and he continued to live at home with his parents as an adolescent and associated only with women and children.

Mental illness. One example was Clark, a man who had moved to Cabbagetown with his wife and children from a small town in northern Georgia a few years earlier. He got a job at the mill, and they rented one of the mill houses. Later, he began drinking and showing signs of sadism, such as beating his wife and children and sleeping with a gun in his bed. His employment became irregular. Then, he abandoned his car, which was towed away by the police, and he did not attempt to reclaim it. The car episode resulted in significant economic loss for the family, making their poverty even worse. For most men their car was a source of pride and status, but he did not respond to the loss. When he made sexual advances to his oldest daughter, his wife and children left, not to return, leaving him alone and unemployed.

Mental retardation. Two Cabbagetown high school students were in EMR (Educable Mentally Retarded) classes in the local high school, and I knew a dozen others in the village who seemed to have impaired cognitive skills. Each of them continued to live with their parents , doing simple household chores within the family.

The "born to lose" attitude applied to social and economic norms, as well as physical and behavioral ones. Although some people dreamed of a better life, most found their occupational skills so limiting that they could not transcend the battery of limitations that walled them into the village. As the men who bought into the "born to lose" mindset dreamed of a better life, most saw it as White, Christian, and patriarchal, and they called for a government that would re-install those conditions for them.

Endnotes

1   Written by Jerry Leiber and Mike Stoller
2   Written by Merle Travis, later interpreted by Tennessee Ernie Ford
3   Joyce Brookshire, the Duchess of Cabbagetown. No date.
4   McDermott and Ferguson 2022:262
5   LaBarre 1962:166
6   Hoverd and Sibley 2013:182 ff
7   Sellars 2018:11
8   Ibid.
9   The permissible exposure limit was set at 1-mg/m3 of total dust
10   Smith 2017:49

CHAPTER FOUR
DON'T BUILD NO FENCES FOR ME:
OUTLAW CULTURE

MEN REVELED IN STORIES ABOUT THEIR DEFIANCE of the government, especially the federal government. These stories seemed to define and re-enforce the alienation they lived. In what might seem like a contradiction in terms, men reveled in their defiance but also called for a strongman who would re-establish traditional values, including White male privilege. The outlaw culture was celebrated in country music by singers like Willie Nelson, Waylon Jennings, and Hank Williams, Jr. Their songs about acting outside of the law were interpreted as being hip and implicitly gave validation to White nationalism. Outlaw culture was one of the building blocks of the MAGA movement.

A man who had broken the law and been in jail was an accepted member of the community and could identify with evangelical social principles.[1] A man could get on the wrong side of the law for many reasons. He might have been wrongly accused or arrested for something that really was not that bad. Or he might have killed a man in a fight without intending to do it. At what point did a crime cross the line into sin? Within the Smith/White family circle many men had been arrested and spent time in jail, including Cecil Smith, his son Johnny, his son-in-law Dewayne, and their neighbor and friend Sam.

Conflict with authorities was a part of life, and it was kept alive in stories. Sometimes it was a domestic dispute, and sometimes male bravado became too much on the street corner. There were fights and even murders, and sometimes a public fight could become a widely discussed spectacle. For some men jail time was a part of their toughness. Defiance of authority got men and boys into trouble on occasion, and some of the stories that men most enjoyed telling were about that defiance.

Crime and Jail Time

Sam Johnson was a peaceful and contemplative man in his 60s, whom I visited on occasion. He had an unusual story. He was a murderer.

He had left Cabbagetown forty years ago to make a better life in California, and during all those years he had never written to his family. His father died not knowing whether Sam was dead or alive. In the meantime, Sam's sister, Betty, married and lived on Kirkwood. After a long life together, her husband died, and not long after Sam returned home as an old man and ill after that forty-year absence. He had completed his sentence in prison for killing a man, and he came home. Betty took him in, and they cared for each other in their old age.

One afternoon sitting on the front porch of their house, Sam voluntarily began to tell me his story. He went to California as a young man to make a better life for himself, but when he was there, he said he got in with the wrong crowd. In a fight he killed a man. He did not see himself as a killer, but he had done it, and he spent the next forty years in prison. Killing a man and being an ex-convict did not make Sam a pariah in Cabbagetown. Having been in prison was even celebrated by some.

The country music singer Johnny Cash was popular in the community, and he sang about getting on the wrong side of the law and going to jail. In his famous concert in Folsom Prison in 1968 he sang "Folsom Prison Blues" about the longing and sadness of prison life, saying "I ain't seen the sunshine in I don't know when, I'm stuck in Folsom Prison and time keeps draggin' on..."[2] He was one of them. He had country roots, and his singing about being in jail struck an emotional chord.

Historian Paul Harvey[3] describes Cash's appeal to the downtrodden as someone like them with darkness within and struggling with personal demons while holding on to the promise of something better. Cash was overtly racist at one point in his life, had drug addiction problems, and had encounters with the law. People in Cabbagetown shared that experience of being racist and having encounters with law enforcement. That made Johnny Cash authentic. He was like them.

Other country performers sang about men not conforming to social expectations. In "Bad Seed" the man said that he could not make his garden with the woman because his seed just would not grow. He was too bad to be

82

redeemed. In "Don't Build No Fences for Me" the man said that he could not be limited by social constraints.

The drinking culture resulted in violence with some regularity, and Johnny Smith explained drinking and men's behavior this way,

There are some boys down here that are my age that cause trouble sometimes. They get to drinkin and get mean. They'll fight a little...I've seen my brother-in-law cuss his own mother to her face, and he lives with her! I'll bet he would hit his own mother. He does a little bootleggin' on the side on the weekends. He always has beer and wine around, and when they get started drinkin, they get mean.

83

One Saturday night I was visiting Johnny Smith and his wife, Anne. During the conversation I told him that a guy named Bean had been trash talking to me on the basketball court and running into me hard beyond what was normal on plays, and Johnny knew him. He said that one of his own older cousins was like Bean, always trying to push people around. He had gotten into trouble a few times and had been arrested. A few years ago, he was caught messing around with a married woman, and the angry husband had shot him. He said Bean might wind up the same way.[4]

In a different case Johnny said that it might happen like it did with his best friend Boog, who was shot to death on the corner near his house. No one knew why. Boog did not have enemies, and he was not involved in drugs or anything that might cause a shooting, but he was killed. Johnny could not explain it. Men who were drunk had the reputation of being potentially violent, either verbally or physically. Although women could also be verbally aggressive, it was not because of drinking. Talking about his father, Cecil, Johnny said that he was not a mean drunk.

Take my ol Dad for instance. He gets drunk every night of the world. But every mornin he gets up and goes to work. And he's good as he can be. He's been that way as long as I have known him. He never does no harm to nobody. He wouldn't hurt a flower. But some people, when they get drunk, they get mean.

Some adults, including mothers, would encourage their sons to fight, encouraging them not only to defend their masculinity but to defend the race. I observed fist fighting among young men and boys, and a fight between White and Black boys had heightened emotions. I saw small boys of five and six years old being encouraged to fight by older boys or men, who would form a circle around them giving instructions and urging them on. This was considered an important element of masculinity, and the idea was that the minor injuries that resulted from the fight helped toughen him and make him a man.

While some younger men were encouraging street fights, older men were complaining that the police were failing to enforce the laws. They wanted government to help keep their kids out of trouble and to control the Black people living in Reynoldstown. They were saying that the government was not re-enforcing Christian standards, and some thought the Ku Klux Klan could do what the police could not do.

Ku Klux Klan and Authority

I heard stories told with admiration about the Ku Klux Klan acting outside of the law to defend local values. To many in the American South, the Civil War was fought over state's rights, and in Cabbagetown people said the federal government should not legislate on issues affecting their local cultural traditions, which they considered state's rights. To them the imposition of integration and the denial of the right to read the Bible and have traditional Christian prayers in school were unjust interferences in their rights as Whites and Southern Protestants. Even non-churchgoers protested the denial of the right to prayer and Bible reading. Referring to governmental decisions, Claude Workman said, "They haven't asked the White man; they don't give a damn about the White man. It seems that way." People said that the federal government had betrayed them, and they did not trust it.

According to Kentucky author Jack Weller,[5] the Appalachian people who turned to working in the textile mills brought individualism and rejection of external authority, especially the government. He argues that Appalachian people had a special culture and history of freedom "from the restrains of law and order". I would hear this rejection of the federal government repeatedly in Cabbagetown. Since government was not providing the needed moral direction for the country, people turned to informal authority, and the Ku Klux Klan[6] was portrayed as being effective.

The KKK[7] was seen as an organization that enforced moral direction and social control. In its manifestations across Georgia, it included preachers along with their church members, as well as law enforcement people, business leaders, and politicians. The KKK was a men's organization, and they identified themselves as Southern White Christians and used the cross as their logo.

Professors John Corrigan and Lynn S. Neal[8] point out that the KKK in the South can only be understood in terms of its close ties to fundamentalist Protestantism. It raises the question to what extent was the KKK an action-oriented extension of the Protestant churches in the South? Their version of Christianity could not tolerate religious or racial diversity, and Jews, Blacks, and Catholics were targets for the KKK.[9]

As I talked with people in Cabbagetown about the KKK, they spoke about it sympathetically, referring to the good it had done. Older men talked about the KKK as an organization that chastised offenders of religious or racial norms, and they said that it was pressure from the federal government had eventually caused it to die out.

85

The famous country singer from Cabbagetown, Fiddlin' John Carson[10] wrote a popular song about the KKK entitled "There Ain't No Bugs on Me". It said, "The night was dark and driz'ly an' the air was full of sleet/my ol man join'd the Klu Klux and' ma she lost 'er sheet."[11] The KKK was an easy theme of conversation in the neighborhood, and the conversation could slip from music to telling tales from the past.

Gene Roberts told me this story about the Klan.

Now you take...I'll say forty years ago. You know what they'd do with somebody like that [i.e., a sex worker]. *They'd go there and warn her one time. If she didn't obey, the Ku Klux would take her out and when they turned her loose, she'd barely be able to walk, and they'd stick fire to that house and burn it down. You didn't see nothin like that goin on then, I know we lived up there close to a little town, Auburn, back this side of Winder, and they's an ol woman up there like that. And you'd see a bunch of men hangin out there day and night. Well, a bunch of them Ku Klux got together one night, went up there and took that ol woman out, and they like to beat her to death. And they give her three days and nights, I think it was to move. She didn't move. Back then you didn't see no electric lights, nothin but lamp light. They went there one night, and they shot out every window light in that house. Shot out all the lamps. And they left a note there and told that ol woman she had better not let the sun rise on her the next mornin. And she left, and she never was heard tell of.*

The authority of the Ku Klux Klan was accepted because it was local and addressed issues of local concern. The KKK would surge into importance when Jews, Blacks, or other unacceptable minorities would seem to threaten the local cultural norms. The vigilante law tradition can be seen in the 4,731 lynchings recorded in the United States between 1882 and 1950.[12]

Most people would speak to me about the KKK in historical terms, but I knew it was active during the time I was in Cabbagetown. Gene-Gabriel Moore, who grew up in Cabbagetown in the 1950s, talked about his adoptive father taking him to KKK meetings at Stone Mountain.[13] A report from the Community Relations Commission of Atlanta described Klan activity in Cabbagetown, and it coincided with my experience. The report said,

> *There appears to be no overt display of Klan activity. However, the majority of the residents are Klan sympathizers. Mr. Calbin Craig, Grand Dragon of the Klan, has been in the community several times and recently conducted a voter registration campaign in which several residents of the community participated.*[14]

Their estimate was that 125 people in Cabbagetown (or 10 percent of the population) were or had been involved in the KKK, and although they did not specify it, men were the members of the KKK.

Defying Federal Authorities

Defiance of authority was a recurring theme in storytelling. Local history was carried on by oral tradition, and no one had written these stories. Men were story tellers. The best tall tales had an element of humor, and the tales that were most appreciated were those in which police officers were outwitted by the agility or inventiveness of the person they were pursuing. The repetition of these anti-government stories suggests a sense of disenfranchisement if not disengagement with the larger American society.

Men told stories of bravado about resisting authority. In contrast, women talked about their religious experiences and dramatic events like conversion. Men recounted youthful escapades as we sat in the dusk of countless evenings as the rocking chairs squeaked on the porch, and they rollicked in telling stories from their past.

Some of these stories come from the rural past and were about making moonshine which was a common illegal activity during prohibition. One afternoon as we sat on the front porch of his house, I recorded the following account by John King, who had grown up in the mountains of northern Georgia. It was a tragicomic story of a man being shot by a "Revenuer", but it included a moment of humor when the wounded man defied the government man.

One time we lived on an ol feller's place; his name was Jeb. He made liquor and sold it, and one night Dad was helping him. And he came in there one night, a little after dark, and he said, 'Bee [the story teller's mother] *let me have a handful of matches.' Well, my mother give him a handful of matches. Naturally, like a kid I was afraid to ask him, but after he got out of the house I asked my mother, I said, 'I wonder what he wanted with them matches.' She said, 'I don't know son.'*

Well, way in the night, it must have been about one o'clock, Pop come in, knocked on the door and said, 'Open the door, Bee, quick.' Said, 'The Revenuer shot Jeb, and he's layin down there in the branch [i.e., creek] *in a puddle of blood.' Well, she got up and opened the door. We didn't have no electric lights, didn't have nothing but lamp light, and he stayed there a few minutes and then he said, 'I'm goin back there and see about helpin get him out of that branch,' and said, 'I'll be back.' Well, he was gone about I guess an hour. He come back, and my mother said, 'Did you get him out?' He said, 'Yeh, they shot him through both legs.'*

They made him one of them big ol boxes and had his feet in it. And two or three days later, that Revenue man that shot him come up there to see how he was gettin along. And his wife's name was Alice, and back them days everybody kept a shotgun layin over the front door or the middle door, loaded all the time. And he walked in there and says, 'Well, how you feelin Jeb.?' And Jeb says, 'Alice, hand me that pokestock up there above that door, I'll show that damn son of a bitch how I'm feelin.'

And that Revenue man run, he run flat out of there. [Laughter] *They called them pokestocks, them blame things, they had a barrel on them as long as that door there, and they'd shoot from here to Grant Park. He'd a killed that Revenuer too…He stayed piled up in that bed for about nearly a year.'*

The Revenuers were particularly hated by the mountain people who saw them as interfering with their traditional legitimate activity. Many of the Revenue agents were friends or neighbors which made the hatred for them even more personal and intense. The men who talked about this told me that the outlawing of home brew was an illegitimate act perpetuated by the liquor industry in collaboration with legislators. Making liquor was a part of a mountain tradition of self-sufficiency, and people were accustomed to a subsistence economy, making what they consumed, including liquor. These stories of resistance to the government could reach heroic proportions.

In a Sunday afternoon visit George Miller told me this story about making moonshine in the country outside of Riverdale, which is south of Atlanta. It continues the tale of violence that marked the feud between the Revenuers and the moonshiners, and in this story, at least, the moonshiners won.

I lived down here in Riverdale, and a feller by the name of Wayne Pye and Sam Allred, Mr. Allred is dead now, and that's all they'd do, just make liquor and sell it, but there wasn't nothin they wouldn't do for you. They was good-hearted. They'd been a makin it down around Riverdale. Some way or another they got in with some Evans boys form around Fayetteville. Went down and put them up a still, and that was back in the thirties. The Revenue from Fayetteville went down there to raid them, and instead of them drivin the car on up close to the still, they call themself a parkin about a mile or two before they got to the still. And Wayne and them had a bunch of men a watchin, and when they seen them Revenues a comin…And back then you didn't have no cards, see to get dynamite. Might everybody had a stick of dynamite. One of them fellows sittin up there in them woods, went down there to that car and put a stick of dynamite in there. Stuck the wire to the spark plug, and this other one run down there to see if Wayne and them was there to give them a signal, so they could run and get away.

They cut the still down all right, but boy when they [Revenuers] come back out [Laughter] and stepped on that starter, it blowed that motor slap out of that brand new A-model Ford, and they found pieces of it two miles over there in that woods, blowed the whole motor out. I don't see what kept it from killin those blame Revenuers, but it just blowed the motor out.

Story tellers also told stories about the foolishness that happened to themselves, even when the laughter was at their own expense. However, the stories were very rarely just comic stories, they were usually comic-heroic or comic-tragic. The following is an example of a comic-heroic story in which the storyteller stupidly falls into the clutches of the law, only to escape through a heroic physical effort.

They come there and put a still about, I guess, about a quarter of a mile below my house, and Wayne, just before they'd be ready to make that liquor, he'd come up there and say, 'Now, Cecil you go down there and get all that beer you want.' He said, 'We're goin to run it off tonight.' Well, I went down there and drunk me a big dipper of that beer. It was in the summertime, and I was plowin out there on the side of the road in front of the house.

I come back by in a little while, and I said, 'Well, I'm goin back down there and get me a little drink of that beer.' Well, I went down there, and I didn't know them blame Revenue officers was down there. They were in there hid, you know, watchin that still. And I had on a bran new jumper and a bran new pair of overalls. I was standin at one of them barrels, just a drinkin beer to beat the band, and all at once I felt something crab me by the jumper at the collar, and I coulda out run a greyhound.

I just throwed my arms back and come out of that coat. The ol Revenuer, he run me, he run me every bit as far as from here to Grant Park. I was barefooted, up through them woods and briar patches. Hell, the further I got, the faster I got. Hell, I run clear over there on a hill, a place they called Pea Ridge. Well, I sat down and listened a little bit. And I said, 'Well, they're gone now. I'll go back over there and go to plowin.' Well, there was a little ol plum orchard out there at the side of the field, and ol John Cook, a feller the name of John Cook, was down there helpin Wayne and them run the liquor. And ol John, where I had run way out yonder, he got over there in that plum orchard and hid. 'Cecil, come here a minute.'

'What the devil you doin up here, John?'

He said, 'How about swappin clothes with me. They like to got me down there a while ago.'

I said, 'Hell, they like to a got me too, I lost my jumper down there.' Crazy fool like, I went on out there in the plum orchard, and John had ol beer spilt all over his clothes, you know. I let him have my overalls, and he let me have his, and he had a gallon of liquor. He said, 'Take you a big drink of this liquor, Cecil.'

And I took me a big drink of that liquor. Well, I'd go back out there and plow a little more, and in a few minutes I heared a car horn, 'honk, honk, honk.' The road come right along where I was plowin, and I'd got just about as fer as from the road goin back out this way towards the other end of the field, and it was them blame Revenue officers, and they had that worm [i.e. the coil from the still] tied on the side of the car and got right there even with me, and he blowed the horn, and he said, 'Go back down there and put you up another one, and we'll cut it down.' I throwed them damn plow lines down and boy, I tore out again. I run about two miles that time and hid over there right in the same place, and I'll be damn...I was hid over there on that big hill they call Pea Ridge, and they circled around and here they come right up that hill with that worm tied on the side of that car.

Such stories of encounters with the Revenuers (i.e. federal officers) were local entertainment and shared with laughter by older men, while younger men told more contemporary stories about not being caught by the police or school teachers after some escapade or minor illegality. In Gal Beckerman's study of social change, he suggested that this overt ridiculing of authority was a starting point for social movements against the established order.[15] His observation suggests that this heritage of disrespect and even hatred of federal government authority would contribute to the readiness of the Proud Boys, Oath Keepers, and other contemporary militia groups to directly attack the federal government.

Bootlegging in Cabbagetown

Bootlegging alcohol was a tradition in Cabbagetown, perhaps one of the Appalachian traditions that survived here. People told me who the bootleggers were during the time I was in the community. They were well know, but no one reported them to the police. They were part of the local culture. The outlawing of alcoholic drinks during Prohibition (1920-1933) did not stop bootleging in Cabbagetown. Historian Cliff Kuhn[16] reported this descrpition from Marion Brown:

Oh, there was white ones [bootleggers], too, a lot of white ones around Cabbagetown. Yeah, there was half a dozen right around in that neighborhood because when all them mill people got out, man they headed for a bootlegger. They sure did. They wanted them to get them a drink when they got out of that dusty cotton mill.

It continued after Prohition ended because under aged people could buy from the bootlegger, or people could buy at night or Sundays when regular liquor stores were closed. The bootlegger was also a neighbor and close by, it was easier to buy locally.

Can't Trust the Federal Government

The emotional disturbance that Claude Workman felt over race relations that we saw in a previous chapter was not only against Black people but against the government. Like many people in the village, he said the best government would be the least government. It would be better to leave people alone to work out their problems locally. This, perhaps, went back to the belief in the imagined mountain tradition of isolated communities living comfortably in isolation with little governmental interference. Their memory of negative experiences with the federal Government ranged from the "War Between the States" to the "Revenuers", civil rights legislation, and the outlawing of Bible reading and prayer in the schools.

Workman said it was the government's violation of a political trust to intervene in the personal matters of how one chose to live. School teachers, and tax agents, politicians were foreign agents of the government that people did not always trust. He shared the words of populist politicians about the breakdown of the political process and the lack of trust in the government.

Claude was talking about his distrust of government, and I asked, "You think the government doesn't understand the problems of the people?"

No, absolutely not. They mean well. I can understand the point they're looking at. Learned men don't know really what they are talking about...Maybe they mean well, maybe most of them, I'll stand on the integrity and honesty of a congressman or senator. They don't see right down into the center of the problem. Well, I can do it myself, I can be just as good a congressman as you got up there... There's nobody up there that sees things and lives in them like I do. They live over yonder in a home worth hundreds of thousands of dollars. What does he know?

Now, this is a wonderful country, really. And I've already put my life on the line a many a times for it, and I'll do it again, but I'll never do it again under the same freedom like I did before. The very heart and the very root of this country is what administrators are tearing down, the people...Deplete the morale, tear down the morale completely. You are killing the backbone, the very livelihood of our society. Tearing down at the seams, and they said they were going to. The very thing that put this country together, that made it the greatest country on earth, they are tearing it down at the very backbone, like damn termites. It is going to go boom...It is the beginning of the end of the United States of America. They're tearing at the very fibers that made this nation great.

I asked him, "Claude, what is the backbone?"

The people that made this country great. The people that mean well. Can't have any more. The people that actually made it. I don't know, you might have looked down and laughed at Robert E. Lee. Or, you might have done vice versa to General Ulysses S. Sherman, or Grant. No two greater men ever lived. But, as far as Grant is concerned, as man to a man, Grant has no standing whatsoever beside Robert E. Lee. Absolutely none whatsoever. As far as a human being is concerned, Lee, he must have been a great man.

92

Workman saw the very foundations of the country under threat. To him the efforts for Black equality had lost perspective, and instead of giving equality to Black people, they had turned it into discrimination against White people. Workman said,

They are trying to make two wrongs make a right. They turn around and instead of trying to get justice for the Negro, they turn right around and discriminate against the White in order to get justice for the Negro. There ain't no way into Hell you can get one wrong and come over here and get another and come up with a right. You can't do it. The only thing you'll wind up with is bitters. You're going to ruin a wonderful country, the only country that ever has been in the world really. You're going to tear this country down right at the foundations; she's going to crumble and fall. United States is on its way out. She's going to kill her own self; she has already started. When you take the very heart out of your heart, you take a rock and lay it out there and you take the very firmness out of that rock then you've killed yourself. Amen.

To Workman, governmental decisions favoring Black rights had been bad ones. He was hostile toward the government and policy makers, as well as the Black people he feared. Although the church and the offices of the most important Black civil rights leader, Dr. Martin Luther King, Jr. were within walking distance of Cabbagetown, he was only mentioned once in these discussions.

Workman said that if he tried to protest the civil rights of Black people, he would be put in prison. He said,

I could get up here and get me a gang of people, and I could start running my mouth, and I can get one of the awfulest riots started you ever seen. I could start here at this church, and I go down to this one, and to that one over yonder...and next thing you know, I've got a bigger following than Martin Luther King did. But before I get that far, you know where I am going to be? In the Federal Pen! My butt is going to be out there in jail...and they will put me in the penitentiary. The very fiber of this nation is falling apart. They have taken out the very backbone behind the thing.

The use of the word "they" is central to understanding the concept of government and political power in Cabbagetown. Workman characteristically said, "They can't solve these problems by passing laws," "They don't understand," or "They don't get down among the people." "They" is an impersonal, amorphous force that cannot be directly controlled, a conspiracy called the "deep state" by some. "They" is not actively challenged in its decisions because it is so complex that a challenge to it seemed impossible.

Maybe it started with the Civil War when the government of the North imposed a new way of life on the people of the South. They did it again with the civil rights legislation and other laws that Workman felt discriminated against White people and the Southern way of life. He mentioned that people in top positions were making poor decisions, but he never assessed blame to any specific politician. He blamed the faulty decisions on unseen and unknown officials who controlled the government, which could not be trusted anyway. To Workman, "they" were seen as making decisions favoring Blacks. "They" were responding only to Black people, making Whites pay the consequences. "They" were not listening to White working-class people.

That has been the appeal of Falwell, Robertson, Reagan, and Trump to speak for those Christians who feel they are the righteous backbone of America who have been ignored by educated, progressive elites. The religious right found people who will speak to their causes, even if they are flawed.

Endnotes

1   Graham and Homans 2024

2   "Folsom Prison Blues" by singer/songwriter Johnny Cash. Written in 1953. Recorded on his live album, "At Folsom Prison" in 1968, it became No. 1 on country music charts, and Cash won the Grammy Award for Best Country Vocal Performance, Male in 1969.

3   Harvey 2019:83

4   Fieldnotes. September 22, 1969

5   Weller 1965:10

6   The contemporary organizations such as Proud Boys, Oath Keepers, and the Traditionalist Workers Party did not exist at that point.

7   Other militia-like groups active in the twenty-first century range from Proud Boys to Three Percenters, Boogaloo Bois, Oath Keepers, and Atomwaffen Division among others.

8   Corrigan and Neal 2020:303

9   Jews and Blacks are still the targets of White supremacist and neo-Nazi organizations.

10   See more about John Carson in Chapter 2.

11   Lyrics assembled and arranged by John Carson. 1928. http://www.bluegrassmessengers.com/there-aint-no-bugs-on-me--fiddlin-john-carson.aspx

12   Statistics provided by the Archives of the Tuskegee Institute. This is twice the number of Jews burned at the stake by the Spanish Inquisition during a comparable period between 1480 and 1550.

13   Moore 1998

14   Cochran N.D.: 1

15   Beckerman 2022:3

16   Kuhn 2005:173

CHAPTER FIVE
DADDY HAS THE DEVIL IN HIM

MEN WERE THE DISSENTERS AND DOUBTERS, sometimes estranged within their own families. Although many if not most men considered church going a facade, most shared the Christian binary view of the cosmic power in the universe divided between God and the Devil and earthly life divided between church-goers and sinners. They regularly told me that America was a White Christian nation and should be ruled by Christian principles, but they opposed what they called the righteousness of their wives and preachers. To them a Christian foundation made America great. They were Christian nationalists who would support a strong man who promised to protect their world.

Masculinity had different expressions, and some men distanced themselves from the Christian paradigm taking on a role of toughness to defy the Devil and Hell itself. Those men would talk about not being weak like church people, and they could drink, curse, and fight to prove their toughness. For such men church was a place for women and children, not for them. The men who attended church and were involved in social obligations tended to be skilled workers or supervisors. The unskilled workers were less inclined to attend church, and these men had little or no social status to uphold by going to church.

It seemed to me that some of the expectations about religious behavior were a barrier to working-class men. In both the Baptist and Holiness churches there were prohibitions on smoking, drinking alcohol, and listening to country music. These were three things that many men enjoyed after work. In making a choice between church attendance and their after-work pleasures, many chose the latter. I frequently heard men saying that God did not mind their drinking and listening to country music, it was the "hypocritical" church members who prohibited it. These men might be anti-clerical, but they were not atheists.

What Were Men Doing?

In her research with White factory workers in Kentucky, Buck[1] argues that factory work contributed to a man's losing his "claim to manhood" as automation made work more monotonous with less need for skill and decision-making. She argues that it heightens the differentiation between the decision makers and workers, reducing the latter to robotic actors. That confirmed my observations of many of the mill workers, who seemed to be losing their roles as decision makers at home and at work, which could explain their expressions of disenfranchisement.

In the three large family networks across the village the older generation of men were either alcoholic, senile, or dead, and none of the older men in those family networks had an active social role in the families. What I observed was that as men abdicated their participation and decision-making roles in the family, women became the primary partner holding the family together. As a result, the older women, the Big Mamas, became the effective heads of each of these families.

Both men and women tended to accept the idea that men were unregenerate, and the result was that people would not make social demands on them. By indulging in anti-social behaviors Cecil and other men effectively projected that they were not available for social obligations. Cecil normally did not attend social gatherings, even those of his own children. The only joint Smith family gathering that I observed in the years I was doing research was a picnic that Billy Joe and his wife gave at their house one summer with Effie, Esther, Johnny, and Anne, and all the grandchildren. Everyone was there except Cecil.[2]

Children tended to be more loyal to the mother, who was the upholder of virtue and religion, leaving no moral space for the man. Alcoholism contributed to the marginalization of some older men, such as Mack Jones. He, his wife Molly, and unmarried daughter Nina lived on Savannah Street just up from the Neighborhood center. He was an older man, an alcoholic, and no longer working. He would go on "drinking benders", being drunk for days at a time. Late one afternoon I was across the street from their house when Molly arrived from work, and Mack was sitting drunk on the front porch of their house. Nina was there too. Molly stood in front of him and lit a cigarette with a wooden match. After the match burned out and curled over, she held it up in his face and said, "There, that's what you're like!" She said, "You're limp, and all shriveled up, just like this ol match. You can't even get it up no more. What kind of man are you anyhow?"

She and Nina laughed at her joke before walking into the house, and he mumbled something to them that I could not hear. Then, I saw them re-appear around the corner of the house with a hose and hosed him down until he was completely wet. They laughed as they called out to him that he was dirty and needed a bath. Even the drenching of water did not seem to pull him out of his stupor. That was the only time that I observed that kind of humiliation of a man for being drunk, but I did observe other scenes of verbal shaming of drunken husbands by women. Although younger men in their 30s or 40s also got drunk, and their wives might protest their drinking, I did not observe this kind of indignity in that age range.

What I observed among the two dozen families that I knew well was that younger men had a more positive engagement with their wives and children while older men tended to be more disengaged. Recognizing that human life is not static, this raises the question to what extent was the strong role of the older women a generational life cycle phenomenon, or was it a unique case for the older generation that I observed? Was it that these older men were at a loss because their gender expectations were no longer applicable when they were losing the male privilege they had experienced in their younger years?[3]

Cecil Smith, the Father

Cecil identified with his work. He was a plumber at the mill, and he talked proudly with me about his ingenuity in solving complex plumbing jobs. From the years that I knew Cecil, I think a good day for him was success in solving the plumbing challenges at work and coming home to sit on the front porch of his house, playing music on the mouth harp, talking with people who passed by, and having a half pint of whiskey until it was time for bed.

Although I visited Cecil and Effie frequently for years, I never saw them sitting together in conversation. Both blamed the distance in their marriage as a struggle between the Lord and the Devil. Their son Johnny, who was closer to his mother, told me that he believed the conflict between his parents was the Devil in Cecil using him to get Effie to backslide into unchristian behaviors.

Although Cecil talked to me about the Lord regularly, he was negative toward churches. He argued that his wife Effie was self-righteous and had a "holier than thou" attitude but was just as sinful as he was. He not only criticized her but also other religious people from the adulterous preacher Brother Adcock to the socially aloof religious neighbor across the street. Interestingly, he did not criticize the religiosity of his daughter Esther.

98

As we were talking one afternoon, Cecil said that he believed in God and felt he had a relationship with God in his own way. He told me that contemporary religion had become corrupted and that too many different sects had been formed. He said that it used to be that people just went to church, but now they were all split up into different kinds of churches that did not make sense to him. "And they're always braggin on their own church and throwin off on somebody else's." He went on to say that Christians were thinking more about other people and less about the Lord, and that could especially be seen in all the attention that was given to the preacher. He said,

> Today, you'll see these ol winos, drunks, bums get out here and never been nothin too low down that they wouldn't do. Well, all at once they'd get saved, and they'd turn out to be a preacher. Well, these people just go wild over Brother this and Brother that, and Brother so-in-so needs a new car. Well, they put him in a church, and give him a car. That ain't right.

Although Cecil would get drunk after work, he did not see himself as one of the "drunks, bums" mentioned above who had become preachers. Cecil's role in the family seemed to have been finally eclipsed during the time the children were entering adolescence. He would have been approaching forty years old at the time. Esther told me that he began drinking more heavily, and that he reacted to the changes in the family with bouts of periodic rage. Esther talked about how demanding he became with her and would not let her see boys. He tried to impose a pattern of rules impossible for her to follow. He would move the hands forward on the clock when she would be out at night then accuse her of arriving late. He gave less attention to the two sons, and they in turn sought little from him.

Cecil called his wife Effie "Mama", which I observed among other men of his age. That seemed a poignant recognition of his dependence on her. Although Cecil was dependent on Effie, he would become hostile toward her when he was drunk. He would come into a room cursing and telling her to leave and leave him alone. I heard him say to her that he did not care what she did because she did not mean anything to him anyway. He would tell her that she was no good. To display his anger, he might throw pans off the table, knock over a chair or turn off the television, depending on his state of inebriation.

99

Cecil showed more emotional attachment to Effie than toward any other person although much of it was negative. She had the primary loyalty of the children, and she had community respect, which he lacked, but he could not live without her. He could not leave; she was "Mama".

When Cecil had money to buy a half pint of whiskey after work, he would drink it that night going to sleep. He would only drink in the bathroom where no one could see him, and I wondered if he had a sense of shame about it, knowing that no one in the family would approve. When he was getting close to going to sleep from his drunkenness, he would stretch out on the bed in the darkness of the middle room still in his overalls from work. He would sing, mumbling softly to himself some song that he made up spontaneously. He might sing about a little bird or other tranquil themes. He would have his eyes closed, and he might appear to be asleep, but he would continue mumbling the song. Even when he appeared to be sleep, he still was aware of what was going on, and he would call out if something seemed amiss.

Cecil aroused emotional conflicts within his children because each was attached to him, but each disapproved of his behavior. They said to me that he was to be pitied but not to be taken seriously. Effie's friends reacted to him negatively, and in a rare show of physical force Effie's good friend and neighbor, Paula, a petite woman, pushed Cecil and knocked him down when he told her that she was no good. Effie's reaction was to say, "You'll just have to understand him, the Devil is in him, and he is just that way."

Johnny Smith, the Son

Cecil's son, Johnny, told me that he believed in the Lord and believed that when he died, he would go to Heaven, even though he did not go to church nor follow any of the socially defined rules of being a Christian. He believed that Christianity was the correct way to live even though he was not ready to follow all its tenets himself. He praised his mother's religious beliefs and practices and condemned his father for being possessed of the Devil.

When his friend, Boog, was senselessly shot to death, just around the corner from his house, Johnny wondered about himself and being right with the Lord if he were to die unexpectedly. He said that his mother, Effie, had told him that when a person was dying that the Lord would know his heart and know if the person were a believer or not. He reasoned that if death were to come suddenly that God would save him. Even with that belief, he continued to be worried.

Although Johnny said that he had tried to abide by Christian rules, he admitted that he had not always been able to do so. He considered it wrong to drink alcoholic beverages, and that a person who drank alcohol could not be "right with the Lord." He promised the Lord that he would stop drinking after their first baby died and again when the second child was to be born.

One day he told me he was conflicted over this because he really enjoyed having a cold beer, especially on hot days. He talked with his mother about his desire to have a beer, and she told him that she thought that the Lord would understand. She said that the Lord understands when we make promises that we cannot keep, and he does not hold it against us. Johnny said that he did not feel that it was wrong to drink a beer, if he did not get drunk and engage in abusive behavior toward others like his father.

In one conversation Johnny told me that the new non-mill families renting houses in the neighborhood were making the "it go down", and their drinking was a major concern. Referring to one of those families, he said,

That Woods family is no account. It's families like that that is makin our neighborhood go down. This used to be a pretty place to live. The Woods have got a house full of kids, two houses full, and they'd all just as soon kill you as look at you. Kids is runnin wild. People seem to have lost control.

There are some boys down here that are my age that cause trouble some-times. They get to drinkin and get mean. They'll fight a little. My in-laws are like that. It's kinda bad livin in the same house with them sometimes. They'll start fightin each other and cussin. It'll sound like they are tearing the place apart. Anne will want to do something because it's her brothers, but I've told her to stay out of it. I don't want to get into that. If she gets her head busted, she'll just have to take whatever happens to her.

I've seen my brother-in-law cuss his own mother to her face. And he lives with her! I'll bet he would hit his own mother. He does a little bootlegging on the side on the weekends. He always has beer and wine around. And when they get started drinkin, they get mean.

I don't mind drinkin a beer or two. I used to get drunk. I told the lord when our first baby died that I'd never touch another drop. And I didn't for a long time. But I really got to missin it...I really don't think that it is so bad to drink. It is not what goes into a man, but what comes out of him.

Johnny's passion was sports, and he would have liked to be a baseball player, and he spent most of his non-working hours playing sports. As much as his mother was devoted to religious practice, Johnny was devoted to sports. Every day the weather permitted he would play the sport that was in season. He listened to sports broadcasts on radio or television and would even listen to two simultaneously.

Johnny was the oldest child and expressed most vividly the role of Effie as the authority figure in the home as in the following,

Most children carry their problems to their mother, cause I guess they just more or less looked up to their mother more so than their dad. When she startin livin right and readin the Bible, she taught us about the Lord. Then she would tell us what we ought to do and what we shouldn't do, and she would say, 'Now. I can't see what you are doing while you're gone, but the All-Seeing-Eye can.' And of course, you know, we was saying, 'Who is the All-Seeing-Eye, Mama?' She would say, 'The Lord.' And then of course, we would say, 'Well, where is He at?' And then she would tell us, you know, explain to us best she could where He was, An, she would say, 'You just remember one thing, even though I can't see you and know what you're doing, the All-Seeing-Eye can, and He'll tell me what you done, if you done anything bad.' And I don't know, it must a soaked in Esther and Billy Joe pretty well, but I sure didn't do nothing that I shouldna done.

She sure did know how to scare me. I mean, you know, tell me about the Lord seein me even though I couldn't see Him. He knew everything I did, knew what I was gonna do before I'd do it, knew what was on my mind, you know. To me, as a kid, it scared me...I thought, what the devil, I ain't got a chance, if I decide I want to do something wrong.

When I asked him about his relationship with his parents, he said,

102

So, I guess, while raisin us, she was more or less our daddy too, even though our Daddy was livin there...Because if you ever done anything that she told you not to, you didn't do it no more after she got through with you. Now, don't get me wrong, she never did beat us, but she just whupped us hard enough to let us know that she meant business, and that we wunnit gonna be the boss. She was the boss, and what she said went, whether we liked it or not. And in other words, not to give her no back talk.

I remember I been slapped one time, just one time. I was eighteen years old. I used to help her around the house. I would wash the dishes and sweep the floor and make up her beds. Cause I quit school, and really, I wunnit tryin to find no job. But she ask me to wash the dishes, and I said, 'Well, I'm not goin to do it.' I said, 'I'm too big to be whupped, and I'm not.' And she backhanded me, boy, and I mean she really cold backhanded me.

And she said, 'Let's you and me get one thing straight, young fellow. As long as you're under your Daddy and my roof and you're not working, you gonna do what I say. You're not big enough yet that you can talk back to me. You're not a man yet, and you won't be a man until you're twenty-one. And let me see how fast you can get them dishes washed, and I don't want them half-washed neither.' And that's the only time that mother ever slapped me. And the onliest time I've ever sassed her. She changes my attitude right quick...So, you couldn't get too much on her, cause she is something else.

After Johnny quit school when he was sixteen, he worked for a time in the mill, but his most consistent employer was Mr. Lake, the owner of a small nearby grocery store where he worked as a clerk. When I asked him about that, he said that he had stayed with Mr. Lake because he had been like a father to him. Mr. Lake always gave advice, loaned him money in crises, and would give him time off work if he needed it. Johnny chose his job, not for the best salary, not for the best future, but because he had a close personal tie with Mr. Lake, and he felt safe with him. This was not unlike the traditional employment at the mill.

He went on to comment that his mother and wife were the other two people most important to him. As an example, he told me that he had been married before, and during the divorce proceedings, he and Anne were seeing each other and decided to get married. He was afraid that his first wife would find out and cause trouble, so to avoid that he suggested to Anne that they "cool it" until the divorce was finalized, but Anne refused. She said that they should continue seeing each other and that she would take care of any trouble caused by the first wife, and that was what they did. If there was trouble with people outside the family, Anne took care of it. Johnny assumed that she was smarter and could address complicated situations more effectively.

He was sad that there was tension between his wife and his mother. Anne did not feel comfortable around Effie, and she continued to call her, "Mrs. Smith," which was unusual in the village since everyone used first names as terms of address and reference. Even though they lived within a couple of blocks of each other, Johnny's calls and visits to his mother gradually diminished after he and Anne were married.

First his mother and later his wife made decisions for Johnny and took responsibilities that he did not want to assume, and that became an integral part of who he was. His mother, his wife, and the Lord give him direction in life. He dropped out of school, balked at the offer to try out for a city-wide baseball team, and refused to accept an offer of vocational training that would have taken him away from home. He backed away from opportunities in preference to staying within the known, comfortable world of the neighborhood.

Talking about the difficulties of his childhood, Johnny said that he failed two grades in elementary school and then failed the seventh grade. That made him the oldest child in his grade, and like most sixteen-year-olds in the village, he decided to drop out of school. He said that school learning was hard for him, and it was better to drop out of school rather than spend another four or five years trying to graduate from high school. He said that by dropping out of school, he could begin working immediately and living as an adult with his own money instead of being a "kid" in school. The choice was easy.

So, I told mother when I turned fifteen or when school was out…I wouldn't have been sixteen til November. School starts back in September, and then you couldn't quit school until you was sixteen. And if I had went on, I would have been in the eighth grade when I was sixteen. I told mother that I wanted to quit and go to work.

Mind you, the people told me, when they found out around there, that I would regret it in years to come if I quit. And so, I told mother that I wanted to quit. One day Esther and Billy Joe was out playing, and daddy was working. She and I sat down, you know, and I was drinking coffee, and she told me how it would be. 'People with good educations gets the good jobs, and the ones not with education breakin their backs and not making no money.'

We had a real long talk about it, and she said, 'If you set your mind to it, you can do anything that you want to do. Any kind of work that you can do, you just have to have confidence in yourself.' She said, 'Now, I'm not going to tell you that you can't quit, and I'm not going to tell you that you can quit.'

So, I decided that I was going to quit. And the first job that I ever had was delivering groceries right up here on Creek and Pleasant Tree, man was named Mr. Reardon. I can truthfully say that I don't regret it a bit. I worked for Mr. Reardon off and on while I was fifteen. I worked there a year and quit and went and worked in the mill for about nine months.

As Johnny talked about school, he told me about sports, authority defying escapades, his teachers, and the social embarrassments he suffered. He remembered not having clothes and not having money and being shamed by the teacher for depending on his sister. He studied little and would frequently get his homework from Esther. Although she started one year after he did, Esther caught up with him because he failed the first grade. However, when he also failed the fourth grade, she passed him, and he was left alone without anyone to depend on.

Johnny dropped out of school as soon as he could. He was aware that his lack of formal education would be a handicap for employment but felt that it was better than staying in school. In contrast to his brother and sister, he did not express regret at having dropped out of school, rather only a fatalistic acceptance of that as a part of his life. He expressed to me this way,

I never was too much on school no way. Why, my dad never went to school but one day in his life. He didn't like it and ran away. They never did make him go back. He can count and add and figure things as good as anybody. He learnt it himself. He educated himself.

I didn't get along too well down at school. I never did like to read too much. Now, I'll read something like the sports in the paper, but nothin like schoolbooks. Those teachers always gave me a lot of trouble. They never did like me down there no way. And I guess you'd say it was mutual. I'd rather a been out playin ball anyhow.

Men Narrating Their Lives: Defying Authority

Masculinity was demonstrated by defying authority, and Johnny and other young men had stories of mocking authority in school. These were always personal stories from the storyteller's own experience, and they were usually told years after the event and accompanied by laughter. These escapade performances were limited to young men and served for masculine identity by showing a disregard for physical injury and authority that women were not expected to show.

Among the more sensational stories told by boys were escaping from school by swinging out of the second story window on a flagpole chain and throwing shot gun shells into the school's furnace. More mundane escapades included smoking in the bathroom, cutting class, throwing food, and shirking responsibilities. An event qualified as an escapade if someone successfully fooled an authority figure, and the best escapade was to outsmart the police without getting caught. There was great hilarity throughout the village when one teenager outwitted fifteen officers from the city, county, and state police forces by escaping when he was surrounded in a house. He was not generally liked because of his budding criminality, but no one informed on him, and he became the hero of the moment. Everyone in the village talked of his exploit.

Johnny told me this story about his escaping from after school punishment when he was in school.

I was in the seventh grade, and I was in Miss Stone's room, and I was talking in class. I guess that was the only time that teachers ever had any trouble with me in school. Miss Stone caught me talking about ten minutes til 3:00, and we got out at 3:00. She said, 'You stay after school.'

I said, 'O.K.' About five minutes til 3:00 I asked if I could be excused [i.e., to go to the bathroom]. She said, 'Yeh.' So, I went on home.

So, the second day, she says...she was waitin for me when we lined up to go in her room, she says, 'Now, you ain't gettin no recess, and you're goin to stay after school.' Said, 'The onliest thing that you get to do is eat your lunch,' Said, 'The rest of them can go out to recess, and you're goin to stay with me.' So, she let me eat lunch, you know. So, when recess time come, I had to sit with Miss Stone.

So, about five minutes to 3:00 she was puttin up on the blackboard what she wanted other people to do for their homework. While she was writin that, well, I eased out the door and went home again. Well, the third day, she said that she was goin to carry me to Miss Sheets' room, that was another teacher across the hall, and she kept me over there. While she was talkin to Miss Sheets, well, I broke and run.

The fourth day she put me at the head of the line and told Willis Day to watch me, and me and Willis were just like that [holding up two fingers together].

So, she went in there and talked to Miss Sheets, and I run again. Then, the fifth day, Mr. Shafford was a teacher then. He's the principal up here now. Well, he come and got me about fifteen minutes before 3:00 and carried me in there to his class, and he stood at the door you know. He dismissed his class.

He said, 'Well, I believe you have been givin Miss Stone a little bit of trouble this week, not wantin to stay after school.' He said, 'Here's what I want you to do. I want you to write 2,000 times, 'I will not talk in class.' He said, 'You think you can remember that?'

I said, 'I don't know.'

He said, 'Well, I'll write it down.' Well, he got the chalk. Now, mind you, we was up on the second floor. Outside that window was a flagpole with a big ol chain. In fact, the chain was layin in the window, and while he was writin I got in the window. This was right before school was out, and while he was writin on the blackboard. I eased on over and got that chain, and down and out of that window I went. When I got...well you could see the playground, we had recess right there you know. I dropped down about middle way of the ground and went up a little bank. There was a big ol high fence there, and I leaped that fence and took off. They never did write mother about it, but Monday mornin Mrs. Paul, our principal, was waitin on me.

She said, 'You risked breakin your neck not to stay in, and I'm not goin to try to keep you in any longer.'

It is a wonder that they didn't write mother about it, and if they had of. Well, I would have been in trouble.

Boys told stories of "putting something over" on a teacher. If the teacher became bitter at having been the victim, that enhanced the emotional value of the escapade. If a teacher seemed to discriminate against a student, the belief in destiny could make it seem that the teacher's dislike was irreversible, and that the student's fate was already determined. Since the dice were already cast, the young man felt free to flaunt the teacher's authority, cutting class or disturbing the class. By challenging the teacher, he challenged the teacher's lack of respect for him. Things were going to be bad for him anyway, and that attitude justified fighting back.

Telling their Story through Music

Music, both religious and secular, had an important presence in the lives of people in Cabbagetown. We will see more about religious music later, but to identify key themes in country music, I analyzed the texts of country music songs selected at random from local radio broadcasts.[4] Like the ballads of the Scotch-Irish mountain communities, country music narrated realistic life events and explored existential themes that resonated with the life experiences of people, such as romantic love, lack of faithfulness in love, work, travel, loneliness, and alcohol.

Although preachers denounced country music as immoral and sinful, country music songs narrated the disenfranchisement and alienation that would feed White nationalism and its Christian variant. The emotional power of tunes and lyrics in country music communicated compelling experiences. I would hear people humming the tunes of songs important to them, they listened to them on the radio, and some men would sit on their front porch and play or sing the songs that echoed in their minds. Historian Clifford Kuhn[5] refers to the early inhabitants of Cabbagetown as having "a rich musical potpourri of hymns, gospel, ballads, folk airs, minstrel tunes, and popular songs." That is consistent with what I observed in the latter part of the twentieth century.

Kwitcherbellyakin Tavern on Memorial Drive was essentially a men's club with country music. Country music played on the jukebox was a key part of the drinking experience, evoking memories of relationships and past experiences. The crux of that was captured by the 1990 hit by the group Alabama which says, "In the corner of my mind stands a jukebox, playing all my favorite memories."[6] The imagery of the jukebox in the bar recaptures the consciousness of such moments. I sat in that tavern many times, hearing the plaintive music of the jukebox with songs about life and love. I listened to men as they became maudlin drinking their beer and talking about their financial difficulties, problems at work, or disagreements with their wives. Often in the background I heard a country music song on the jukebox telling a story like the one they were telling me.

Older men, like Cecil Smith, did not go to bars, but they would sit on the front porch of their house and play their favorite songs on the mouth harp, the harmonica, with the tune calling forth the lyrics. Country music was a medium that expressed a belief system about the realities of life, starting with the difference in character between men and women. One of the largest genres of country music was about love, its loss, conflict between men and women, and the longing for what might have been. Country music appealed to the underdog, and some songs spoke to tension between workers and the authority figures who had power over their lives. Others spoke of nostalgia of small town or rural life, which was seen as having been better than urban life. Although country music was produced by a wealthy entertainment industry, it spoke to the working-class with authenticity and validity.

Anthropologist Aaron Fox[7] studied the role of country music in a working-class town in Texas, and he said that, "Country music is...an essential resource for the preservation of community and the expression of white...working-class identity." Like Fox's experience in Texas, country music was ubiquitous in Cabbagetown despite preachers denouncing it. In conversations men would make references to country songs, which I understood to mean the songs had some significance for them. The sharpness of a nagging sadness in one's mind could perhaps be eased as one listened to a country song, realizing that sadness was normal and shared with other people. In these songs people found feelings packaged and made beautifully real by country music singers.

Ninety percent of Cabbagetown residents regularly listened to radio, and thirty percent listened primarily to the country music station WPLO. The rest were divided between other types of popular music and religious programs. Country music and religious music were often intertwined in an almost indistinguishable flow in daily experience. People listened to the radio while doing household chores, eating a meal, or resting after work. People watched television programs that featured country music, and most people knew the tunes of country or religious songs which they would sing, whistle or hum during their normal activities. Parents would sing for children, relying on lullabies or their own favorite songs. Men who were drinking would sing melancholic songs that had lingered in their minds.

Men in Cabbagetown did not talk about romantic love, but country music could verbalize the stories of love and longing that they could not personally articulate. When men were sentimental about their families, they talked about how sweet and tender their children were, but they talked about their wives in an indifferent, off-handed way and would refer to them as "my old lady".

Ethnomusicologist Vanessa Paloma Elbaz[8] talks about the use of songs in describing life experiences, and I found that country music does that. Most songs were about the frustration and suffering over a lost love, sung in a plaintive tone and frequently referring to the man shedding tears. In these songs the man was portrayed as a passive victim of a capricious woman who left him, having no compassion for his longing for her. Filled with self-pity the song could become mawkish about his suffering. A country song could talk about a man's humiliation of being left by a woman, but it would be more difficult for the man to express those same feelings in his own words.

Songs such as "I Know You're Married, But I Love You Still", "If You're Lookin for a Fool", "Statue of a Fool", "Blackboard of your Heart", "Oh, Lonesome Me", "Flushed from the Bathroom of Your Heart" and "Two Arms, Two Lips, Too Lonely, Too Long" were examples of the man suffering over a lost love. In "From Heaven to Heartache" by Eddie Arnold the man assumed the responsibility for having done foolish things that caused the woman to leave. Now he was repentant and said that if he had another chance, he would never do it again.

In "Allegheny" the woman was furious because the man had made false promises to her, and then when she was asleep, he stole her money and left. Adolescent males sometimes projected this exploitive attitude toward women and talked about their sexual adventures with girls in which they hinted at getting the sexual favors they wanted and condescendingly left when finished. The familial control of young women suggests that such stories told by boys were more displays of their pretense and boasting than reality.

In "I Can't Believe That You've Stopped Loving Me" by Charlie Pride the man could not understand how such a perfect love was ended, and he was at a loss for what to do. Charlie Pride was the lone Black singer in the White world of country music, and there was an interesting dissonance in that people would listen to his songs, but they would not have invited him into their house to eat. It showed that a Black man could be accepted if he entered their world on their terms and sang their songs.

Work songs such as "Sock It to 'Em J.P. Blues" talked about small town policemen and justices of the peace exploiting truck drivers who were caught speeding. "Big Wheel Cannonball" was in the heroic mold of the old railroad songs from the past, claiming that the truck drivers who move the transportation network of this nation are the real patriotic heroes. "Little Johnny from Down the Street" was a patriotic song about a little boy who grew up to be a soldier and died in defense of the country.

"Louisiana Man" was about a more traditional struggle for existence by a fisherman in Louisiana. Two songs about a coal miner and an elevator operator emphasized the happiness that existed despite poverty. The heroic nature of these songs about work paralleled the everyday work experience of these men who knew long hours of back-aching drudgery at the looms and loading docks.

Travel songs had long been in the repertoire of country music, and they played on the chosen alienation felt by the traveling person who was far from his family. Four songs were recorded with this theme, all describing bus and train travel. In "Sitting in Atlanta Station" and "Atlanta Georgia Stray" the songs described drifting from town to town with no one important enough for the singer to stop and stay in one place. The subject was travel, but it was about loneliness and lack of community. This was made emphatically clear by Tom Hall's "Now I Sleep Good and Miss a Lot of Trains" which was about finding love and ending his traveling days. Few of the older people traveled any distance from Cabbagetown, but they understood the pathos of loneliness. Some of those who did travel, frequently returned with stories of the emotional pain and loneliness described in the travel songs.

Loneliness was a common theme, and it usually dealt with a man who had to leave his family to go to the city to find a job. It addressed the problem of the unemployed in rural areas and small towns that led to migration to cities. Since these men had to look for unskilled work, they usually did not have enough money to bring their families with them. Hank Snow sang of the loneliness of the man away from home working in "Come the Morning". "In Sunday Morning Sidewalk" Johnny Cash sang of being alone in a city on Sunday morning and becoming nostalgic about Sunday mornings at home with the family and church. "New York City" by Buck Owens mourned the crowdedness, impersonality, and pollution of big city life and dreamed of home with nostalgia.

I documented several songs on the use of alcohol, which was referred to alternately as a tranquilizer and as a sexual stimulant, suggesting a link between the two. Some songs referred to alcohol as a tranquilizer for the anxieties aroused by their marginal economic existence and austere lives. In "If I Had One More Dime, I'd Have Peace of Mind" the man was standing on a street corner begging for money to buy cheap wine, as the only way to calm his anxieties and enjoy himself. In "Gotta Be Right Back to Lovin You Again" the man says that he was going to drink more so that he would be sexually aroused to make love with the woman. Since sexual inhibitions were strong, alcohol was portrayed as helping people express sexuality.

"All of My Hard Times" talks about poverty and jail and the lack of anyone to help. In two more heroic songs "Cross the Brazos at Waco" and "El Paso" the man's love for a woman gets intertwined with criminality and eventually leads to his own doom. Petty criminality was not uncommon among the men of Cabbagetown. Since many men had the experience of spending a night in jail and putting up bail and paying fines, they could listen to those songs and empathize with the sense of hopelessness that was portrayed.

Country music romanticized the rural past and religion. The past often acquired an aura of sublimeness when it was portrayed in such songs as "Sunday Morning Sidewalk" which spoke of family and church in a small town and "Snowbird" which talked of innocent youth and "Times Were Good While They Lasted", which talked about a lost idyllic past. An idealized state of religion was presented in "Daddy Was an Old Time Preacher Man", which told about the simplicity and success of religious meetings in the old days. "On the Wings of a Dove" referred to an ideal religious state of God's love and protection, and "Let the Sunshine on the People" was how God could make daily life better.

There were humorous songs such as "Here Comes the Preacher" which was about a wayward preacher being chased up a tree by a bear and "Welfare Cadillac", which was about milking the welfare system and having a Cadillac. The stories emphasized the bravado of minor scrapes with the law, making fun of established authority and learning to fight.

Country music was rooted in the earthiness of the rural past of the people of Cabbagetown. It was bawdy when they could not be bawdy. It talked about love when they could not. It brought all the dirty laundry of one's emotions out of the house and put it on public display, frequently with such caricature and frankness that it could be uproariously funny, and no one denied the truths so openly portrayed.

This complex of evangelical superiority, masculine defiance of authority, disenfranchisement, and alienation became building blocks for Christian nationalism in Cabbagetown. The theme of defiance of authority, especially the federal government, was important in men's traditions, re-enforced in stories and song. If a politician spoke to their victimhood, men were listening, and they would not oppose someone who promised to support the sacred trust of keeping America Christian and making it great again, the metaphorical expression for maintaining White dominance.

Endnotes

1   Buck 2001:132-133

2   Fieldnotes. July 2, 1969

3   I observed four different behavioral patterns among men. In the older family (Cecil and Effie) Cecil had a secondary role. The older son, Johnny and his wife Anne, had a relationship in which Anne was the stronger force but without Johnny drinking or using harsh language against his wife like Cecil. The sister, Esther, had a conflictive relationship with her husband in which he would drink heavily to drunkenness and became verbally abusive. She terminated the marriage. The younger son, Billy Joe, and his wife had a less conflictive relationship, but he was clearly the "head of the household", and he would make condescending remarks to his wife on occasion.

4   There were 94 different singers of the 100 songs that I studied, 75 men and 19 women.

5   Kuhn 1993:45

6   "Juke Box in My Mind" by Dave Gibson and Ronnie Rodgers. © Copyright 1991. Maypop Music (a Division of Wild country, Inc.)

7   Fox 2004:21

8   Elbaz 2021

PART TWO:
THE EVANGELICAL BASE:
FIGHTING FOR THE SOUL OF AMERICA

Evangelical exceptionalism provided the ideological structure of beliefs and behaviors for the people of Cabbagetown. It ranged from the binary perception of the world divided between God and the Devil to the distrust of federal authority. This ideological structure justified Christian nationalism with its absolutism.

The evangelical preachers were the leaders advocating Christian leadership in government and laws based on biblical principles. Most preachers in Cabbagetown made politicized statements in their sermons, supporting Christian nationalism. They regularly spoke with racist and xenophobic overtones and called for a government that would impose Christian values on the land. Religious belief and practice in Cabbagetown included ethnic and racial discrimination, advocacy of religious superiority, and the call for family values, a euphemism for the rejection of women's liberation.

Chapter Six
Mama Was our Daddy Too

The campaign to make America Great and Christian started in the family. As we saw in the last chapter entitled, "Daddy Has the Devil in Him", some men did not go to church, had anti-clerical attitudes, and indulged behavior unacceptable to churchgoers. Many families had some internal church/anti-church divide. Women in those families often perceived their relationship with such husbands as a struggle between "the Lord" and the "Devil". Women were more identified with being religious and attending church, and they repeatedly reclaimed their Christian behavior was superior to men's anti-clerical attitudes.

These binary family relationships were parallel to the larger society around them. In this evangelical world, life was divided into good and bad influences, Christian and non-Christian. Ultimately that would mean that political differences were also either Christian or non-Christian, giving a foundation for the need to make America Christian. As the belief in evangelical exceptionalism morphed into the political movement of Christian nationalism in the 1970s it became inherently linked to the idea that America could only be great if it were Christian.

Women churchgoers frequently talked about their cause being righteous and God given, but many men did not accept that religious narrative. Those men did not have room for being "church good" within their masculinity, and tended to be skeptical about churches and preachers. Men often shared the Christian cosmology of a dualistic supernatural of God and the Devil and Heaven and Hell with women. Both were commonly supporters of the idea that government should be Christian, and they would vote for the candidate who supported Christian values.

The familial and religious behaviors of women were nuanced, and some were more religious than others and some more outspoken. Since women were the primary churchgoers, we will look at their experience to see how Christianity functioned in the gender divide from their perspective.

Women and Family Networks

There were three large mill worker family networks in the neighborhood, each composed of two or three extended families, which were the focus of daily life.[1] When someone needed critical support, they turned to family members. These family networks were three or four generations deep, and each could trace its descent back to someone who came looking for work in the mill in past decades.

- The Williams family network was associated with the director of the Neighborhood House.
- The Jones family was a smaller family with a problem of alcoholism in the family.
- The White family was a larger family network.[2] Corey White was the grandmother and great-grandmother of this family, and the extended families of her daughters Effie and Ruthie and their fifteen children formed the nucleus of this family network. This family was the center of my research.

The central person in each of the three family networks was an older woman. It seemed that women had developed managerial and decision-making skills through the years of child-rearing and household management while men working in the mill were largely involved in routine, repetitive work with few decision-making opportunities. Just as middle-aged women were flourishing as managers, some husbands were drifting away from them into an alcohol induced never-land.

Social life was largely focused on visiting relatives in the extended family, and conversations were focused on family members and what they were doing. Children visited easily from the house of one family member to another and could virtually live with their cousins, and they had frequent contact throughout childhood with these extended family cousin groups. Kerri Arsenault[3] described her experience of growing up in a mill town saying that they had a large family, but there was always enough food, secondhand clothes, and affection to make a good life. Like Arsenault's description, social relationships in Cabbagetown were based on extensive family ties of trust and shared experiences.

The extended family was a major factor in village organizations, and it seemingly was the only factor that could sustain organizations, such as small Holiness churches. When Bubba, Ruthie's son and Effie Smith's nephew, organized The Lighthouse Church of God's Truth he turned to his family for support. Of the twenty or so people who formed the nucleus of his new congregation, all but three were family members. Effie had been attending Brother Adcock's church initially, but when she was criticized by one of Bubba's brothers, she began attending Bubba's new church.

When someone needed help, they turned to family members. When a woman was widowed, she frequently lived with one of her daughters, like Corey White did after her second husband died. The extended family group provided the primary emotional support for people within the family.[4] The family provided the most important emotional experiences, and the most positive and rewarding relationships that people reported were between brothers and sisters and children and mothers.

As religion permeated family life, it created a rhizosphere of beliefs, practices and assumptions about life, an environment conducive to a world view of the centrality of religion and the need to protect it.

The Mother: Effie White Smith

Effie's life was focused around evangelical values. She talked regularly about her beliefs; she lived a modest life; she when to church regularly; she read the Bible daily; she helped those in need; she prayed for the sick. She was known to have the "gift of gab", meaning that she was articulate and liked to talk. She spoke with me extensively about her life, the lives of her family and neighbors, and her religious beliefs. She was passionate about religion and could be combative with her husband Cecil because of his drinking and anti-clerical attitudes. She accused him of having the Devil in him, and their children agreed with her. It was a house divided, and Effie was more verbally aggressive. She had the superiority of religious identity and used it against Cecil and his unchristian behavior.

One afternoon Effie Smith was explaining to me that things had not changed since the beginning of time when God created people. She said that although we are God's creatures, we had lost the pureness and innocence that

Adam and Eve had at creation. Now, people are sinners and evil and only by special effort can we keep ourselves in God's path. Some people are rich, some poor, some healthy, some sick, some Black, some White, but the most important dichotomy was between saints and sinners, those who were "saved" and would go to Heaven and those who were "lost" and would go to Hell.

As proof of what she was saying, she referred to Genesis 1 in the Bible. She said,

In the beginning God created the heaven and the earth...every one of them is made in God's own image, and He gave them a mind. He gave them so much faith, and He gave them eyes to see with, and He gave them everything they needed. When he created man, he put so much faith in their bodies and in their heart, soul, and mind. He gave them that understandin. He did that when he blowed the breath in Adam's nostrils. He gave them everything they needed.

Effie was explaining to me her belief that the human character was inherently flawed as evidenced by Adam and Eve in the Garden of Eden. When God placed the primeval couple in the Garden and prohibited them from eating of the Tree of Knowledge of Good and Bad, the Devil was also present, and he convinced them to disobey the commandment of God. When Adam and Eve disobeyed and ate of the forbidden fruit, they condemned all future people to be born sinners, setting the essential human character to be evil.

People in Cabbagetown regularly referred to the Adam and Eve story in Genesis as setting their destiny. Some people repent and are "saved" from an evil life and follow the Lord, but those who refuse are accused of following the Devil. For true believers, life has two choices, either good or bad, God or the Devil. The differences were absolute, not allowing for nuance or flexibility.

Christianity and the belief in its unquestioned superiority gave Effie legitimacy as the moral spokesperson for the family. Christianity was the dimension of her life that she talked about most. In every conversation she would mention ideas she recently read in the Bible, or talk about a sermon she heard, or speculate about the rightness or wrongness of a neighbor's behavior. Christianity was the authority in her life, and she followed the teachings of her church, as well as negotiating to shape them. Her strict observance of the Christian lifestyle assured her social and self-respect.

Her son Johnny told me one day, "Our Mama was our Daddy too," and that was a telling observation. As I observed the two generations of life in this family, first the parents (Effie and Cecil) and then their adult children (Johnny, Esther, and Billy Joe), I came to understand that the older generation of women were the stronger figures in their families, a role legitimatized by their religious identification.

When Cecil avoided assuming responsibilities and social obligations, Effie assumed them. Effie maintained the social relationships through visits and conversations, took care of sick relatives, paid the bills, bought the groceries, loaned food or money when someone was in need, and prayed for the sick. As the children reached adolescence and adulthood, Effie's role evolved into an authority figure for the emerging extended family of children, spouses, and grandchildren. Like most Cabbagetown families Effie was the emotional keystone that held the Smith family together. She influenced the behavioral decisions of her children through advice and approval or disapproval.

When Johnny, Effie's oldest child, was about to get married to Anne, Effie told Anne not to marry him because he was too much like his father and would not be a good husband. Anne married him anyway. During the years I was in the village, I observed Effie continuing to advise, if not instruct her children, on multiple occasions.

Effie's father had died when she was young and when her mother Corey re-married, Effie was initially shocked and opposed it, but she quickly followed suit, getting married to Cecil, the son of the man her mother had just married. Effie was twenty-four and two years older than Cecil when they were married, both anomalies in the village. Effie's sister Ruthie was married at thirteen, and her own daughter Esther was married at fourteen, so being married at the age of twenty-four was unusual for a woman.[5]

When I met Effie and her husband Cecil, they had been married for more than 30 years. Effie was 56 then and Cecil was 54. While both were about 5 feet, 6 inches tall, Effie was slightly plump, weighing perhaps 150 pounds, and Cecil was thin at perhaps 130 pounds. Cecil was called "Little Dad", and Effie was called either "Mama" or "Big Mama" or even "Mean Mama", and those terms seemed to define the difference between them.

No religious woman would smoke or have alcoholic drinks, which must have led to better nutrition and health for them, compared to their husbands.

Meals heavy with potatoes, beans, and cornbread could lead to "middle age spread" for women who became more physically imposing as they grew older. Cecil's nickname not only referred to the fact that he was physically smaller, but I think it also referred to his smaller role in the family. Effie had been a bit older and more mature than Cecil when they got married and that difference seems to have continued with age.

The third person in the household was Corey, Effie's mother. When I met her, she was 72 years old having been born in 1896. They called her "Little Mama" because she was barely 5 feet tall and slim, weighing little more than 100 pounds. I saw Corey regularly when visiting Cecil and Effie. She talked to me about arriving to Cabbagetown and told me about the gossip in the community. She would speak in soft asides to Effie, but she was largely a silent presence. She helped clean the house and do kitchen work, but when Effie and Cecil fought, she would take the Bible and sit quietly to one side and read. Corey was a small, wistful person who seemed to be bundled in a shawl summer and winter. She liked to dip snuff, and in the evenings after dinner, I would see her with snuff in her lower lip, and she would occasionally lean over and spit into a can she kept by her chair.

When Effie's children made important life passage decisions, they regularly consulted with her. When Johnny and Esther chose to drop out of school, they turned to Effie to discuss it. Favorite teachers, best friends or other secondary relationships seemed to be relatively unimportant at such times. In fact, the reasons for quitting school were normally related to the familial situation, such as the need for another worker in the family or the decision to get married, which for young women seemed to be as much about leaving her parents' home as it was toward setting up her own married family.

Esther: The Religious Daughter

Esther was the daughter of Effie and Cecil Smith, and she and her husband Dewayne continued the pattern of religiously based gender conflict into their generation. At the time of these interviews, she was thirty years old and divorced with four children. In her early twenties she had a dramatic conversion experience, and afterwards, she devoted herself faithfully to acting out the religious tenets of the Holiness way.

Lewis Rambo[6] argues that a conversion experience can only be understood within the personal and family experience that the person is living, and we can see that with Esther. Her husband's lifestyle included drinking, spending considerable time in bars, playing pool, and associating with people who were not religious. Before her conversion she had experimented with her husband's world, smoking cigarettes, wearing pants, using make-up, and even going once to a tavern to drink beer trying to connect with him. She told it this way,

My husband, he would drink and go out every weekend and dance and all that. I would more less try to fight him or try to make him think that if I was gonna turn out like he was that would change him. But that's really bad. 'Course I was with him. I think it's shameful, but the Lord knows this, so I don't care to tell it.

123

But he was at this beer joint, and I've never been in a beer joint in my life. But I started in there. And naturally he would 't dare have me to go in that beer joint. So, he said [later], 'If you ever go in there again...' And he nearly hit me.

But I was just gonna be real smart that night and...A man told him, he says, 'Dewayne, here comes your wife.'

And he says, 'What are you doin?'

And I said, 'I come for some beer.' And of course, he had the can of beer in his hand. And so, he says, 'Well, if you want it here it is.' And so, the throws my head back and puts it in my mouth. And when he did, it humiliated me. Oh, it made me awful mad. And it embarrasses me to death. And then it just flies all over me and makes me awful mad. And then, I just take it and drank it. And so, then he went back and got another one, and he kept on til I had drank three or four, and I was lit. I was really looped. And so, then he takes me home and feeds me soup and all and says that he wouldn't have me die like that for nothin in the world.

But I made up my mind that night. I said, 'My God, if it takes me changing like you to change you, I'm afraid you'll have to die like you are. Cause this is it. I'm sure not goin to do this anymore.' And I didn't. So, he was always rough.

With her conversion Esther adopted religion as the organizing focus for her life much like her mother, and she became a moral spokesperson within her network of friends and relatives. Her children were loyal to her, and she encouraged them to rely on her and her judgments. She did not believe that her ex-husband was capable of socially responsible behavior because the Devil was in him, just like her father. With her children the gender pattern of behavior seemed to be repeating itself into the third generation.

Sarah, her fourteen-year-old daughter was doing well in school, and Esther gave her considerable responsibility in managing household affairs, and she hoped that her daughter might graduate from high school and go to college. In contrast, her three younger sons were doing poorly in school, and she did not expect them to graduate, but she hoped that they would stay in school at least long enough to get a basic education. She feared that since they were boys, they were susceptible to going the way of the Devil like their father and grandfather.

She was establishing her own moral authority and gaining the respect of her family and friends and the loyalty of her children. Her ex-husband's arm tattoo, "Born to Lose" accurately depicted his role in that family. Esther grew up with low expectations about men even though she dreamed that it would be different in her life. Then, her own married life became like her parents' marriage. The difference was that she divorced her husband, which her mother never did. By marginalizing her ex-husband and eventually divorcing him, Esther became the primary influence in the lives of her children.

Esther was one of the few Cabbagetown people who never failed a grade in school even though she dropped out to get married when she was fourteen.[7] As Esther spoke with me about her life, she felt that she had a smoother relationship with her mother Effie over the years than her two brothers had. Effie did not approve of Esther's decision to get married, but contrary to her attempted interference with Johnny's marriage, she did nothing to stop her. Esther had strong conflicts with her husband, Dewayne, over the role Effie had played in their lives, and he said that Effie "put things" in Esther's mind. Eventually the conflict became so strong that Esther got a divorce, with Effie's blessing.

Esther told me the following,

Well, I remember when I first went to school...We'd go up to the front of the room and sit in a little circle and have reading. I liked reading. I liked writing. I liked school in general. I loved my teacher, Miss Simpson. I never had a teacher that I didn't love.

And then I was real happy when I passed into the second grade, and Miss Kahn was my teacher. She used to get me up every morning, and I'd read out of the Bible. We used to have Bible reading every morning, first thing every morning. Brother [i.e., Johnny] failed the first grade, and I started the next year. I'd take his lunch money to him every day, and just seems like I kept progressing and getting a little better and a little better.

I was always real conscientious about my work, and if I was to come to a problem that I didn't understand, I'd go to the teacher, and she'd explain it to me. And seemed like after she explained it to me as an individual, I could understand it better than when she explained it to the whole class.

125

Esther's account of her school experiences dealt with skill development, starting with learning to read and write. Her comments were sprinkled with references to good grades and being conscientious about her work. She had difficulty with geometry and rejected science because it challenged her religious training. She most liked art and home economics classes.

Then in geometry...I never did understand much in geometry when I was in the seventh grade. I just figured well, I don't understand this, I can just write anything down. Now, that was a bad mistake that I made because if I had really dwelt on it and studied it, I would have learned it. I always made fairly good grades, even when I went to high school. I liked all of that, and I'd a went on to school, I guess, and finished if I hadn't a met that scalawag that I married.

She said girls were more intelligent than boys but felt that eventually they sacrificed their own better abilities in preference for a husband and family. With real pathos she regretted getting married at fourteen rather than completing her education. She felt that fate had her locked into her current way of life with no possibility for escape, and she had four children to care for, and she was divorced from her husband.

I went seven years to grammar school. I finished two years of high school, then I dropped out. I just thought, 'Well, now is a good time to get married and be your own boss.'

When daddy heard about it, he hit the ceiling! But he was always real strict, he didn't want me to go with any boys at all. When I asked mother about it, she said, 'Is that what you want?' I'd tell mother anything, and she'd tell me anything. If I had a penny, I'd go to the store and buy a piece of bubble gun and bite it half in two and take the other piece to my mother. So, I would confide in her just like you would a very dearest friend.

I wanted to get out of school and set up my own house and get married and have a little girl, and I'm goin to get nice furniture and stay home and tend the house and take care of my little girl.

126 *My mother told me, 'Honey, you'll be lucky if things turn out like that. You're better off not to get married too soon. Some ol boy'll tell you nice things at first and when he gets you where he wants you he won't be no good to you no more. He won't give you nothin but headaches and a house full of kids. Then, he'll stay drunk all the time, and you'll have to support him too. Johnny if you get married I better never catch you or your brother either treatin your wives like that. You do, and I'll tell em what to do with you. Your Daddy was goin to be a good man and look at him in there on that bed. But if you pray to the Lord, even if your lot gets hard, he'll take care of you. Don't ever forget what your Mama tells you. Stick with the Lord.'*

So, she asked me if that's what I really wanted. I said, 'Mother, I would hate to run away and get married. I know that would hurt you awfully bad.' And so, I said, 'I want to be married, and if you will, I want you to sign for me.'

So, she signed for me. She said, 'You know that you are mighty young and that it'll always be my fault if things don't go right for you.' And so, I said, 'No, you mustn't look at it like that. This is a chance that I'm takin. If things don't work out fine, you'll never, never hear me say, 'Well, mother if you hadn't signed for me.' Cause if she hadn't a signed I probably would have run off.

Esther learned her role as a woman after the model set by her mother with whom she closely identified. As early as four years old she had already learned to take care of her five-year-old brother, Johnny. Instead of a mutual collaboration, their relationship was one of the stronger sister protecting and caring for the weaker brother. By the time she entered adolescence she could no longer tolerate the confines of her subordinate position in her parents' family, and she sacrificed further education for the need for independence that she would have as a married woman. As a mother, she had continued the pattern of being the strong figure, re-enforced by her adherence to religious principles.

Well, this is the way most women look at it, they think, 'Well, I won't want to go to work anyway, and all I want to do is set up housekeeping and start a family.' That was my heart's desire to grow up, marry and have a little girl, and all my life that's what I wanted. But I should have waited, but a girl, they'll think, 'Well, education is not really important to me. I know enough to get by, and I don't really want to go to work anyway.' And so why not just go ahead and get married and be a tending to your own house and then you can keep house while the husband is out working.

127

According to Esther, she had always shown respect for the authority figures around her including her mother, her teachers, and her minister, and she never mentioned conflicts with her mother, even when she was marrying and leaving home. She and Effie discussed the matter of marriage, and Effie signed the permission for her to get married under the legal age. She always sought her mother's companionship and shared everything with her. With her teachers and currently with her minister her attitude had always been acceptance of authority.

Esther described her dramatic conversion experience when she received the "gift of the Spirit." Although she had been raised in a Christian setting, she had not considered herself a Christian until that climactic day when she was "born again" in her conversion experience. Her husband, who was not a Christian, had insisted that they go to church. She told it this way,

He said, 'I'm goin to take my sister home, and when I get back, you be ready, and we're goin to take the children and go to church.' It was Mother's Day. I said-, 'No, I don't care to go to church. Besides, our clothes is not fixed, and it seems funny ironin clothes on Sunday to go to church. And nevertheless, he said, 'You be ready when I get back, and we are goin. So nothin would do him, but...And I had painted my fingernails and toenails that mornin...When he come back, he said, 'Come on, let's go.' So, we went.

The street by the church was three parts, and we didn't know it. And it was a new church. He's always known Brother James, the pastor of my church. He's always really loved him, but anyway they had moved the church. And the church

was on Bass Street, and it had three parts to it. And we didn't know it, and so we went down the first street. And that wasn't it. And we rode down another street, and then it picks up and that wasn't it. And he said, 'Well, if it's the Lord's Will for us to find the church this'll be right down here.' So, sure enough we turned down that other street, and he saw Brother James' little ol Chevrolet. He said, 'Yep,' said, 'there it is.'

Once they were in the church, she said that her only thought was to leave and go home, but something else was to happen that night.

And I was wantin to hurry and get home and get out, of Sunday clothes, cause I wore pedal pushers and slim jims about all the time. And wanted to hurry and get me a cigarette and get out of that hot dress.

And it was real hot that night, and anyway we went on in, and he preached. And I don't remember much about what he preached about. I just remember he said something about a ship and blood, but anyway when he started to give the altar call, you know, that's where they invite you to come down and pray if you want to, and he said, 'Is there anyone here who is lost, and they know if they die they would go out to meet God unprepared?' Well, that didn't faze me at all, you know. I just thought, 'Well, I've never committed any big crimes. I've always been a pretty good girl, trustworthy, and all that. Really, I don't need prayer, and that's what I thought. And he said, 'If you know that you are lost and on your way to Hell, and when we pray, if you would like for us to call your name in prayer and ask mercy on you as a sinner, and be merciful unto you,' he said, 'just let it be known by raisin your hand.' Well, my husband raised his hand!

And I'm tellin you that just went all over me. I just thought, 'Now, some-body as mean and wicked as he is acknowledgin the fact that he needs prayer, and I'm so high and mighty that I don't think I need prayer.' And brother, I run down to that altar. I didn't wait then, I run down there, and of all the cryin and prayin and askin God for forgiveness. And then, I saw myself like I really was.

And so, I just cried and prayed and asked God to forgive me, and then I was real sorry for the things that I had done to crucify the Lord. And I was just cryin, and I just got so happy. And somehow my shoes come off, and I looked down at them big ten toenails, and I knew that it was wrong. I said, 'Lord, if you'll forgive me for puttin that stuff on my nails, I'll never do it again the longest day I live.'

And something just come all over me. And I was a shiverin and a shakin, and I just couldn't control it. There wasn't no way that I could control it, and I didn't know that much about the Holy Ghost. And I know that the Bible says that all manner of sins shall be forgiven to man. You can even blaspheme God and get forgiveness for it, but there is no forgiveness for blaspheming the Holy Ghost, not in this world, never, in the world to come, never. And so, I thought that I had felt so good because I had got converted. I felt like if Jesus had left Heaven and come down and sat in my lap. I couldn't be any happier, and so, I thought that was why I was so happy. I could tell that I had really been changed, and I could tell that a new life had come in me, and that old man was dead, and now I was a new creature. I felt like that I lifted my feet off the floor that I would just start flyin. That's just how I felt.

For Esther conversion was a dramatic, personal experience with God, a direct connection with the supernatural that some defined as a scintillating feeling overwhelming the body. It was a mystical experience that was accompanied by intense emotional states. The psychological effect was to give her a sense of meaning and moral focus and confidence in her new religious life. Her conversion also symbolized social identification with religious people and making a public declaration of giving up immoral behaviors. The anthropologist Simon Coleman[8] describes charismatic Protestant conversion as totally surrendering oneself to the all-encompassing spiritual presence of God, followed by glossolalia and spirit possession, and that is what Esther described.

Her conversion was a dramatic psychological event that brought a marked reorganization to her life and gave her a new focus and purpose. She became a member of the Fire Baptized Holiness Church, and after she was divorced from her husband, she and her children lived on the second floor of the church building. The church was small, and she was close friends with all the members. She attended the three regular church meetings each week and any special one that occurred.

Robert Jones[9] explains "sin and salvation" as permeating Protestant life, and this can be seen in Esther's experience. Before Esther's conversion, conflicts in her life were becoming increasingly tense. Her husband Dewayne lived an "ungodly" life, and she had been raised to believe that kind of be-

129

havior was wrong, yet the emotional ties of marriage pulled her toward her husband. She decided that she could not go his way, and shortly afterwards, she had the conversion experience.

Her conversion seems to have been part of the gender conflict with Dewayne. She said that she did not think about being saved until her husband raised his hand asking for prayer, and she said, "that just went all over me." She ran to the altar and asked God for forgiveness.

She tried to establish a better relationship with her husband after her conversion by having more children which she interpreted as being God's will. She explained it saying,

> But then right after that I felt that it was my duty to give birth to another child. I never did believe in birth control. And I knew that birth control was wrong. And so, nine months to the day, well four or five days after, I had Sarah...
>
> He didn't change at all, and that's hard to understand...He wanted them to pray for him, but he wasn't willin to pay the cost himself, to give up the things that he had been doin. And you do have to give up things. We was married thirteen years... Aw, he would give anything in the world to be back. But I haven't seen him four weeks come Tuesday, and I better not see him.

Esther's mother Effie seems to have eliminated intimate relations with Cecil after their third and final child was born five years after they were married. She would have been twenty-nine or thirty years old at that point. Her conversion experience coincided with that time period, and she began to be actively religious. That conjunction of becoming religious and cutting off intimacy in the marriage at the same time seems to have left a mark in Cecil's mind because he regularly accused Effie of having an affair with her pastor even when I knew them. I saw a version of this clash between sex, gender, and religion in a number of families.

Esther had a different experience after her conversion, rather than curtailing intimate relations with her husband, she had two additional children. She said that she thought it was God's will to be intimate with her husband to help the marriage and having the additional children would help bond him to the family. When she saw that the marriage was not improving, she lost hope, stopped the marital relationship, and got a divorce.

Her attempt to rebuild the marriage was ill-fated because the husband did not change, nor did the marriage relationship, and she was no longer willing to live with him unless he joined her in becoming a Christian. For Esther Christianity differentiated herself from Dewayne and that led to the divorce.

The principles of right and wrong with which Esther had been raised were highlighted at the moment of her conversion. When she saw her red toenails after she had prayed for forgiveness, she knew that it was a sin. At that moment she promised God that she would never again use make-up of any kind. She dropped other sinful behaviors such as wearing pants and smoking cigarettes, and she started attending church, reading the Bible, and praying. Elaine Lawless[10] talks about the importance of the dress code for women and the almost total control of life by religion in Pentecostal churches, which I observed in women in Cabbagetown.

131

At the time of her conversion, Esther was almost twenty-one years old, and she had been married six years and had two children. She was beginning to be uncomfortable with her way of life, and it seems that her experience was part of her entering a new more mature period. After her conversion Esther talked about re-ordering the priorities in her life.

The anthropologist Diane Austin-Broos[11] discussion of conversion as a life passage seems to define Esther's process in which the person is negotiating their personal identity and their place in the world around them. She had been negotiating with her husband about the lifestyle they would share between his bar-oriented drinking culture and her desire toward a home-oriented family life. The linchpin to the way of life she wanted was religious practice, and her conversion was a public announcement of commitment to that way of life.

Esther's spiritual life story about her married life and conversion was richer in detail and substance than I had in any other interview.[12] Esther explained to me that as a woman she was more intelligent and morally superior to the men around her. Although she experienced considerable conflict within her marriage and eventually divorce, after her conversion she was at ease within herself. She was a Christian. She was on the right path and would go to Heaven.

Family Values in Popular Culture

Popular culture from country music to television shows portrayed women as mothers, the moral center of the family, and preferably religious. Country music was not necessarily a reflection of the life of the people in Cabbagetown, but the idealized or stylized images of love, religion, and the rural past portrayed in the music seemed to resonate with people.

Many of the country music songs I heard in Cabbagetown by women singers elicited feelings of distress about bad relationships with men and the importance of moral rectitude for women. Anthropologist Aaron Fox discusses the feelings elicited by country music, and he suggests that it stimulates memories of similar experiences that people have had.[13] There were women's songs about ideal love, but more were about unfaithful husbands and lovers. In "Giving Out of Givin In", "Still Love You" and "When You Want Something Different" the woman is telling her wayward husband that she is waiting at home for him. The song portrayed women in charge of the situation, knowing that the man would come back to them. The man was even referred to as a "pampered child".

In the song "Allegheny" the woman chased her deserting lover with dogs to recover her honor and her money. The attitude of the women in these songs was one of strength and self-control. The songs "Endlessly", "Forever Yours", "You'll Never Take Your Love Away from Me", "Still Love You" and mentioned the ideal of perfect love while "Man and Wife Time" and "We'll Build a Third World" spoke of collaboration between the husband and wife.

Women often sang about their indignation at the recklessness and irresponsibility of men, particularly in matters of love. The women were portrayed as suffering because of those experiences but expecting to win in the end. Although women in Cabbagetown tended to be more articulate about matters of love than men, I think these songs enabled them to remember feelings and desires that the harsh conflicts of their marriages had blurred out. The woman's role as moral arbiter was dramatically presented in several songs about "Fallen Women," in which their plight was bemoaned. Such songs served to warn women that they did not have the freedom that men had.

Except for the mill, women rarely worked outside of the home. The mill was safe because it was accepted as a traditional village workplace, essentially an extension of community life. The fear of a woman working other than the mill was that she would sacrifice the high moral standards women were expected to maintain. This fear was a dominant theme in honky tonk tunes. In "Queen of the Honky Tonks" a man says that he took his girlfriend to a bar, only to lose her to immoral ways. In "Honky Tonk Angels" Kitty Wells blames men for causing women to go bad, introducing them to the "wild side of life". But in contrast, "After Closing Time" defends the new generation of women working as waitresses and barmaids, telling of a woman who was faithful to her man even though she uses her attractiveness to get more tips. Waitressing was the theme in "Something to Brag About" in which the woman retains her virtue in a dreary cafe.

Music and singing can be a form of sexual control of women,[14] and country music explores the experiences of women that might be denounced in the church but not be explored there. The woman's voice in the church was to express her religiousness not her sexuality, which country music could express. The melancholic, plaintive tone of country songs conveyed a sorrow and unsureness about life that sometimes turned to religious themes. It was a marginal existence, where one could always be sure of suffering but never be sure of comfort.

The fact that sexual liberation was not acceptable for women is reflected in the country song "Mama, I Won't Be Wearin a Ring" by Peggy Little in which a young woman who went to the city only to come home pregnant and unmarried, a shame to herself and her family. The song starts by saying,

Mama, this big ole city is just like you said it would be. Heaven knows, I should have listened to you. It's hard to tell you all the things that happened to me, but trouble is so easy to fall into. Mama, I won't be wearin a ring...

"When I Reach the Bottom, You'd Better Be There" was about a woman who was adopting immoral behaviors to please her man, and she warns him not to abandon her. The woman who was morally corrupt was portrayed in "The House of the Rising Sun" and "Bed of Roses", songs about prostitution and promiscuity. These songs were done with heavy pathos, suggesting that the woman's life was ruined, and she could no longer live in acceptable society. Since women were expected to be the bulwark of community standards, it was a great tragedy if a woman passed over to the world of immorality.

Television

Although not as emotionally powerful as country music, television programs provided entertainment, a conservative view of the role of women, and religious programs. Women watched television more than men, and they selected programs consistent with their lifestyle and heritage. In the 1960s and 70s there were a number of programs reflecting life in the South that people watched most frequently in Cabbagetown.

One program was "The Beverly Hillbillies", a sitcom that ran through much of the 1960s, ending in 1971. It was a spoof on Appalachian people who discovered oil on their land and became rich, moving to Beverly Hills in Los Angeles. It included the dream of becoming rich, but more importantly it contrasted the hill country people with their human values with the pretensions of wealthy Californians. Cabbagetown people could identify with the Hillbillies, and the fantasy of becoming super wealthy and dealing with people of "high society" was entertaining.

Another popular program was "The Johnny Cash Show" a music variety show, featuring Johnny Cash and the Tennessee Three band that backed him. It was taped at the Ryman Auditorium in Nashville, the home of country music, and his guests ranged from country music favorites to Bob Dylan. Occasionally he sang gospel songs which was a popular part of the program, as were the times when he sang with his wife June Carter. The program ran from 1969 to 1971 and was among the most popular in Cabbagetown during that time, as it was across the American South.

Religious radio broadcasts became important in the 1930s with Father Coughlin, a Catholic priest who had a weekly radio program that attracted an audience of 30 million people. By the 1960s the airwaves provided a plethora of religious programming. Televangelists such as Rex Humbard, Billy Graham, and Oral Roberts drew audiences in the millions, and people in Cabbagetown watched them. Large churches in

Atlanta were broadcasting their Sunday morning services on television, watched by older or sick people who could not easily attend services. I noticed on occasion that a religious program would be playing on the television while people were mending or doing minor household chores, splitting their attention between the two activities. In the 1970s and 80s the televangelists from the religious right Jerry Falwell and Pat Robertson were drawing large audiences, and we will discuss their impact in the Epilogue.

Religious life and the family were important for Cabbagetown women, and their sense of Christian superiority gave basis for Christian nationalism in politics. They called for politicians who would support their values from racist ones to Christian ones. A politician who claimed to support Christianity in government was honored and valued like motherhood. Who could oppose a Christian politician? Even the anti-clerical men would support the idea of making America great with a leader who would support Christian values.

Endnotes

1   Beaver 1976
2   See Appendix Two for more information about the White family and the individuals with whom I had the closest contact.
3   Arsenault 2020:8
4   Weller 1965:59
5   Blank, Sallee and Charles (2007:1) point out that in mid-twentieth century in the United States girls could be married with parental consent at 12 or 14 years old in many states. By the mid-1970s most states had increased that age to 16 years old.
6   Rambo 1993:20
7   Block, Sallee and Charles 2007:1. In the 1940s and 1950s many states, including Georgia, permitted a girl to be married with parental consent at 12 and 14 years old. Later, the State of Georgia raised that to 16 years old, and in 2019 Georgia raised it to 17 years old. As of this writing there is no federal law banning child marriage in the United States, and individual states set different age limits.
8   Coleman 2003:16
9   Jones 2020:95
10   Lawless 1988:7
11   Austin-Broos 2003:2
12   Lawless 1989. Elaine Lawless also mentions similar life stories in her study of Pentecostal women in Indiana and Missouri.
13   Fox 2004:171-177
14   Elbaz 2016

Chapter Seven
I Will Walk among You and be Your God,
and You Will be my People

Long before MAGA, the combination of racism, the born to lose attitude, outlaw culture, and belief in Christian superiority were cultural elements shaping the linkage of Evangelicals with the prequel of that movement. They were advocating the establishment of a Christian government that would enact laws in accordance with Evangelical beliefs. To the fundamentalists among the evangelical people of Cabbagetown their God was the absolute truth that anchored all of existence, and they were true believers. They talked about Christian absolutism in government, created by a strong ruler who could guarantee that the country would be Christian.

The people of Cabbagetown saw themselves as God's chosen people, they reported the physical presence of God among them. Their experiences with God confirmed to them that their version of Christianity was the true one. The sense of superiority I encountered in Cabbagetown was that White people were better than Blacks. Holiness people were better than Baptists, who were better than communists and Jews.

Johnny Smith expressed it this way:

I've never had nothin', never did expect nothin', and the good Lord has taken care of me. Riches are a burden to the spirit, and I guess the Lord knows what he was doing by never giving us much...We've always had plenty of beans in the pot and cornbread in the oven and clothes on our backs. We've never really been wantin' for nothin'. The Lord has been good to us.

To author Joan Williams[1] the working-class poor were not focused on joining the more prosperous middle class, which is a foreign culture to them. They are more interested in staying in their own communities and culture although they would like to have more money.

Two-thirds of the people in Cabbagetown identified themselves as churchgoers, and all seven congregations they attended were evangelical. Sixty-five percent of the people surveyed said they attended either the Baptist church (40 percent) or one of the Holiness congregations (25 percent). With few exceptions every adult woman in Cabbagetown identified with a local evangelical church.

Prejudice Against the Other

Christianity has a deep history of rejecting people who do not accept its superiority, starting with Jews. Prof. Luke Johnson[2] points out that Jews were repeatedly slandered in the Christian Gospels, especially in the books of Matthew and John. Prof. Johnson has documented twenty-three different negative statements about Jews, with references to Jews as the people of the Devil and to the synagogue of Satan. In Matthew (23:1-39) the writer has Jesus saying that the scribes and Pharisees are hypocrites, blind guides, serpents, a brood of vipers, and children of hell. In the same chapter he says that Jews are vainglorious, pretentious, preoccupied with trivia and do not observe true religious practice.

The writer of Matthew goes on to accuse Jews of killing the prophets and the emissaries sent by Jesus. That writer also says that in the trial of Jesus before Pontius Pilate, Jews asked that the blood of Jesus be on them and their children. This de-humanization of Jews in the Christian Bible is parallel to the language Nazis used as justification for their mass murder of Jews as undesirable elements in the Third Reich.

In the God/Devil binary, Christians were on the side of God, and non-Christians, including Jews, were on the side of the Devil. Preachers in Cabbagetown repeatedly referred to Jews as foreigners, neither American nor Christian. Jews were said to be the people behind the Supreme Court rulings banning prayer and Bible reading in the schools. The euphemism of "communists" was regularly applied to Jews, a broader reference to anyone who was not Christian.

The Presence of God

In Cabbagetown the Lord and the Devil, the good and the bad supernatural beings, were opposing cosmic forces locked in conflict over the nature of humankind. People frequently referred to the Lord and the Devil in the same sentence, the eternal dialectic of good and evil in life. From preachers to common mill hands, men and women talked about these dueling cosmic forces going back to the beginning of life itself. God gave free will to humans at creation, and during their lives they are pushed and pulled between the Lord and the Devil in the exercise of that will. Even the most religious people had demons to control, and the Lord could help them do that.

I heard Rev. Davis, the Baptist preacher, and Brothers Adcock and Hoagy, Holiness preachers, re-assure the congregants that God was ever present, and his spirit lived inside of those who were true Christians. In interviews people confirmed that they felt God living within them, and that life was a struggle with the Devil. They saw the natural and supernatural worlds as being fused into a unitary existence. The personal experience of God in visions, faith healing, conversion, and charismatic states was the hallmark of religious identity. I understood this as the true believers being fused with the supernatural. Their oneness with God gave them a sense of superiority.

Christians told me of their being possessed by the spirit of God, and I observed many people being possessed or going into an altered state of consciousness in church services. Although Church-going people frequently talked about the Devil being in non-Christians, I did not observe Devil possession, nor did any non-Christian report being possessed by the spirit of the Devil.

God was a physical presence "walking" among them, and Johnny Smith reported God physically touching him. People reported God "speaking" to them. They talked about the afterlife in heaven and hell in physical terms. People would "burn" in hell and live a life of leisure and pleasure in heaven where people would meet each other and renew their human relationships. As I understood their concept of God, it was not the abstract supernatural that the philosopher Spinoza described but a human-like male figure who could physically interact with them.

The Banality of the Lord

People talked about their lives being in the hands of the Lord, and whatever happened to them was the "Lord's will". "If it's the Lord's will" punctuated daily conversations of church goer and non-church goer alike. People made the simplest promises contingent on it being the "Lord's will". People would describe unfortunate events (sickness, death, and poverty) and say, "The Lord

139

knows best", "The Lord has a plan", "It must be the Lord's will". For those who believed, Christianity and daily life were a closed system directed by God. Those who were religious seemed to think that their fragile existence on the edge of the economy could only be maintained by unquestioning loyalty to the Lord. In my conversations with people the "Lord" or God was the common reference point for the definition of good. "Thus, sayeth the Lord" was the dependable, absolute truth, and the churchgoers in Cabbagetown were true believers. People did not question God's truth.

The Lord/Devil duality was also used to explain social situations and even to threaten opponents if necessary. I was at the community sing one Friday night when a small group of people, mostly churchgoers of the White extended family, wanted to start a prayer service before the Sing. They said the selection of songs had become too secular and was influenced by the Devil, so it needed gospel songs to counteract the secularism. When the organizer of the Sing objected, Mary Ann Brown stood and warned all those present that they should be careful because the judgment of the Lord was going to strike them for standing in the way of his work. At that point she and those with her walked out, not to return. Mary Ann was a gospel singer and wanted the community sing as an outlet for her music. Rather than attack the organizers directly for denying her the role she wanted, she threatened them with the wrath of God. In her words, when the Devil was winning, God would strike back in anger.

The God of Cabbagetown was a wrathful God, especially in his combat with the Devil. Sermons were invariably marked by warnings from the preachers that the Lord would punish those who strayed to the ways of the Devil. In the face of sin, God could become angry,[3] and it was the image of this wrathful, vengeful God that mothers used to threaten their children as a means of social control, warning them that God would see any wrong they might do. No one could escape the ever-watching eye of God. In his book *The Cabbagetown Years* Eddie Sellars talks about growing up being taught the fear of God. He wrote,

As a little boy I was afraid of God...But God was made out to be something of a terror, always a watching eye, seeing if you were doing anything wrong.[4]

Spirits Walking among Us

Effie Smith told me about people having direct experiences with the supernatural, which went beyond the limits of human understanding. She had seen a spirit herself. Like Effie, other people expressed to me the belief that spirits could walk among the living and bring messages with spiritual insight. Folklorist John Burrison[5] says that experiencing supernatural figures and spirits of the dead was not unusual in Georgia, and it was important for a person to know how to deal with such events.

The presence of spiritual beings could bring fear or comfort, and Effie told me of her experience of seeing a dead woman when she was a girl. She and another girl were waiting for their boyfriends when Effie saw a woman she did not recognize walking near them. She pointed the woman out to her girl friend who began to scream, saying that it was her aunt who had bled to death on the steps of the house where they were standing. The girl ran away in fright, but Effie was so scared that she could not run. She stood there frozen while the dead woman walked up to the kitchen window of the house and looked in, and then she disappeared.

Shortly afterwards the same spirit woman came to Effie at night in a dream and led her down a path to the well near their house and had Effie draw a circle on the ground. The next day Effie was at the house alone when the other family members were out working. She went out to get water, but as she was arriving to the well, she saw her own footprints in the soft ground and the circle that she had drawn in her dream. She was so frightened that she ran back to the house without the water because she realized that the woman had brought her spirit there the night before.

Effie's son, Johnny, also told me about a vision he had when he was a teenager. He saw his deceased grandmother standing in the street in front of the house where she used to live, and he was so frightened that he would not go back to that street for weeks. People told stories of visions and miracles with some regularity. Although such events were extraordinary, they were seen as feasible because the Bible recounted incidences of spirits walking among the living.

Miraculous Healing

In addition to experiencing spirits, people in Holiness circles told me about miracles of faith healing. Almost everyone knew of miraculous healing that had occurred, usually involving cures of internal illnesses such as leukemia, cancers, tumors, and nervous conditions. Many people also attributed their being healed of influenza and body aches and pains to God's intervention. All miraculous healing people described to me occurred with illnesses that were in progress but that had not led to any physical damage to the person. But if an illness had done permanent physical damage, no faith healing could return the person to the pre-illness condition. For example, brown lung,[6] limbs disfigured by polio, or serious scarification were never corrected. Johnny Smith told of a serious health problem his wife had when she was pregnant that could not be healed by prayer.

When my wife was pregnant with him [4-year-old son] *her teeth got brittle and whitish, and it wasn't long before they started coming out. She is almost as toothless as her old mother now.*

Health was a matter of faith and religion, not necessarily of scientific medicine. Many people would say that it was only the Lord who could heal, and in some extreme cases people would say that medical doctors were completely useless. I heard people say, "Doctors only take your money. They don't care if you are healed, but the Lord does." According to this perception of health, all healing was ultimately achieved by divine intervention, giving rise to the countless stories of miracles, which were frequently enhanced by the claim that the medical doctor was totally amazed at the recovery, and occasionally the doctor was even said to have converted to being a Christian because of the miraculous healing that he or she had observed.

Some people who were "close to the Lord" were perceived as having the gift of healing, and people would seek their prayers for minor illnesses. Effie and her sister, Ruthie, were frequently called on by the people to pray for fevers, aches, and influenza, and in such cases the person did not even go to a medical doctor. The prayers of neighborhood people were often preferred because they would be available at night and on weekends, and no one charged a fee for praying for a sick person. Although these requests for prayer for healing would frequently go to a trusted woman in the community, men who were religious leaders, especially preachers, were also asked to pray over people who were ill.

The prayer of a local person was an act of religious kindness, and it would be repaid later by sending a cake of cornbread or other exchange of food. Furthermore, no social tensions were endured, as would have been the case in dealing with an upper middle class medical doctor. If the illness did not get worse, it was generally considered that God answered the prayer and stopped the illness, even though actual recovery might take days. If the illness was of a more serious nature or did not disappear within a reasonable period, the person might go to another person for additional prayer. Often the last option was to visit a medical doctor. If the intervention by the doctor were futile and the illness continued its progress, people would say that it was God's will that the person suffered with the illness. If it stopped, the power of God was re-affirmed.

Believing in miracles, people also expressed that "the Lord would provide" in any situation. I heard that phrase daily, and it could be used to explain almost anything. Even the impenetrable mysteries of life and death or power and wealth could be explained as the Lord's will. The belief that the Lord would provide what was needed assuaged the difficult periods of being sick or not having money.

Being Touched by the Hand of God

Johnny Smith told me that the Lord could be trusted for help. He told me about his personal experience when he and Anne lost their first baby, and it seemed as if she might also die. Although the doctors assured him that she would be all right, he was not convinced, and he called his mother to come and pray. He described it in these terms.

So, I got quiet for a few minutes, and mother got real quiet, and I knew that she was praying the whole time. So, she assured me that Anne was goin to be all right, and I got to believin that she was goin to be all right, and I got all right. Then, I guess that it was about an hour after that talk that the ol Devil jus got into me, and he says, 'Your wife is goin to die.' So, I asked mother, 'Anne is goin to be all right, ain't she?' Mother knew that the Devil was tryin to make me believe different, and she gritted her teeth and said, 'Yes, she is.'

143

Johnny said, "I got to believing that she was goin to be all right…" With that belief his anxiety was eased. He trusted his mother's prayer, and then he believed that Jesus would heal his wife. Johnny said that the Devil worked to destroy for the sheer sake of destroying, often with more success than the Lord had in creating good. If faith were lost, the Lord could not work. So, when the Devil almost destroyed Johnny's faith, Anne's life was in the balance. He was caught in this colossal struggle between the Lord and the Devil and only through personal fortitude and the social re-enforcement of his mother's prayers could he restore his faith in God, and he believed that saved Anne's life.

On the night that his wife seemed to be dying, he felt the physical touch of God's hand on his back. He told me,

I felt his hand on my back just like that [and he laid his hand on my back], *and I know that it was his hand because there ain't nothin no sweeter that ever touched me, and then I knew that she was goin to be all right.*

He was the only person to tell of having the experience of physical contact with God. Although the spirits of the dead people were frightening, the personal experience was perceived as a real and comforting presence. Effie Smith told me that being in the Holiness Way meant receiving the Spirit [i.e., spirit possession], living a clean life, and eliminating any intermediaries between yourself and the Lord. I interpreted the latter comment to refer to the long tradition of rejecting external authority among these descendants of mountain people. It meant that the clergy and the church should not interfere with a person's direct communication with God in the form of prayer, receiving the Spirit, hearing voices, and having visions.

Cabbagetown Churches

In Cabbagetown people attended seven different churches, not all of which were in the village itself. With an estimated population of 1,200 in the neighborhood, this gave an average of one church for every 171 residents.[7] The South has more churches per capita than any other region of the United

States at 15 churches per 10,000 people, one church for every 666 persons. Cabbagetown had 3.9 times that number of churches per capita, an abnormally high concentration of religious institutions.

One explanation for such a high number is the definition of "church". Most of these were more transitory congregations than churches. None of the Holiness congregations had an established church building, and four of the five were small "family" congregations, some with only a dozen or so adults, and they were not permanent organizations. They would last as long the family group could support it or hold it together. So, this phenomenon of small, transitory family-based congregations created this unusually high number of churches per capita.

The psychologist R.I.M. Dunbar[8] suggests that the religious fragmentation like I saw in Cabbagetown functions to re-enforce the internal cohesion of small groups, and that it is adaptive to nuanced differences in world view, but its contribution to cohesion and solidarity had the counter effect of intolerance against those outside the group, resulting in xenophobia, all of which I saw in these churches. For the Baptist and Holiness traditions each local congregation was a law unto itself, and each local preacher and church were free to develop their own messaging program.

I attended dozens of religious services, documenting the differences in religious practice, belief, and economic standing between the larger Baptist church and smaller Holiness congregations. The Baptist church attracted people of higher economic status,[9] and its members advocated more self-reliance, proclaiming that "The Lord helps them that help themselves."

This divide between churches and congregations was comparable to what Kenneth Morland found in Appalachian mill villages.[10] The church had been a central institution in the lives of the ancestors of these former mountain people before they came to Atlanta. Some reminisced about the happy religious days of their grandparents or great-grandparents in the rural past when church and religious meetings were important social gatherings. They imagined that life as being more secure, enjoying relaxed days with friends at religious meetings. One afternoon John King began telling me how he remembered churches from his youth in the Piedmont region of northern Georgia, and he described those halcyon days as follows,

145

Well, they had about the same type of churches that they have now but wouldn't ever see no brick churches. Back then, they was all wood buildings. In the summertime they would have meetings, have what they would call big, protracted meetings, and then out in front of the church they'd have big tables, and they wouldn't baptize like they do now all through the year. They wouldn't baptize but one month in the year, and they didn't know what a baptizin pool was like they got now in these churches. They'd go to a creek, a clear creek or branch, and they'd take ol slabs from a sawmill and dam that branch or creek up. Then, they let that water stay damned up you know way up until the summer when it would get good and warm. Then, they'd go there to that creek or branch and baptize them people.

Then, they'd have meetings, all day singings, big dinners on the ground. And boy, you talk about...you didn't see people go to church back then, today or tonight and come back a cussin and a fussin and a rarin and fightin like they do now. Everybody got along just as smooth and good.

In *Thank God for the Cotton: Memoir of a Mill Worker's Daughter*, Sybil Smith[11] tells her personal story of growing up with Christianity and the mill. Her grandparents came from the mountains of North Carolina and north Georgia, and they found jobs in a South Carolina cotton mill where she grew up. For her Christianity was interwoven with mill village life, and she says, "Cotton was a means used by God to anchor my life in His life-giving ways."

Becoming a preacher was one of the more glamorous means of making good. It was the most visible professional occupation in the village, and it represented considerable social and economic mobility with minimal formal preparation. As a preacher, a man could jump instantly from being a mill hand to being a white-collar professional with considerable prestige because of the religious nature of their work. Being a preacher did not require any specific education, but it required the ability to speak in public and to read the Bible. The two most popular and successful preachers from Cabbagetown had not graduated from high school. All the pastors of local churches were economically comfortable. Five lived outside of the village, and the one, who did live there, had one of the best houses.

Anti-Clerical Men

On the other side of the religious and gender divide were the anti-clerical men, who did not attend services because of negative attitudes toward the church as an institution. Cecil Smith, his two sons Johnny and Billy Joe, Claude Workman, and other men talked to me about religion as a matter of personal feeling, not church attendance. Religious people often accused them of belonging to the Devil because of their negativity toward churches and ministers. They, in turn, criticized religious people as being more interested in seeing who was in church, rather than the true spiritual quality of the experience. In contrast, the religious people replied to these anti-church accusations saying that the worse sin was to know about God and not accept him.

147

Cecil Smith criticized preachers saying they were only interested in money, and he also accused them of preying on women. Everyone knew the gossip about Brother Adcock, the popular, Holiness free-lance preacher. He was a tall, well-dressed man, who attracted women's attention. A few years ago, he ran away with the neighbor's wife and the two had to flee because the estranged husband pursued them with a shotgun. After a year he returned from his pilgrimage of fornication (as it was called locally) and sin, and his wife took him back. The neighbor woman with whom he left could not return to the village. She was shunned. He returned to preaching, regained his popularity, and had the largest Holiness congregation in the area. Most of his congregants were women, and husbands could become irate with jealousy over their wives' devotion to him. To Brother Adcock's followers, his sinful past enhanced his position as a warrior of the Lord because he had struggled personally with the Devil and sin, and he had won.

The preacher who was most criticized for taking money was also Brother Adcock, who could be called a religious entrepreneur. His services regularly attracted seventy-five people, and he collected money in all the services. In addition to the Sunday morning services, sometimes he held nighttime revival meetings in a tent during the week, which meant he was preaching seven days a week at times and collecting donations at every service. Since he personally received all the money from donations, he was economically successful.

During the winter he would make "mission trips" to Jamaica and other Caribbean locations to preach the gospel to the "natives who did not know about God", and he would ask for special donations from his congregants to pay for his trips. That seemed to appeal to the sense of Christian superiority and racism to Cabbagetown people, and they donated for him to take the gospel to the "ungodly people" in the Caribbean. For many who donated for his "mission" trips, visiting the north side of Atlanta would have been a rarity, and his winter trips to the Caribbean for a godly purpose must have been a dream-like fantasy.

148

Being Christian in Cabbagetown

Being Christian in Cabbagetown meant belonging to a church, having correct beliefs, practicing proper behavior, and having rightful intention.[12] Christian practice generally included belonging to a congregation and making donations to support it, reading the Bible, praying, and living a moral life.[13] The anthropologist Weston LaBarre,[14] who studied religious behavior among Appalachian Mountain people, commented on this submission to God as a lifestyle that was puritanical, fundamentalist, and intolerant. Religious practice and believing in Jesus as God were the path to salvation from an afterlife in Hell.[15]

The big fear in the community was that the Christian way of life was being threatened by the alien forces, the "Jews and communists", who had taken away Bible reading and prayer in the schools. They feared that those forces would outlaw Christianity itself and their survival was at stake.

On the other hand, Ed Kilgore[16] notes that the mixing of Christianity with nationalism is a formula for fascism. The evangelical belief in miracles and God's direct presence in human life led people to believe that God could create a miracle in government. Godly power was absolute. That raises the question of whether absolutism in evangelical thought would be comfortable with Christian fascism, if required, to realize the goals of making America Christian again.

Endnotes

1   Williams 2017
2   Johnson 1989:420. Prof. Johnson is the Woodruff Professor of New Testament at Emory University's Candler School of Theology.
3   Lefever 1970:32
4   Sellars 2018:118
5   Burrison 1991:11
6   Brown lung is a disease that developed from years of working in a cotton mill inhaling cotton fibers.
7   Indianapolis, Indiana is the city in the United States that has the highest density of churches per capita, and there it is one church for every 288 persons. https://www.businessinsider.com/cities-with-most-church-es-2015-6. Cabbagetown is 340 percent higher density of churches.
8   Dunbar 2012:59-60
9   Liston Pope documented similar information in Gaston County, North Carolina among mill workers. Pope 1965:96-116.
10   Morland 1958:108f
11   Smith 2017:13
12   Powell and Clarke 2013:10
13   Morality was defined by many as leading a simple life, if not austere, without smoking, drinking, dancing, cursing, fighting, attending movies, listening to secular music, having sex outside of marriage, or other hedonistic indulgences.
14   Labarre 1962:166
15   Morland 1958:137
16   Kilgore 2022

CHAPTER EIGHT
THE MYSTICAL PATH OF THE HOLINESS WAY

THE PENTECOSTAL HOLINESS PEOPLE brought a mystical element into the evangelical linkage to the MAGA movement. Their belief in faith healing and seeing spirits prepared them for supra-natural thinking and expectations. This pattern of thinking, not limited to the natural world, can open the believer to believing in conspiracy theories or the dream of God making America into a completely Christian nation.

Effie Smith was active in the Holiness church, and she said that it was a place where she could strengthen herself spiritually. The church was the most important regular gathering place in the community. Just as women defined and enforced norms within the family, so the preacher defined norms within Cabbagetown and could enforce them from the pulpit. Religious people used their church attendance to symbolize the uprightness of their roles as the possessors of truth.

In the evangelical congregations, both Baptist and Holiness, people referred to each other as "brother" and "sister". Holiness churches were more egalitarian with more direct participation than the Baptist church. People dressed more casually. Men wore their normal daily clothes rather than a suit or tie, and women tended to wear more common cotton dresses. More women depended on car-pooling, and the men who had a car were expected to take women to services. A man with a large car was a valued member of the group. The Holiness churches were smaller, poorer, and less stable, and they were organized around the person of the preacher and were made up of his family members or a following that he had developed. Since these congregations had fewer economic resources, most Holiness preachers were bi-vocational with other jobs during the week.

In both Baptist and Holiness churches the sermon was the core of the service, and it represented God's message to the people. Susan Harding[1] mentions that the "Word", as in the Bible or a sermon, could cause the unbeliever to convert when they hear it. Whether spoken or read, the "Word" has the power of God behind it. In the Baptist church the sermons were primarily evangelical, designed to convert a "lost" person who might be in the congregation. These sermons emphasized the dangers faced by those who were "lost", those who had not accepted the religious path in their lives. The sermons I observed in the Holiness churches were more about exhorting people to live according to Christian principles, and they were more about personal healing than proselytizing new members.

Church was also important for life passage rites, the two most important being conversion (seen as a re-birth in this life) and the funeral. When a person was converted to accept belief in Jesus as God, he or she was said to be "born again", and then the person was baptized to symbolize the new spiritual life they were to lead. These were happy events in which the baptized person was warmly congratulated and welcomed into the community of the church. I did not observe any wedding ceremony in a church in those years. No one could afford a church wedding, and young people often eloped before legalizing their marriage. So, a simple court-based ceremony was the norm.

The funeral services were marked by dramatic outpourings of grief, and the life of the dead person was recounted making emphasis on the positive or negative aspects of the example that the person had set. In the funeral an evangelizing plea would frequently be added, using death as a prod to those who were not "saved" to remind them that if they did not accept Jesus when they died, they would live for eternity in fiery punishment.

Evangelicals were divided among themselves, and Baptist and Holiness people believed their version of Protestant belief and practice was the correct, God-given path. Baptists were aggressive proselytizers, trying to bring people back to God. Holiness people thought the Baptist churches were not on the God-given path because they had a human hierarchy, which meant that full time clergy and administrators came between the people and God. The Pentecostal Holiness people were more local in organization with fewer layers of human influence. Both Baptists and Holiness people said that Catholics were not real Christians, the old Protestant belief from the time of Martin Luther.

The Pentecostal Holiness Way

One day I was talking with Effie Smith about religion, and she said, "Ron, I don't know nothin but Holiness." Although Evangelicals tended to be more politically active, Pentecostal Holiness people supported Christian nationalism as a means of protecting their way of life. Holiness preachers represented a range of opinion on the mixing of politics and religion. Some talked more about the need for the government to impose Christian values on the country to prevent it from being doomed while others tended to emphasize more mystical values from faith healing to spirit possession.

Effie went on to explain the Holiness way was a matter of being close with the Lord. She said that church attendance was not the only element in religious practice, but believing in Jesus and being right with God were. Although she said it did not matter which church a person attended, she made it clear that the mystical experiences of the Holiness church were the superior Christian path.

153

To Effie, Christians were God's chosen people. Christianity had replaced the Jews, who were benighted, because they had not accepted Jesus as Messiah when he lived on earth. The Holiness path was God's way. Nothing was better. She told me about encountering an old friend of twenty years at a revival meeting with Brother Adcock one night. The friend had always been a Baptist, but recently she had gotten the gift of the Holy Spirit and was now in the Holiness Way. Effie was happy because the woman would be closer to the Lord.

In his book *Millhands and Preachers*, Liston Pope[2] also mentioned that mill workers tended to move from Baptist churches to the Pentecostal Holiness congregations in North Carolina and that Holiness preachers tended to ridicule the character of denominational churches. I found the same in the Cabbagetown community.

Effie said that if a person claimed to be a Christian, he or she ought to be a walking sermon, being careful about what he or she said or did because sinners were constantly watching. She said,

That's the reason I try to do the things that is right. Sometimes I'm tempted, but my Lord was tempted too. That don't make me feel so bad. The inward man checks the outward man.

She liked to say that there were two of her, one a man [i.e., human] and the other a woman, and the more moral woman part could check the more secular human aspect of her soul, which could only be brought to moral observance through religious practice. As Effie continued, she said that through prayer the person could feel the Lord and commune with Him about one's most intimate and most important feelings. The Lord maintained direct contact with the person if the Holiness Way, and the person could feel inwardly what the Lord was saying. Sometimes the Lord spoke quite overtly. She recalled one instance,

When I told this lie, something spoke to me and said, 'Every lie you tell, I know about.' I got up and went all over my house looking to see who that was talking to me...I realized it was God.

According to Holiness belief I recorded in Cabbagetown, the natural man was evil and controlled by the Devil, but by converting to follow Jesus, people could attain a measure of goodness. Although they did not always understand why they had to be poor, somewhere in the Lord's unfathomable plan, there was a divine reason for things. People would say that the Lord knew better, and he would take care of their life in the way that was best according to his plan.

Holiness groups interpreted biblical texts literally as written. They were binding for adherents and were to be obeyed strictly in their daily behavior.[3] The Holiness movement prohibited smoking, drinking alcoholic beverages, dancing, or listening to non-religious music. Women were prohibited from wearing make-up or jewelry and their clothing should be plain and loose fitting to hide their figures, covering their body as completely as possible. They were not allowed to wear pants.

Although daily life was closely choreographed by religious principles, in the Holiness churches, emotional spontaneity was encouraged. The order of comments, songs and prayers that made up the service were determined by the intuitive feeling, as opposed to the more formal "order of service" in the Baptist church. In the Holiness church the Holy Spirit moved people, and whoever was moved by the Spirit to preach the sermon might go to the front of the church and preach. Women could also be preachers in some Holiness churches, and generally they played important roles.

The Holiness Way refers to a branch of Pentecostalism that can be traced back to the Holiness movement in the Methodist tradition. Rather than a denomination, it is a conservative movement focused on mystical and otherworldly experiences, including capture of the soul by the Holy Spirit, glossolalia (speaking in tongues), faith healing, and the gift of prophecy.[4] It was a movement emphasizing the spiritual purity of the church by minimizing the human organizational structure.[5]

The Holiness congregations were attended mostly by older people. In Brother Adcock's church the proportion of older to younger people was 6 to 1. The smaller family congregation of Brother Hoagy did not have any young people, only adults over fifty years old. Women also outnumbered men four or even five to one. Women over 40 years old outnumbered all other churchgoers.

Healing in the
Charismatic Holiness Church

The Charismatic Holiness Church had the largest attendance of the Holiness churches. The leader, Brother John Adcock, was the most popular preacher in Cabbagetown, and a personality cult surrounded him as a strong, spiritual leader who had the power of healing.

Charismatic states and healing from illnesses were important in the Holiness church, and the Holiness religious practice that I observed was more mystical and otherworldly than the Baptist churches. In Holiness churches references to current politics and social trends were less strident, and the focus was on mystical experiences that linked individuals directly to God.

In one service he took out a stack of "prayer cloths", pieces of ribbon measuring one and one-half inches square. Some were white and others were light blue, and they had a red dot (like blood the preacher said) in the center. He asked the persons sitting in the first two rows to come up and pray over the prayer cloths to ask God to bless them and give them healing power. After that, he invited everyone in the church to come up and get one of the squares of ribbon, and most of the people did. He told how one woman who had "milk leg" put a prayer cloth in her shoe, and she was healed. People were invited to take as many as they wanted, and some people took several. One man who had just testified about having tuberculosis took a dozen or so and put them in his shirt pocket over his chest.[6]

Brother Adcock was singing loudly and with microphone in hand walked up and down the aisle. He stopped next to four or five people and prayed to the Lord to heal them of their various ailments, one was a kidney infection, and another was the "evil spirit of the flu". As everyone was standing and clapping with high emotion, three women were possessed by the spirit of God and began speaking in tongues with rapid-fire, unintelligible staccato sounds like I had heard in other services.[7] Later, I asked people about the experience of speaking in tongues, and they explained that when the spirit of God was inside of a person, God could begin speaking through the person with involuntary sounds that they did not understand. If the person were a true and pure believer, God would use their voice to speak.

Brother Adcock went up to one woman who had been speaking in tongues and took her by the hand and pulled her out into the aisle. Another woman came and stood behind her. He put his hand on her head and began to pray in a low pitched voice; his tone increased intensity and loudness, becoming more rhythmic as his grip grew stronger. As the physical tension in his face increased, he prayed to the Lord almost shouting to strengthen her and give her the Spirit. Then, he released his pressure with a dramatic sweep of the hand up toward the ceiling.

156

She collapsed backwards into the arms of the woman behind her emitting soft groaning sounds. She was eased to the floor, and someone offered a covering for her and pulled her skirt down since her legs had become exposed in the process. She lay on her back in the middle of the aisle for the next ten minutes as the service went on around her, and she periodically shuddered as if having a chill. Then, she got up quietly and returned to her seat and sat as if she were emotionally drained or exhausted. Most of the people attending the service were women, and they were the ones in most of the healing and trance induction sequences.[8]

A middle-aged woman and a couple of the younger women asked to be healed of physical problems, and a young mother had a fear about the well-being of her baby and asked to have the fear removed. A middle-aged man had broken ribs, and another middle-aged man had been through a lot the last week and asked for God's help with his heavy burdens.

At one point Adcock stopped to tell about a man who had come to him with a piece of steel next to his heart. It was so dangerous that the doctors would not operate. He prayed for the man, and the steel disappeared. He said that it was strange that some people could believe that man could go to the moon and would not believe in something so simple as being healed by prayer. After he had prayed with each person, he would leave them and go on to the next. Frequently the person would stand there a short while, seeming to savor the euphoria before moving back to their seat.[9]

Possessed by the Holy Spirit

God demonstrated his presence by his spirit possessing believers in church services and causing those possessed to speak in "unknown tongues". No one ever saw God himself, but many reported feeling his spirit entering them. Esther Smith Durham described spirit possession to me as the Holy Spirit entering her and possessing her with the resulting infusion of divinity flooding her entire being with elation. Her normal state of consciousness was altered, and she felt herself being saturated with happiness within the grip of an overwhelming benign force. She reported tingling feelings run up and down her back and arms and legs, and she talked about jerking and shivering without being able to control her body. Some reported feeling faint and having to lie down on the floor because of not having strength in their legs.

Getting the Spirit was a mystical experience that was the essence of true bonding with the Lord. To receive the Spirit a person must first be in a state of complete surrender to God, having completely denied self. In that vacuum when all analytical judgments had been consciously suspended, feelings were permitted free rein, and the Holy Spirit could possess the person.

Esther[10] said that the first time she was possessed by God, she did not know about the Holy Spirit (or Holy Ghost), but she later realized that it was the Holy Spirit that had possessed her. After conversion Esther began to recognize her new abilities of receiving the Spirit, entering trance states, and speaking in unknown tongues.[11] All of which confirmed the genuineness of her union with God.

Esther expressed that experience in these terms:

So, they was havin service on Tuesday, but I got the stammerin of the lips that night, and my lips was just goin up and down and up and down, quiverin like. And I had never had anything like that to happen to me before, and I didn't know what was takin place. And then, I just knew that it felt so good that I didn't never want it to stop feelin like that. But anyway, I just thought that's why I am feelin so wonderful because I have been converted, and I know that Jesus lives within my heart. And so, they was havin service on Tuesday night, and so they asked me, they said, 'Would you be back Tuesday night?' And I said, 'I'll be back if I'm livin, cause I know that it will be the Lord's will.' And so that next Tuesday, we had startin, and after we got to singin songs I got to feelin like that again, and the Devil kept tellin me, 'Now, you're cold, you're cold, that's why them chill bumps is on you.' You could just look down and see chill bumps all over me, and you would just be wipin sweat all off me, and you wouldn't be jumpin up and down or anything to work up all that sweat. And so, I could just feel that electrifying power start all over, start at your head and just start goin down, and it feels real good, you know.

But you can't, you just can't explain it, but that's the best way I know how to explain it. But anyway, we was singin songs, and my lips got to quiverin again, just to where I couldn't stop them, and the Devil would say...Now, when I say the Devil, like if you were to say, 'Now, I'm goin to go outside and steal me somethin,' you know that would be the Devil talkin to you. If you walk by a piano or something, and you saw something that you thought you could get by with, 'Hell,' he says, 'Go ahead and take it nobody's looking at you.' Well, that's the Devil talkin to you. And then, when somethin says, 'Naw, you wouldn't do that for nothin, that's wrong.' You know that's the Lord talkin to you. Well, how can you tell the difference? Well, the Lord won't tell you anything bad, and the Devil sure won't tell you anything good.

But anyway, I had started feelin like that again, and my lips had started quiverin. My mouth was just goin up and down, up and down, and he said, 'Now you're cold, and you better not act like you got the Holy Ghost. If you do,' he said, 'you know the penalty for that.' And I was afraid you know. I was afraid if I startin talkin in tongues, that it wouldn't be the Lord, you know. And so, I just lifted my hand to heaven, and I said, 'Now, Lord you know that I'm ignorant about this Holy Ghost, but You know that I want it with all my whole mind, heart, soul and strength.' And I said, 'If that's what it is, give it to me.' And He just come down, and I started speakin in tongues and dancing, and ever since then I've knowed what it really was. And it is just like stickin your hand in that light socket up there, you can really feel it. Just that real, but it doesn't hurt.

The Lighthouse Church of God's Truth

Like most Holiness churches, the Lighthouse Church of God's Truth was made up of working-class people with few resources.[12] This was a small church made up mostly by older women from the White extended family. The church was started a couple of years earlier by Bubba, one of Ruthie's sons who was Effie Smith's nephew. After one year he quit, and the leadership was taken by Hoagy, one of Ruthie's sons-in-law. Hoagy was not a preacher, but he had a station wagon to take several women to services, and he played the guitar. He became the preacher.

The Lighthouse Church of God's Truth met in the concession stand of an abandoned drive-in movie theater. It was a surreal dream like setting with the old and broken movie screen towering over an empty field of metal posts where speakers once hung for the cars parked for the movie, a stark reminder of poverty, abandonment, and of the illusions of what might have been.

I attended services there several times, and one winter Sunday[13] there were twenty members present, and all but three were members of the White family or related in some way through marriage. Excluding me, three men attended along with nine women and eight children. The twelve adults were all over fifty years old. Two of the three men worked in the mill, and most of the women had either a husband, father, brother, or son who had worked in the mill. Some of the women had also worked there in past years. Brother Hoagy Jones was a middle-aged man. He was a supervisor at the mill which was considered a good job, and he devoted evenings and weekends to the church.

If he and his wife were to stop, the church would cease to exist. His wife worked closely with him in the congregational activities, and they seemed to enjoy it. His kinship ties pulled in most of the people. There was no official church organization, no officers, no membership, and no formal rules. The morning was divided between Bible study and preaching. We started with singing. There were no songbooks, but people seemed to know the songs by memory.

After a couple of songs Brother Hoagy began Bible teaching, and he chose the fifth chapter of Galatians in the New Testament. In verse 14 he read, "Love thy neighbor," and he said that Christians should help their neighbors. He gave the example of a non-Christian man who worked at the mill and lived next door to another mill worker. The neighbor got sick and could not work, and some members of his family were also sick. As long as that man was out of work, the sinner man bought groceries for that family. When he would go out to get groceries, he would get as much for his neighbor as for himself, and he was just a sinner man who did not go to church or believe in God! He was an example for all Christians. Effie spoke up and said that even though he was a sinner, he still had good in him.

159

Verses sixteen through eighteen were about the spirit and the flesh. He said that people were more and more ruled by things of the flesh, and as an example he said that women were taking their clothes off and throwing them out on the highways which is a sinful thing to do. He said that he knew because when he would drive to work in the morning, he would see their clothes along the street. Just the other night a woman was killed in a wreck on the Interstate, and when the police got there, they found her with no clothes on. He said that the spirit and the flesh were contrary to each other, so if you do the things of the spirit, you will not have time for things of the flesh. Miniskirts and shorts were bad. A woman could not bare herself and be right with the Lord.

After that the Bible study was over, and people stood up, some got a drink, others went to the bathroom before the preaching service was to start. As we warmed our hands over a gas stove in the interim between Bible study and the preaching service, Hoagy talked about Christians losing their freedoms because Christianity was under threat. He said the only way to preserve America was through Christian teachings and practice. He was specifically concerned that Bible reading had been taken out of the schools. He said that in the time of the founding fathers of our country, there was a law that Bibles had to be in every school, and that people learned to read from the Bible. He said that it was a Jewish woman[14] who had gotten that decision from the courts and that she would soon want to outlaw the Bible completely, and he predicted that within eight to ten years the Bible would be completely prohibited for the American people to read. He said that we should be using our time to get to know the Bible, so that we will be able to know it after it is taken away from us.

In the interactive spirit of this small, family congregation, Effie said that we should concern ourselves with that part that cannot be taken away, i.e., the spirit inside of us. Someone else mentioned that we should be glad that we can worship as freely as we do without persecution.

Everyone returned to their seats for the preaching service, and Hoagy took his guitar and led the group in two songs. Sister Creek stood and sang a song that she had composed, followed by prayer during which most people knelt by the pews and prayed out loud, creating a cacophony of voices in the small space. After the prayer Hoagy asked Brother Clarence to come up and lead the testimonies.[15] All of the women and two of the men stood and spoke, one after the other, thanking the Lord for what he had done for them during the week, frequently naming specific blessings. In contrast to the Baptist church, I noticed that everyone present in this small family run congregation participated actively in the service by praying aloud, singing, and speaking, giving their testimony about how God had helped them.

Then, there was more singing during which Hoagy's mother became possessed by the Spirit. She waved her arms in the air, shouting and praising God, and danced in a small circle in the aisle, chanting unintelligible syllables. After more singing Brother Clarence's wife also went into trance with eyes closed, convulsing, and singing out loud staccato-like syllables. Later, I asked them what they felt speaking in tongues, and they described it as losing control over speech and beginning to speak compulsively in sounds that they did not understand. They said they were channeling the sounds that God was giving to them.

As they finished the last song, Hoagy asked Brother Creek to come and preach. When he got to the front, he asked for those who were right with the Lord to come around him and pray with him for a good sermon. The twelve adults clustered around him and prayed that the Spirit would come to them. As they returned to their seats, Brother Creek opened his Bible to Acts 7:38 which was the text he chose to preach about. He read,

Moses was with our ancestors, the assembly of God's people in the wilderness, when the angel spoke to him at Mount Sinai. And there Moses received life-giving words to pass on to us.

He said that he felt that the Lord's Spirit was present today, and in fact, he felt closer to the Lord than he had ever felt. He moved quickly from one side of the room to the other talking about schools being a bad influence on young people because ungodly teachers were teaching them ungodly things. He recalled the first day that he had gotten the Spirit. He was in church, and the next thing he knew he was standing in a corner at the front of the church and screaming out, "Lord, I am completely yours." It was an experience that he would never forget. He used to go to a denominational church, but after he got the Spirit, he followed the Holiness Way.

As he continued to speak, his fists were clenched, and he waved them above his head and pounded the pulpit to make his points. The room was hot and stuffy now from the fires of the gas heaters. He shouted with loud, chaotic force. He frowned. He stomped. He said that denominations were bad, and he would not go to a Baptist or Methodist church because it meant humans were in control of the running of the church when it should be God. Denominational preachers were influenced too much by what people say and think and their superiors in the church. They did not have a free spirit like the Holiness people. Since denominations were man-made and man was basically sinful and evil, such organizations could not be good. Eliminating the human hierarchy would minimize the evil influence inherently brought by people.[16]

162

After he finished preaching, he asked for anyone who needed prayer to come forward, but no one did. There was a final prayer, and the service was over. Afterwards adults stood milling around, talking, shaking hands, and exchanging greetings while the children stood and watched or went outside for a few minutes of play. Everyone commented that it had been a good service because they had felt the Spirit move among them and because two of the "sisters" (i.e., women of the group) had received the Spirit. Each encouraged the other to come back for the next service. Brother Creek's sermon was unusually dramatic beyond the range of what I had observed in other services. Later, in a rare critical comment toward a fellow church member, Effie told me he did not control the Spirit in his sermon, which a person should know how to do when gifted with the spirit.

Slowly, the group moved out the door to the cold gray of the overcast day, dispersing to the cars under the towering movie screen of the abandoned drive-in theater.

Beliefs Expressed that Sunday

Spirit possession. A central belief was the mystical connection to God, which was manifest when a person was possessed by God's spirit, the Holy Spirit. This was an ethereal spirituality with less emphasis on the morality of the country than I observed in the Baptist church. It was more personal and immediate with people being possessed by the spirit and speaking in tongues. The spirit possession of the preacher's mother and wife was an indication that God's spirit was present, and it assured the sacredness of the service.

Miraculous healing of the body. The theme of healing runs through the daily lives of people who practice Holiness belief, and it was a feature of religious services. People said that God could intervene directly to heal the person of illnesses. It was like spiritual radiation that could move through an intermediary who was spiritually in tune with God and burn out whatever was causing the malady.

Bible reading and prayer in schools. Losing Bible reading and prayer in the schools was evidence of the failure of American society. Brother Hoagy blamed Jews for the Supreme Court rulings on devotional prayer and Bible reading.[17] A Jewish man did bring the case of devotional prayer, but Brother Hoagy thought it was a Jewish woman, which seemed to reflect the misogyny I commonly heard in these services. Because of those rulings, he defended Christian nationalism as the only way to avoid the breakdown of American society.

163

Replacement Theory. Brother Hoagy argued that Jews and atheists had taken away their right to pray and read the Bible in school, and the values of Jews and atheists were replacing Holiness Christian values. He was afraid they would totally outlaw the Bible and being Christian.

The religious life in Cabbagetown was one example of the culture out of which Christian nationalism emerged with its emphasis on religious practice, Bible reading, prayer, and the centrality of women as preservers of the moral center of the family. Holiness people like Brother Hoagy and his followers were Christian nationalists because they perceived it as necessary to preserve their right to live as Christians and study the Bible.

Endnotes

1   Harding 2000:36
2   Pope 1965:133-134
3   Russell 2010:121
4   Larger Pentecostal churches, such as the Assemblies of God, are
not holiness, nor share the same religious practices with the Holiness Movement. There was no Assembly of God church in Cabbagetown, only the
smaller and poorer Holiness churches.
5   Harvey 2019:75
6   The use of prayer cloths was a magical practice, and, as in other
cultures, religion and magic could be practiced together at the same time.
Magic refers to using supernatural powers through human intervention,
such as contagious magic transferring supernatural power through contact
with the magical source (i.e. prayer cloths).
7   Glossolalia. Speaking in unintelligible syllables.
8   Lawless 1989. Elaine Lawless describes these dramatic speech
events and gesturing in her study of the Pentecostal service. She uses the
term "folkloristics" to refer to analyzing the special speech events, gestures,
and posturing used in Pentecostal services in southern Indiana.
9   In all, eight women and two men went up for prayer, ranging from
twenty years old to about fifty. These people were not getting saved or spiritually redeemed. They were getting personal therapy. For thirty seconds or
one minute while they spoke to him and for a couple of minutes as he spoke
to the congregation and to God, they were the center of attention, receiving
social support and divine help.
10   The Holy Ghost is the third part of the trinity including God the
father and God the son, who was Jesus. The Holy Ghost is that aspect of
God that interacts directly with people.
11   For a further discussion of religion as a somatic experience and the
swooning experience see Austin-Broos 2003:6-8.
12   Miller, Donald 1999:5
13   In the winter of 1969-1970.
14   The Supreme Court case on Bible reading in schools was not
brought by a Jewish woman as Hoagy believed, but it is notable that he was
blaming Jews directly for taking away the Bible in contrast to Rev. Allen
in the Baptist church who used the euphemism of "communist" to refer to
Jews.

15   Testimonies were first-person narratives usually about recent events in their lives giving praise and credit to God for good things that had happened to them.

16   This comment also applied to government. Since it was an organization created by people, it was inherently evil and should be minimized. This was a theological argument for state's rights in government.

17   A common belief in Cabbagetown was that Jews had taken away the right to read the Bible and pray in school, resulting in antisemitic attitudes being frequently expressed. The specific Supreme Court rulings in question were the rulings on devotional prayer (Engle vs. Vitale 1962) and Bible reading (Abington School District vs. Schempp 1963) in which the Court ruled that the practices were unconstitutional. In fact, in the case of the devotional prayer, Steven Engel, who was Jewish, challenged the constitutionality of imposing a standardized prayer on all the students in the school district. Ellery Schempp, who brought the legal challenge to reading the Bible in schools, was a Unitarian high school student, not Jewish.

CHAPTER NINE
ONWARD CHRISTIAN SOLDIERS: THE BAPTIST CHURCH

THE BAPTISTS IN CABBAGETOWN TENDED TO BE politically at-tuned to the national discourse. When meeting with Baptists, I regularly heard statements of evangelical exceptionalism and the immutability of Christian beliefs. The Baptist sense of Christian superiority provided the ideological foundation for their belief in Christian nationalism and an intolerance of non-Christian, non-evangelical behaviors.[1]

The Baptist pastor was probably the most important opinion maker in Cabbagetown. What he said from the pulpit on Sunday morning had the weight of moral authority. Although preachers in the community might vary somewhat in their messages, they agreed that their America was White, Anglo-Saxon, and Protestant, and they protested that America was losing its religious essence. The sense of alienation from the federal government was deep seated, and people regularly commented that the government no longer represented them.[2]

The Baptist pastor blamed federal government decisions for destroying Christian values and advocated Christian control of governmental policies, a Christian nationalist argument. He said that Christianity was the way of God and that America should be Christian. Anthropologist Sarah Riccardi-Swartz[3] has called this melding of religion and politics "hybrid fascism" because of its totalitarian assumption that the political system should be based on obedience to Christian values.

Anthropologist James Peacock called this appeal of authoritarianism the "Southern Protestant ethic disease."[4] He suggested that the culture of Southern Protestants permitted them to express more uncensored feelings, and consequently, they relied on an external authority to establish limits to their behavior. This need to set boundaries was an opening to authoritarianism, and it made fascism palatable if it would guarantee Christian values.

The historian Roel Reyes[5] classified political thinking among Protestants in the Civil War era South as proto-fascist for the same reason. When people thought the society faced decay, they were willing to accept absolutist solutions because it protected their way of life.

Heritage of Christian Militancy

Some church hymns had overtly militant messages, and one was "Onward Christian Soldiers",[6] a song with military imagery. It was in the song book of the Baptist church, and people sang it on occasion. It suggests the idea of life being a battleground between God and the Devil in direct combat for the lives of people. Implicit is the idea of an army for righteousness which people should join. Life was a battle between good and evil.

Onward, Christian soldiers,	*Like a mighty army*
Marching as to war,	*Moves the church of God;*
With the cross of Jesus	*Brothers, we are treading*
Going on before!	*Where the saints have trod.*
Christ, the royal Master,	*We are not divided;*
Leads against the foe;	*All one body we,*
Forward into battle,	*One in hope and doctrine,*
See His banner go!	*One in charity.*
(Refrain)	*(Refrain)*
At the sign of triumph	*Onward then, ye people,*
Satan's host doth flee;	*Join our happy throng,*
On, then, Christian soldiers,	*Blend with ours your voices*
On to victory!	*In the triumph song;*
Hell's foundations quiver	*Glory, laud, and honor*
At the shout of praise;	*Unto Christ the King;*
Brothers, lift your voices,	*This thro' countless ages*
Loud your anthems raise!	*Men and angels sing.*
(Refrain)	*(Refrain)*

Refrain:
Onward, Christian soldiers,
Marching as to war,
With the cross of Jesus
Going on before!

This song celebrates the militancy of Christianity, justified by its infallibility.

Attending a Baptist Church Service

Rev. Arthur Davis, the pastor of the Baptist Church had grown up in Cabbagetown and was well-liked by local people. He had worked in the mill like them. He was one of their own who had made good. The members of the Baptist church tended to be skilled and clerical workers and supervisory personnel from the mill. There was a higher frequency of the family attending church together, and there were more men and more cars. Women outnumbered men two to one, and the age divide between people over forty and under forty was in the range of three (older) to one (younger). Although young people were a distinct minority in all churches, some did attend the Baptist church which seemed to be a meeting place for those of marriageable age.

This church had a Sunday morning attendance of approximately 100 people, and it had more human and financial resources than the Holiness churches. It could pay the pastor a full-time salary. This difference could be seen in dress and the mode of transport for people arriving to the Sunday service. All the men wore suits and ties, and the women wore fashionable dresses with purses and sometimes hats. Most men had a car or truck and drove their family to services.

The church was a simple wooden building that opened directly onto the sidewalk.[7] At the door I was greeted by a man who welcomed me to the service, and I entered into a spacious auditorium with church pews lining a central aisle. It could easily seat 150 people or more. I sat near the back to observe the congregation. I saw couples and women friends gathering to take their seats together. It was summer, and the windows along both sides of the auditorium were opened and fans were used to circulate the air.

The pastor was wearing a dark suit and tie, and he opened the service calling on one of the men to lead the congregation in prayer. From the songbook the song leader asked the people to open their hymnbooks to "Tell Me the Story of Jesus" and to sing with him. After the song the pastor asked about anyone who was sick and in need of prayer. That was followed by a prayer for the collecting of money for the work of the church, and the pianist playing softly in the background while ushers passed through the auditorium row by row to collect donations. Then, the choir sang a "special song" and following that, the song leader asked the congregation to stand and sing with him the hymn "Amazing Grace". Then, the pastor came forward and led everyone in prayer to begin the sermon.

The text he chose to speak about was Jeremiah 12:1-13, and he read from the King James Version of the Bible[8] verse five which says,

If thou hast run with the footmen, and they have wearied thee, then how canst thou contend with horses? And if in the land of peace, wherein thou trustedst, they wearied thee, then how wilt thou do in the swelling of Jordan?

170   As he spoke, he stood behind the pulpit. He was animated and started saying that the family and the children should always be united and loving, and the only way to do that was through the church. Then, he went on to discuss the threat to Christianity.[9]

The problem today is that we are losin the children to the Devil. Negroes[10] and Whites are together, and it ain't right. It's the communists who are behind it; they are bringin about the degeneration of our youth. Television has been a damnation to our children. They see all of the sinful songs and dances and long hair of the singers, and they go out and do the same thing. All of these kids that hang out on the street can't be locked up anymore, and you know why? It is because everything is corrupt from the President to every office in the land.

Taxes have gone up. The kids dancin is bad because after they get through then they get in the car together alone and pretty soon they are in a motel room. Sex is takin over; the Devil is takin over. The communists said that they would take over the United States ... without ever firin a shot, and they're going to do it by takin over our kids.

What can be done? Hitler and Stalin did something. The communists killed 50 million Chinese Christians when they took over. They were tortured and killed. What will we do when we are tortured by communists to reject Christ? When the communists take over, there is no more home life. There is no marriage. They just breed people. The children who are raised in communism are trained to believe in it, and they are just like Catholics because they hardly ever change once they have been raised to believe that way. There are more communists in the United States today than ever before, and they are all armed. They have a plan to kill the President of the United States and every other high official within 15 minutes when they get the signal.

You might say that I am not preachin the Bible this mornin, but I am because I am warnin you what is to come. We have to watch out for ourselves as Christians before the Devil and the communists take over everything. What is wrong with us in this day and age? What has happened to us that this has become so bad? When I was young, people were God-fearin, and they believed in the Lord and in His church, but they don't anymore. I like havin a nice car and a nice house like we have today, but I would rather have things like they were in 1934. The only thing that the Devil needs to take over this country for the good Christian people to do nothin. Are you doin what you ought to do for the Lord?

As the pastor ended the sermon, he bowed his head and prayed asking forgiveness from God for anything he might have done wrong. Starting the ritual of the "altar call", he called for those who were not Christians to come forward and accept Jesus to save their souls and for any Christian who had sinned to confess and re-dedicate themselves to sin no more. They sang the invitational hymn, "There is a Fountain Filled with Blood" that could cleanse people of their sins.

The pastor stood in front of the pulpit and pleaded with the people to examine their lives and see if they were right with the Lord and if they had done everything they could do as Christians to fight the Devil. Two women went forward to talk with the pastor and ask for prayer for problems they were having in their lives. He knelt with each in turn at the foot of the pulpit and prayed that the Lord would help them.

At the end the pastor said another prayer thanking the Lord for the service of the morning. With that people began standing and talking in small groups with those around them. Outside on the sidewalk in gender separate groups men stopped to talk with other men, women got in their last comments to their women friends, and children chased each other in and out of parked cars.

Finally, each family group formed, and they walked off together to the waiting car or truck. They would go home or to the house of a friend or relative to have the special Sunday lunch. They would spend the afternoon in casual conversation on the front porch of the house, weather permitting, enjoying the pleasantness of an afternoon of rest with friends and family in the afterglow of a filling meal.

Gospel Music

In addition to the beliefs expressed by the preacher in the sermon, the songs also carried messages of the power and superiority of Christianity. The song "Tell Me the Story of Jesus" has the following lyrics:

Tell me the story of Jesus,
write on my heart every word;
tell me the story most precious,
sweetest that ever was heard.
172 *Tell how the angels, in chorus,*
sang as they welcomed His birth,
"Glory to God in the highest!
Peace and good tidings to earth.

This is an affirmation of the Jesus-centric belief system, which is re-enforced with key emotive words such as "heart", "precious", "sweetest", "angels", "peace", and "good tidings".

The classic Protestant hymn "Amazing Grace" was popular, and it was regularly sung in church services. Its lyrics are:

Amazing grace! how sweet the sound,
That saved a wretch; like me!
I once was lost, but now am found,
Was blind, but now I see.
'Twas grace that taught my heart to fear,
And grace my fears relieved;
How precious did that grace appear
The hour I first believed!
The Lord hath promised good to me,
His word my hope secures;
He will my shield and portion be
As long as life endures.
When we've been there ten thousand years,
Bright shining as the sun,
We've no less days to sing God's praise
Than when we first begun.

This 250-year-old hymn is about the effectiveness of Christianity to transform the worst of people into a good person. Written by John Newton, a former captain of a slave ship, who explains how he was a "wretch" who was "blind", but with salvation he was transformed into a good person who could see the truth. Salvation brought "grace" to him, which in late eighteenth-century English referred to good behavior. God becomes a "shield" protecting the person, and the end concludes that Christians must sing praise to God for the "grace" that they have found, and the protection God guarantees.

The hymn "There is a Fountain Filled with Blood" provides the imagery of a pool of blood into which people can submerge themselves and be cleansed of their past bad behavior. The first and last verses were commonly sung, and they are:

There is a fountain filled with blood
Drawn from Immanuel's veins;
And sinners, plunged beneath that flood,
Lose all their guilty stains:
Lose all their guilty stains,
And sinners, plunged beneath that flood,
Lose all their guilty stains.
When this poor lisping, stammering tongue
Lies silent in the grave,
Then in a nobler, sweeter song,
I'll sing Thy power to save:
I'll sing Thy power to save,
Then in a nobler, sweeter song,
I'll sing Thy power to save.

The lyrics of this song are magical, promising a cleansing of all past misdeeds and a safe and secure future under God's protection even after death. The blood imagery in this song raises the imagery of this being a primeval reference to human sacrifice. The "sacrifice" of Jesus, and his blood in death cleansing people of their past misdeeds was a common theme from the pulpits of Cabbagetown. Although human sacrifice ended dramatically with the story of Abraham and the binding of Isaac in the Bible in Genesis, Christians seem to have retained this imagery by turning the death of Jesus into a ritual sacrifice, not unlike the animal sacrifices common in the ancient Jewish, Greek, and Roman worlds. The harshness of blood imagery and adamant evangelism combined with a message of love and gentleness seemed like an incongruous mixture in the messaging of evangelical preachers.

The sequence of the songs was interesting. From the sweetness of the "Story of Jesus" in the opening song to the melancholy of "Amazing Grace" and the immersion in the flood of blood in the latter hymn, the songs give a promise of salvation and a good future for those who believed in Jesus as God. These songs promise guarantees that range from being saved to a life of good behavior on this earth to protection in a life after death. The strict moral codes imposed by the religion and accompanied by threats of eternal damnation produce a religious music that was somber and cautious, even fearful that God, like a strict parent, could punish a person for their moral indiscretions.

Core Elements in the Sermon

Christian nationalism. The country is in decline because of a loss of Christian principles. In the first part of the sermon, he argued that the country was being lost to non-Christian forces. Then, his condemnation moved on to the rock-n-roll culture and the corruption of the political class from the President of the U.S. on down. His argument was that only Christian nationalism could save the country when governing would be based on Christian principles.

Replacement Theory. The Devil and the Communists will replace Christians. The reference to the Devil was the evil half of the supernatural and was equated with "communist", a euphemism for the "progressive" influences in America, such as Jews, colored people, and immigrants that he saw as foreign to Christian hegemony.

Christian fascism is biblical. When he said, "You might not think that I am preaching the Bible this morning," he went on to say that this is a biblical matter because Christianity is on the verge of disappearing. He was advocating militant Christian action to fight to preserve Christian dominance. It was a rallying cry to defend Christian superiority in American life.

Authoritarianism. Strong men rulers like Hitler or Stalin achieved dramatic changes in their societies. The underlying suggestion is that such a ruler might be needed to establish the hegemony of Christianity in America.

Antisemitism. The pastor's fear was that Jews and other non-Christian foreigners would take over the country and outlaw all Christian practices. Much like the expressions of hatred against Black people, antisemitic references were not about individual Jews, rather they were about an imagined cabal of Jewish power brokers taking over the country and destroying its Christian roots. This sounded like a trope reflecting ideas from *The Protocols of the Elders of Zion*. The fear of Black people was the immediate daily concern in the neighborhood, but Jews were a distant reality, subject to vague conspiracy theories. Jews and Blacks were competitors with Christians for control of the country.

Anti-government. He said that all levels of government were bad, "everything is corrupt from the President to every office in the land." In the next sentences in sequence, he mentions kids dancing, motel rooms and sex, the Devil, and the communists. The linkage is interesting, connecting immoral behavior (dancing and sex) to the Devil and the communists (foreigners and non-Christians). He was suggesting that only an authoritarian government organized around Christian values could solve these problems that he saw in society.

Omissions. What stood out to me as missing in the social commentary of the sermon was any reference to the morality of the economics of corporate/worker relationships. Although national politics were regularly referenced in the dozens of sermons I heard, I did not document any references to the mill or labor conditions. Preachers focused on the distant federal government rather than local conditions.

Baptists were the largest religious denomination in Cabbagetown, in Atlanta, in Georgia, and in the United States. When calls were made in the 1970s from some 30,000 Baptist pulpits across the country to reclaim America for Christianity, it was one of the most important influences on public political opinion. After the evangelical/Republican alliance with Christian nationalism was forged in that decade, Baptists have been leading voices among Evangelicals supporting political candidates of the Republican Party with the aim of bringing evangelical principles into government.

Endnotes

1   Powell and Clarke 2013:7-8
2   See Chapters Two and Four
3   Sarah Riccardi-Swartz 2021:3
4   Peacock 1971:10ff
5   Roel Reyes 2021:88
6   "Onward Christian Soldiers" was written by Sabine Baring-Gould in 1865 in England. It eventually became a staple hymn of Christian militancy among Southern Baptists and other evangelical groups.
7   The auditorium had a single central aisle leading to the pulpit in the front. A section was reserved next to the pulpit for a small choir, and a piano was located to one side. Ten to twelve pews were lined up on the left and the right with an aisle down the middle. Date: September, 1969.
8   The King James Version of the Bible was used by both Baptist and Holiness preachers, and it was the Bible that people had in their homes. The more affluent Baptist church had a piano and specialized song leader, whereas music in the Holiness church was with a guitar and no song leader.
9   I had my small tape recorder with me and recorded the sermon.
10   A slur term for a Black person was used.

Chapter Ten
Evangelicals and Christian Nationalism

THE PEOPLE WHO ARE TRUE BELIEVERS IN EVANGELICAL exceptionalism tend to share attitudes about morality, race, society, and religious practice that feed into Christian nationalism and the MAGA movement. Believers in the absolute correctness of their religion tend to not accept the validity of other religious systems. How does that intolerance impact the larger society in a pluralistic, multi-cultural nation like America? How did the politics of grievance that I observed in Cabbagetown feed into the largest religious political movement in the country linking Christian nationalism and evangelical churches to the Republican Party and the MAGA movement?

177

When Christian Nationalism Emerged

The roots of this movement have been present through much of American history. The most immediate example from the 1950s and 1960s was the John Birch Society that gained support across broad sectors of American life. The Bircher positions for state's rights and a small federal government and their opposition to civil rights, set the stage for Christian nationalism. It promoted Communist and Jewish conspiracy theories, which supposedly were undermining traditional White American Christian principles. The Birch Society decried the moral decline and loss of "family values" in America, which it argued were evidenced in abortion, drugs, feminism, the sexual revolution, and same-sex relationships, all issues that would become prominent in Christian nationalism.

Evangelical preachers that I heard in Cabbagetown were repeating the Birch Society view of America almost point by point. Chris Lehmann[1] suggests that the Birchers transformed and re-invigorated political conservatism with its emphasis on Christian, American life values, and its opposition to cultural relativity and moral nuances. With its opposition to issues from abortion to gay marriage, it seems to have been a prequel to the socially conservative politics of recent decades.

During this research, Lester Maddox was governor of Georgia and George Wallace was governor of the neighboring state of Alabama, and both expressed racist and segregationist views. Maddox refused to serve Black customers at his restaurant in Atlanta in violation of federal law, and he even handed out pickax handles to White customers to threaten any Black people who might try to enter. Maddox created GUTS (Georgians Unwilling to Surrender) to fight against integration which was a parallel organization to MASE (Metropolitan Association for Segregated Education), which was fighting integration in Atlanta schools.

178   When Dr. Martin Luther King, Jr. was assassinated, Gov. Maddox refused to allow him to be honored by lying in state in the Georgia State Capitol and went further to order state troopers to cordon off the Capitol during the funeral procession for Dr. King to avoid mourners entering the building. Wallace famously proclaimed in his inauguration as governor in 1963 "segregation now, segregation tomorrow, segregation forever." Wallace said that Black people were an inferior criminal race in which venereal disease, rape, assault, and murder were common. He went on to argue that intermarriage between Whites and Blacks would lead to the degeneration of the White race.[2]

As anti-Vietnam War protests grew in intensity in the late 1960s, the America First and the White supremacist movements were also growing. Historian Kathleen Belew[3] links the opposition to anti-Vietnam protests by the political right to the rise of White supremacy. Civil rights, immigration legislation, and the Vietnam War changed the face of America, and those grievances reached Cabbagetown.

Although Congress approved the Equal Rights Amendment[4] in 1972 and the Supreme Court ruled in favor abortion services in the Roe v. Wade decision in 1973, the ERA and Roe decisions sealed the end of an era. They proved to be the final straw galvanizing Christian conservatives[5] into a national force that would eventually defeat both measures. Conservatives successfully stopped the ratification of ERA and launched their decades long fight against abortion rights. Although the Democrat Jimmy Carter won the 1976 election, the country and the federal government were shifting to the political right. Starting with Ronald Reagan in 1980 four out of the next six Presidents of the country would be Republican, each elected with overwhelming support from Evangelicals.

Intolerance
and White Christian Superiority

Religion in general and Christianity in particular have made important contributions to human life in spirituality, hope, and moral focus, not to mention richness in the visual arts and music. In Cabbagetown religious faith gave hope and moral focus to people. But the conundrum is that religion can include the antithesis, a culture of religious absolutism when those who believe they have an exclusive, God-given truth can go to ignoble lengths to guarantee it. Scholars from the anthropologist Harvey Whitehouse[6] to philosophers Russell Powell and Steve Clarke[7] and psychologist Daniel Batson[8] have described these two faces of religion, the one of spiritual quest and concern for others, and the other, a darker face of intolerance and bigotry. In Cabbagetown I saw both faces of Christianity.

Religion based on spiritual quest tends to be more open and questioning, and this openness to alternatives tends to permit tolerance of differences. In contrast, religion based on creed and its definition of boundaries tends to be focused inward on the group and less tolerant of differences.

Is intolerance endemic to any kind of ideological purity, whether religious or not? Steve Clarke, Russell Powell, and Julian Savulescu[9] point out that the tendency toward intolerance has been greater among religious groups focused on creed. The psychologist Daniel Batson[10] points out that existing research among White Christians in the United States shows that religious people tend to be more racially prejudiced, antisemitic, and ethnocentric than non-religious people. Yet, it should be noted that some religious groups have had a history of promoting social justice and tolerance between groups.[11] Religion and intolerance can correlate with each other, but does religion cause intolerance?

The concern about the connection between religious belief and violence gained attention after the attacks on the twin towers of the World Trade Center in 2001 and stimulated research and commentary on the subject. In 2007 I attended a conference at the Abdelmalek Essaâdi University in Tetuan, Morocco, and one evening my wife, daughter, and I were having dinner with two local professors from the university, one a sociologist and the other a professor of Islamic literature.[12] In the discussion over dinner we talked about tolerance in religion, and the literature professor commented that tolerance was dangerous and unacceptable for Islam. He went on to argue that Muslims had to be intolerant of foreign influences that could contaminate the purity of Islam. His comments led me to think about the linkage of ideological purity and intolerance in all religious systems, including Christianity.

The violent attacks on synagogues and Black churches in the United States would soon re-focus attention on White extremism in this country. I thought about the long history of intolerance in the name of purity in Christendom. We can see the oppression and eradication of the Other, the impure, repeatedly in European history from the Crusades against "infidels" in the Holy Land in 1098 to the Inquisition burning Jews at the stake in Spain and Portugal, the slave trade, the history of lynchings in the United States, and the state sponsored genocide that was the Holocaust. That history raised the question to me whether this perceived threat of Jews, Blacks, and other "foreigners" in Cabbagetown was a recurrence of this European tradition of religious intolerance.[13]

Although the ancestors of Black people have been Christians for centuries and living in the Americas since the early 1600s, they were still considered the "Other" by people in Cabbagetown. Their Black neighbors in Reynoldstown were not considered equally Christian and not allowed to attend White churches in Cabbagetown. This world view of White Christianity did not allow equality for non-White, Anglo-Saxon Protestants.

Author Magda Teter[14] argues that the theological structure for Christian supremacy can be traced back to the time when it became the official religion of the Roman Empire. The original Roman version of Christian superiority became more deeply entrenched in law, theology, and culture during the Medieval period. Later, during slavery and colonialism, it added the racial component, becoming the doctrine of White Christian superiority.

Christianity was a centerpiece of European thinking with the beginning of the European expansion in the 1500s. Europeans saw themselves as civilized and the possessors of the Christian truth, and they saw it as their obligation to take the truth to uncivilized peoples.[15] During the conquest of the indigenous civilizations in the Americas and the beginning of African slavery, it was widely accepted among Europeans that the conquered and enslaved peoples should be subject to their superiority.[16] Christian missionaries spread out around the world to take the message of their superior religion to colonized people.

How do we distinguish between Christian superiority or exceptionalism and Eurocentrism? Is the latter the educated version of the former? In *A System of Synthetic Philosophy* (1896) Herbert Spencer introduced the concept of "Social Darwinism" by which he meant that social, economic, and political success were based on the "survival of the fittest", a phrase that he coined. He conceptualized that some people and some societies were more successful because they were the "fittest". These Eurocentric theories provided the intellectual justification for European supremacy and racism, and these assumptions existed covertly in early versions of Christian nationalism.[17]

181

Race, Politics, and Christian Nationalism

Christian nationalists argue that the United States was founded by White men with the intention that it be a Christian nation with laws based on Christian biblical principles. Some argue that God has made America a powerful nation and has given it a special role in the world because it was founded as a Christian nation.[18] Andrew Whitehead and Samuel Perry[19] have documented that Christian nationalists tend to belong to White evangelical churches.

White nationalists and Christian nationalists have tended to share conservative values on race, gender, sexuality, family, and gun control. Journalist Anna Merlan[20] has shown that the racist and antisemitic rhetoric that I saw in Cabbagetown continues in White nationalist groups with the stated purpose of guaranteeing the future of the White race.

Southern Baptists, the largest Protestant denomination in the United States, have had a history of segregation and racism. Anthropologist Miles Richardson[21] pointed out that during the era of civil rights protests in the American South, Black Baptist churches were where civil rights marches started, while White Baptist churches were where the White Citizen's Councils were organized to stop them.

Following the assassination of Dr. King and the ensuing riots in 1968, the Southern Baptist Convention did make some efforts to modify its historic positions on race and segregation. "Messengers" or representatives of the denomination met in Houston and issued a statement on the problem of racism and their denomination's involvement in it, entitled "A Statement Concerning the Crisis in Our Nation."[22] It read in part,

> *Our nation is enveloped in a social and cultural revolution. We are shocked by the potential for anarchy in a land dedicated to democracy and freedom. There are ominous sounds of hate and violence among men of unbelief and rebellion toward God...*
>
> *As Southern Baptists, representative of one of the largest bodies of Christians in our nation and claiming special ties of spiritual unity with the large conventions of Negro Baptists in our land, we have come far short of our privilege in Christian brotherhood.*
>
> *Humbling ourselves before God, we implore Him to create in us a right spirit of repentance and to make us instruments of His redemption, His righteousness, his peace, and His love toward all men...*
>
> *We will strive to obtain and secure for every person equality of human and legal rights. We will undertake to secure opportunities in matters of citizenship, public services, education, employment, and personal habitation that every man may achieve his highest potential as a person. We will accept and exercise our civic responsibility as Christians to defend people against injustice.*

With that statement, moderate forces among Southern Baptists were trying to disassociate the denomination from its traditional linkage to slavery, segregation, racism, and discrimination. Although these Baptist leaders were recognizing the problem of division within American society, not all Baptist state groups, local pastors, and churches agreed with that statement.[23] The denomination did not call on its member churches and families to stop using the Confederate battle flag until 2015, forty-seven years later.

In Atlanta, church leaders held a conference after the assassination of Dr. King to address the role of churches in response to the racism and violence.[24] The report entitled "Atlanta Area Study on the Churches' Response to Violence" came out in March 1969. It stated that segregation was the norm in churches in Atlanta and that segregationist sentiment had been exploited by politicians. It concluded that church integration was not happening because it was irrelevant to many Black people, and that White moderates believed that race relations were good, and nothing more could be done.[25]

As the White Christian movement became more sophisticated, sociologists Gorski and Perry[26] found that the overt racial comments that were still used in the 1960s were changed in the 1970s and 1980s to metaphorical references to "states'-rights", "illegals", or "immigrants". The use of the word "communist" was eventually be replaced by "immigrants" as a metaphor for non-WASP foreign influences threatening the Christian racial purity of the society. Anthropologist Jane H. Hill[27] points out that the racial and ethnic metaphors are for public speech while much of the everyday language of White supremacy has continued to be used privately, often under the cover of anonymity, and is dismissed as a "gaffe" if it became public.

183

In the racial world view of Cabbagetown, White people saw segregation as having been ordained by God as part of the divine plan for human life. Rev. Arthur Davis was an outspoken advocate of Christian primacy, and he would say that the federal government should be subject to God's laws, and White Christians should determine the political, economic, and social direction of American society. People said that segregation and Christian prevalence were their God-given civil rights, and the federal government had broken God's will for a White, Christian America. Christian primacy was the protective cultural cocoon enveloping local values from xenophobia to racism.

From the preachers to mill workers like Claude Workman, I heard people saying that God had created Whites and Blacks as different peoples, and he did not intend them to be equal. I did not hear one dissident voice. The belief that Black people, especially men and boys, were dangerous was a powerful influence on the thinking of people in Cabbagetown. Emotion and belief interacted to produce behaviors, such as Workman carrying his 38 Special pistol for weeks on end, ready to use it against any threatening Black person. Such racist beliefs could induce a family to keep "a man-eating dog" out of their fear of Black people.

Jane H. Hill[28] defines what I observed in Cabbagetown as the "folk theory" of race. It claims that "race" is biologically real, and that everyone can be assigned a status based on color and other phenotypical characteristics. The second component of racial folk theory is that "colored" people are "biologically inferior". Hill goes on to argue that the "White racist culture" dominates American institutional life and that most White people are complicit.[29]

Religion and Christian Nationalism

As I listened to people in Cabbagetown, I heard the belief in White Christian rights and entitlement embedded in Christian nationalism. Although they could accept poverty as a part of God's plan for their lives, they could not accept the federal government forcing them to live with Black people and prohibiting prayer and Bible reading in the schools. Rev. Arthur Davis, Brother Hoagy, and Brother Adcock were religious voices in Cabbagetown arguing for White supremacy and Christian control of the government. They spoke to the cultural trauma of their community that they saw resulting from the integration of the races, the outlawing of Christian practices in the schools, and the loss of "family values", according to their definition.

184

Yuval Noah Harari[30] talks about a collective fiction shaping the behavior of people, and we can see it in Cabbagetown. The social collective became the validation of the truth of Christian supremacy, and each person re-enforced their belief by repeating it to others. The collective confirmed validity of Christian exceptionalism and superiority.[31]

Explaining their poverty, Effie Smith told me that God had a divine plan for the world, and he intended for some of his children to be poor to test them. Their riches were to come in the afterlife. Frequently a person would point out the paradox for Christians that the people most blessed on earth were the rich who were often non-Christians. That was explained by the biblical verse about it being more difficult for the rich to enter Heaven than for a camel to pass through the eye of a needle.[32] To become rich meant to neglect the things of the spirit, violating the Lord's will, and ending up in Hell. In contrast, religious people in Cabbagetown saw themselves as the privileged ones who would go to Heaven.

It seemed to me that their belief in an afterlife in Heaven gave people hope and helped them accept the hardships of poverty and their marginalization in society. Religious belief gave them a sense of well-being.[33] To think that they had an exclusive and absolute religious truth leveled the playing field with those who were more economically and politically successful. They might be poor, but they had the trump card. They would have the better life in the afterworld.

Until the 1950s the people of Cabbagetown lived in a bubble of White Protestant superiority, a protected world of Jim Crow entitlement, not unlike the world of 1917 when Corey White first arrived to work in the mill. As their traditional practices of religion and race were outlawed between 1954 to 1973, the historical moment that I recorded was one of cultural trauma for the adults who had grown up with segregation, Bible reading and prayer in the schools, and an ideal of the woman who stayed home and stood by her man. They had lost what they perceived as their God ordained world and lifestyle, and they were protesting.

The fusion of the belief in Christian superiority and Christian nationalism with America First groups would produce a political movement convinced that it had God-ordained absolute rights to their way of life. In this unitary belief system, the pluralism of democracy was a threat. Christian authoritarianism would be the only way to guarantee the dominance of Christian values in society even if it required the old alliance between authoritarianism and the church. As historian Heather Cox Richardson[34] explains, Donald Trump "married" authoritarianism to his political message to racists, anti-feminists, and the religious right.

Although the identification as a Christian dropped from 90 percent to 70 percent[35] in the United States in the fifty years between 1970 and 2020, the more conservative Protestant denominations (Southern Baptists, Assemblies of God, and Church of the Nazarene) grew between 15 and 20 percent during the same period. The mainline Protestant denominations (Episcopal, Presbyterian, Lutheran, United Methodist) dropped to approximately half their former membership. Southern Baptists now outnumber Methodists by two to one and have become an even more dominant force in American religious life.

In *The End of White Christian America*,[36] Robert Jones sees these declining numbers as a turning point in American life with the loss of influence of Christianity, something that de Tocqueville could never have imagined when he visited the new American republic.[37] As overall Christian identity has declined, Evangelicals have become the dominant religious group, and their alliance with the Republican Party has given them the access to political power that they had never had previously.

Outlaw Culture and Morality

The growth and influence of conservative religious groups in recent decades has emboldened some on the religious right to "take back America", joining movements that they think will restore an America that is "Christian" according to their definition. Professors John Corrigan and Lynn Neal[38] argue that the growth in the power of the religious right has led to the interweaving of religion and intolerance, contributing to the "religious zealotry" of hate groups.

In Cabbagetown I observed White Protestant exclusivity and the belief in White "racial" superiority embedded in religious experience. Social reality fit into a framework of fixed binary categories: God and the Devil, good and evil, black and white, male and female, winners and losers, government and non-government. The system of morality for religious people in Cabbagetown was validated by the opposite behaviors of those who were not religious.[39] When Cecil Smith got drunk at night and became verbally aggressive, those around him explained it as his being possessed by the Devil. In contrast, his wife Effie never got drunk. Her non-drunkenness and his drunkenness created a completed moral circle of right and wrong, saint and sinner.

Given the absolute binary of evangelical belief in Cabbagetown about the world with the God/Devil and good/evil contrasts, there were in-between areas of moral ambiguity.[40] Criminal activity could be a moral netherland, not good but not necessarily sinful. Taking the life of a person in murder was a sin, but I never heard anyone say that shooting at a Black man was a sin. I did not hear any preacher denounce carrying a gun with the intent to kill as a sin. Integration was denounced as wrong, but no one said it was sinful. Although many would approve of these acts, I did not hear anyone denounce the violence of the Ku Klux Klan or the bombing of a Black church or of a Jewish synagogue as a sin.

Rev. Arthur Davis, the Baptist preacher, defined sin as "songs and dances and long hair of the singers", and he linked the songs and dances with the sexual behavior of the young as caused by the Devil and communists. The concept of sin could refer to a variety of behaviors under the umbrella of unacceptable community behaviors from drinking alcohol and sexual conduct outside of marriage to using curse words, not attending church, and speaking badly about God or God's people.

These were behaviors affecting close interpersonal relationships, mostly within families. Inebriation could lead to domestic violence and family conflict. Defying the holiness of God, the church, and churchgoers were seen as perhaps the most heinous of sins. This was the breakdown of society that Rev. Davis, Brother Hoagy, and others said could only be corrected by having a government guided by their Christian principles.

Rev. Davis referred to corruption starting with the office of the President of the United States. He was referring to the government of the Kennedy/Johnson years that had passed civil rights legislation and prohibited Bible reading and prayer in the schools. He also referred to foreign, non-Christian forces, such as Jews, taking over the country, and he warned that they would outlaw the Bible and even Christianity. He even hinted that they might kill Christians. According to Rev. Davis, the Devil and the non-Christian alliance was destroying the Christian nature of society. He saw society as a zero sum system in which the rights being given to Black people and women were being taken away from White Christian men, eroding the White Christian patriarchal social order. 187

Family Values:
The Veil of Patriarchy and Women's Liberation

Family values were a re-occurring theme in Cabbagetown, and that discussion focused on the role of women. In the Charismatic Holiness Church when Brother John Adcock talked in a sermon about the three messengers who visited Abraham, he referenced the Bible verse about Sarah's role. The Bible says that after she prepared food for the visitors,

Sarah was listening at the entrance of the tent, which was behind him [i.e. Abraham]. Genesis 18:10

Brother Adcock pointed out that Sarah prepared the food and stood behind Abraham at the entrance of the tent listening. Her role in correct Biblical patriarchy was to serve and stand back quietly. Brother Adcock smiled after making that comment, saying that he knew he had ruffled some feelings. He knew that women in the congregation, which included some in their thirties and forties, did not agree with him about their role as being quiet servers. Beyond Brother Adcock, other preachers in the community, all men, also made comments about the role of women as servers and not decision makers. Women could listen to the men surreptitiously as Sarah did but no more. This example of Abraham and Sarah would suggest that the opposition to women's liberation was about patriarchal authority under the euphemism of family values.

In The Lighthouse Church of God's Truth when Brother Hoagy condemned what he perceived as the increased sexual freedom of young women today, the women in his congregation, all of whom were over fifty years old, gave him verbal support with loud "amens" in approval. Women wanted a voice in decision making but publicly disapproved of sexual freedom. Brother Hoagy was concerned that the changing roles of women meant a loss of the spiritual connection with God within the family. Women were identified as the upholders of religious values, and their social role in the family and as mothers was seen as the moral core of the society. Women's rights, abortion, and increased freedoms were seen as threats to family values.

The control of women by men was an aspect of "patriarchal" authority that was falling into question with the feminism movement and set off alarm bells with abortion rights and Roe vs Wade. Esther Smith talks about the change in her father, Cecil, and his attitude toward her as she entered adolescence. He would not allow her to be seen with boys, and if she were out at night he would alter the setting on the clock to falsely blame her of arriving late. To escape that harassment, she got married when she was fourteen years old. When Cecil was drinking and angry, his recurring accusation against his wife was that she was having an affair with her preacher, even though at the time, her preacher was her cousin's husband in a tightly knit family, which made his claim highly unlikely. In Cecil's case he was setting the boundaries of the sexuality of women in the family by verbal harassment and control.

In the interlaced male and female roles, men were nominally the head of the family, and their family name was passed on to children, a patriarchal practice. Yet, women were important decision makers in family life. As mentioned in chapter six, women were the effective leaders of all of the extended family networks in the community. In the case of each family the men were either dead, alcoholic, senile, or had abandoned the family, and by default women were the *de facto* heads of those families. In what might seem contradictory, older women were major supporters of the "family values" movement, even though it included the myth of patriarchy. That might be explained by switching between public and private spheres. Women could acknowledge the public illusion of patriarchy because in practice they had more control of the less recognized private sphere of the family.

What I observed in Cabbagetown tended to coincide with the premise by authors Corrigan and Neal[41] that fears of gender equality and of sexuality were two of the hallmarks of religious intolerance. The opposition to the Equal Rights Amendment and abortion rights became a platform around which the religious right coalesced in subsequent decades, focusing on maintaining the traditional role of women as the moral core of society.

Autocratic Leadership and Christian Nationalism

White Christians feared that their very existence was threatened, and the Baptist minister, Rev. Davis said "Hitler and Stalin did something," he was highlighting autocratic rulers successfully achieving their goals. Implicit in his comment was the success of autocratic rule.

Rev. Davis and others saw their way of life being threatened by a Communist conspiracy of Jews, Blacks, and other foreigners. Religious leaders blamed the federal Government for the loss of the Christian character of the country. The line dividing religion and politics disappeared when it came to discussing the rights to public prayer, Bible reading, and segregation. To many in America those were public policy issues, but to people in Cabbagetown, they were religious issues. People told me that the federal government was undermining the United States as the greatest country on earth, and that it would lead to its doom.

The people arguing for a strong government to impose Christian values thought of themselves as being patriotic and defending a God-inspired cause. That argument was not new; the American South had a history of would-be strongman leaders, ranging from Huey Long to George Wallace, who promised autocratic leadership in support of traditional values. They had failed, but the rise of Christian nationalism once again promised hope for states' rights and local culture over national norms.

189

Christian Nationalism and MAGA Themes

I observed cultural practices and beliefs in Cabbagetown that I would later recognize as elements in Christian nationalism. Some of those are:

- **Unquestioned Belief.** As a creedal religion, Christianity is based on belief. For the true believers in Cabbagetown creed was absolute, and questioning it would be heretical.
- **White Christian Superiority and Authoritarianism.** Both preachers and their followers talked about their superiority as Christians, which was used to justify authoritarian rule to establish a White, Christian society.
- **Racism.** Christian superiority emphasized "whiteness" and did not include Black people.
- **Conspiracy and Fear of Replacement.** People feared that the trends of the transformative decades would lead to the outlawing of Christianity and their being replaced by Jews, Blacks, and other foreigners. They saw themselves as fighting for survival.
- **Disenfranchisement.** Many felt that the judicial decisions and legislation between 1954 and 1973 had left them without power to influence political decisions.
- **Morality and Family Values.** Women's Liberation, the Equal Rights Amendment, and Roe vs Wade offered women's rights that were interpreted in Cabbagetown as threatening traditional family values and women's roles as moral arbiters.
- **Defiance and Outlaw Morality.** If an authority or a law were interpreted to be culturally invalid, then they were non-binding, giving validity to acting outside of the law. The tradition of resisting federal authority from the Civil War to the KKK, justified whatever means might be necessary to make America Christian.
- **Xenophobia and antisemitism.** Jews were seen as non-Christians, who were foreign in Christian America and threatened its existence. The euphemism of communism was used against Jews and other immigrants who were seen as displacing White, Anglo-Saxon Protestants as the backbone of America.

As mentioned earlier in the book, the evangelical world is fragmented by gender, region, and religious differences. The evangelical base of true believers and church goers, who are mostly women, might be passionately dedicated to creating America in their Christian image, and they might turn out to vote in significant numbers, but they will probably not turn to violence. Men in the dissenting base, the born to lose and disenfranchised, might be more willing to carry guns and use physical violence, but both men and women were responding to the same wellspring of grievances within the evangelical universe.

Evangelicals and Politics   191

In the early twenty-first century Christian hegemony is no longer absolute in American society, as the preachers in Cabbagetown predicted fifty years ago, but Evangelicals have become a dominant political force. Many evangelical people believe in the superiority of their religious path and their God-given responsibility to establish Christian rule and guarantee a Christian America. For many, preservation of evangelical exceptionalism can justify the extraordinary measures of supporting fascist-leaning candidates with the alluring promise of a Christian government.

As religious people in the United States have turned to the right politically in recent decades, Evangelicals have coalesced to support Christian nationalist causes and candidates. They have become the largest voting bloc electing Republican politicians to office. That has created a mutually re-enforcing right wing religious political coalition suspicious of pluralism and democracy and increasingly willing to favor a strong man leader to lead them to the promised land of a Christian America.

Endnotes

1   Lehmann: 2021
2   Carter 1995:237-238
3   Belew 2018:3
4   Equal Rights Amendment to the U.S. Constitution, which was submitted to the states for ratification. It guaranteed equal rights to women and required approval by two-thirds of the states. Christian conservatives opposed the amendment, and it was not ratified by the states in the time frame allowed.

5   Whitehead and Perry 2020:73-77. These authors give a lengthy discussion of this issue in conservative politics.
6   Whitehouse 2013:36-47
7   Powell and Clarke 2013: 11-13
8   Batson 2013:88f
9   Clarke, Powell, Savulescu 2013:vi
10   Batson 2013:89
11   Clarke, Powell, Savulescu 2013:vi
12   Although both were Moroccan professors, the sociologist had a Ph.D. from an American university, but the literature professor had his degree from a Middle Eastern university.
13   Telfair Sharpe 2000:604ff
14   Teter 2023:3
15   Ibid.
16   Hanke 1974:67. See also Hernandez 2021:95ff and Adorno 2014
17   Whitehead and Perry 2020:7-9
18   Gorski and Perry 2022:4
19   Whitehead and Perry 2020:xx
20   Merlan 2019:171-198
21   Richardson 1998:viii
22   http://baptiststudiesonline.com/wp-content/uploads/2008/08/a-statement-concerning-the-crisis-in-our-nation-_1968_.pdf
23   Newman 1997:294. Historian Mark Newman has documented the decisions promoting race and segregation in the Arkansas Baptist State Convention during the 1950s and 1960s. Following national leadership, it finally passed a civil rights resolution calling on Baptists to comply with civil rights laws in 1968.
24   "Atlanta Area Study on the Churches' Response to Violence." Unpublished mimeographed manuscript. March 1969. Georgia State university Library.

25   Hein 1972:214

26   Gorski and Perry 2022:21

27   Jane Hill 2008:177

28   Jane Hill 2008:6

29   Jane Hill 2008:4

30   Harari, 2015

31   Bidney 1967:xxii. Theoretical anthropologist David Bidney suggests that as individuals we shape our behavior, and we make our experience of the world understandable through our organization of symbolic categories. He goes on to say that even if we accept the collective fiction of our social group, we are not passive recipients.

32   This verse is from Matthew 19:24, Mark 10:25, and Luke 18:25.

33   This parallels the research results by Hoverd and Sibley (2013) in New Zealand that religious belief gave a sense of well-being to people who lived in poverty.

34   Cox Richardson 2023:84

35   Whitehead and Perry 2022:44-45

36   Jones 2016

37   Alexis de Tocqueville 2002:334 and 335

38   Corrigan and Neal 2020:303

39   The philosophers Ingmar Persson and Julian Savulescu (2013:248) say that the credibility of the moral precepts of a person will depend on the firmness of his or her belief in the supernatural.

40   Austin-Broos 2003:4. Anthropologist Diane Austin-Broos delineates some of those differences in her discussion of the contrasting concepts of Christian sin with indigenous definitions of wrongdoing in Peru, highlighting the local categories such as depravity, damage to another, malicious intent, and malevolent deception, as opposed to the Christian missionary definitions focused on belief.

41   Corrigan and Neal 2010:305

EPILOGUE:
EVANGELICALS IN THE TWENTY-FIRST CENTURY

THE EVANGELICAL CALL TO MAKE AMERICA GREAT and Christian
has evolved over the last fifty years from Rev. Arthur Davis in Cabbagetown to
Jerry Falwell, Pat Robertson, Ronald Reagan, and Donald Trump. The MAGA
movement has had special appeal in the South with its nativistic call from the
religious right to re-create a White Christian America, and it has appealed to
other disaffected groups, making it an important social and political movement
across the United States. In 1970, evangelical Cabbagetown was a microcosm
of working-class America. From that base over the last half century, the evangelical alliance with the Republican Party has made "culture wars" a centerpiece
of building a Christian country, focusing on abortion, public prayer and Bible reading, and immigration among other issues. Their politics of grievance
have focused on the ebbing of Christian values in the country and re-creating
the lost evangelical dominance from the 1800s through much of the 1900s. It
might seem like the struggle of Sisyphus because the United States is no longer
the White, Anglo-Saxon Protestant country that it was during that time in history. As Evangelicals protest the growing religious and ethnic diversity of the
United States, they are calling for an America in which their grandparents and
great-grandparents once lived.

Christian Nationalism

As we have seen in Cabbagetown, by the late 1960s and early 1970s Evangelicals were pushing back against the legal changes of the transformative decades, and they developed mechanisms to blunt those changes. Schools were
the first focus in re-establishing segregation, prayer, and Bible reading, and
that was achieved by establishing private schools. By 1965 one million students were in private schools across the South supported by legislation from
state legislatures.[1] By 1990 there were 25,000 private schools in the United
States, one-quarter of all schools, and they had almost five million students.[2]
Home schooling became popular, and increasingly families were able to avoid
integrated schools. Between private religious schools and home schooling,

Evangelicals counteracted the effects of the Supreme Court decisions of segregation and Bible reading and prayer in schools.

Evangelicals opposed the Equal Rights Amendment, and it was not ratified. Then, in 2022 Roe vs Wade was overturned at the federal level in a key victory for Evangelicals in the culture wars of recent decades. Although the core of civil rights legislation has remained largely intact, voting rights have been regularly challenged. Immigration and culture wars continue to be important targets of Evangelical groups with a focus on the re-reinforcement of Eurocentric views in education and opposition to discussions of race and slavery. Evangelicals have seen Republican politicians as their pathway to a White Christian America, and Republicans have responded by supporting Christian nationalism.

The Pew Research Center's 2022 report on religion[3] in the United States found that 70 percent of adults identified as Christian (182 million) and a quarter of that group identified as White Evangelicals, more than 45 million. Based on those numbers, White Evangelicals are the largest voting bloc in the country.[4] Twenty-nine percent of Americans identified as Christian nationalists or sympathetic to the cause,[5] and among White Evangelicals that number goes up to 65 percent.[6]

The Pew report[7] also found that 81 percent of White Evangelicals believe that the founders of America originally intended for the United States to be Christian and that it should be a Christian nation today. Forty-eight percent believe the Bible should be the standard to be followed in law-making and should have more influence on U.S. laws than the will of the people.[8] This evangelical ideology of Christian nationalism has merged with the Make American Great Again movement,[9] and Donald Trump has publicly identified with their cause and has oriented much of the 2024 campaign toward Evangelicals.

In a study of evangelical churches and political preferences by Pew[10] identified the percentage of Republican-leaning membership in the seven evangelical churches: Southern Baptist (64 percent), Church of the Nazarene (63 percent Republican), Presbyterian Church in America (60 percent), Lutheran Church-Missouri Synod (59 percent), Assemblies of God (57 percent), Church of God (52 percent), Churches of Christ (50 percent).

People in the evangelical world differ widely from group to group and from region to region. Evangelicals in the American Southeast have a unique culture from those who live further west in Texas or those in the Midwest. Asian and Spanish speaking evangelical communities have their own cultural uniqueness. Not all Evangelicals are Christian nationalists or supporters of MAGAism. The Center for Religion and Civic Culture of the University of Southern California has divided Evangelicals into five different groups.[11] There are other classifications, but this one is instructive. The first two tend to be active or sympathetic supporters of MAGA, and the other groups are so in varying degrees.

- Trump-vangelicals. This group is politically aligned with Trumpism to achieve the goals of banning abortion and gaining increased religious freedoms. This group tends to identify with Christian nationalism.
- Neo-fundamentalist. These people are not as politically active as Trump-vangelicals, but they are sympathetic to the achievement of evangelical goals in government and Christian nationalism.
- iVangelicals. The megachurch movement focuses on outreach through popular worship services and focusing on social programs for people.
- Kingdom Christians. They work toward a spiritual goal of creating the "Kingdom of God" in the larger community around them.
- Peace and Justice. These are Evangelicals who focus on social issues from poverty to immigration, racism, and gender issues among others.

Writing for *New York Magazine*, Ed Kilgore[12] argues that Evangelical Christian nationalists see Donald Trump as an irreplaceable figure who would implement God's plan for a Christian America. Ruth Graham and Charles Homans reporting for *The New York Times* quoted one evangelical voter saying, "Trump is our David and our Goliath."[13] Tens of thousands of evangelical preachers have supported Donald Trump over the last decade, including evangelical superstars such as Franklin Graham and Robert Jeffress, who have been leading supporters.

Rev. Jeffress is pastor of the First Baptist Church of Dallas, Texas, a megachurch of 16,000 members and arguably the most important evangelical church in America. After Trump announced that he was running for President in 2015, Jeffress and a group of evangelical preachers went to Trump

Tower to meet with him. They laid their hands on Trump and prayed for him giving their Christian blessing. The "laying on of hands" was particularly important because it implied they were giving God's blessing. They were calling for an end to abortion among other evangelical goals. Jeffress was a frequent visitor to the White House during Trump's term in office and is a regular commentator on Fox News. He has invited Trump to speak at his church and has continued to support him for president. As the civil and criminal indictments grew against Trump in 2023, evangelical support for him continued because people said Trump was suffering for them like Jesus did.[14]

198   Southern Baptists are the largest evangelical church in America with 15,000,000 members in 47,000 churches, and they have been leaders in the Evangelical/MAGA alliance. They were historically an all White denomination, and today continue being 85 percent White with only 6 percent Black membership. As its title suggests, 81 percent of its members are in southern states. They tend to be politically conservative, and 64 percent are either Republican or favor Republicans.[15]

The rightward drift of the Southern Baptist Convention has caused cracks among Baptists. The White Cooperative Baptist Fellowship, broke with Southern Baptists in 1990 over their rightward movement on matters such as the freedom of choice, rejection of LGBTQ people, rejection of women in the clergy, and its position on Christian nationalism. Southern Baptists have not been tolerant of dissent voices, and critics of denominational policies or Christian nationalism have been exiled from the body.

Dr. Robert P. Jones, *The New York Times* best selling author on white supremacy and Christian nationalism and founder of the Public Religion Research Institute, is such an exile. Dr. Russell Moore, the dean of the Southern Baptist Theological Seminary and director of the denomination's Ethics and Religious Liberty Commission left or was pushed out of his position after criticizing Trump for claiming to be endorsed by God. Moore had also criticized the apparent creeping White nationalism within the denomination. This exiling of critical thinkers in evangelical churches seems to be consistent with the binary, black/white belief systems in fundamentalist circles which are not conducive to nuanced discussions.

In 2021 the Pew Research Council issued a report on the continuing support of Evangelicals for Donald Trump. In the 2016 presidential election he received 77 percent of the White Evangelical vote to Hillary Clinton's 16 percent. According to the Pew report, White Evangelicals who voted for Trump in 2020 held strong at 78 percent.[16]

With this outsized influence of Evangelicals in the electorate, Trump has emphasized his religious connections more in 2024 than in previous campaigns, building his campaign to appeal to them. The ending minutes of his 2024 rallies have the character of an evangelical altar call. With soft music playing in the background, Trump invites people to dedicate themselves to the fight to save the country and support him. *The New York Times* writer Michael C. Bender says that he seems to be building a "Church of Trump" with himself as the head of it.[17] Trump's social media platform has multiple images of Jesus, and one shows Trump sitting next to Jesus with a message saying "You Can Judge a Person By the Company He Keeps."[18]

As the MAGA movement has grown from Reagan in 1980 to Trump in 2024, Evangelicals have pushed Republican politicians to the right. Given the shrinking White electorate, Republican candidates need overwhelming evangelical support to be elected, giving White nationalists and Christian nationalists major influence in early twenty-first century American politics.

About the Author

RON DUNCAN HART IS A CULTURAL ANTHROPOLOGIST (Ph.D. Indiana University) with postdoctoral study at the Centre for Hebrew and Jewish Studies, University of Oxford. The focus of his research has been on religion and culture, ranging from this study of Evangelicals to the Catholic Church and the Inquisition, and Sephardi Jewish life and practice.

He is a former Dean of Academic Affairs at InterAmerican University and Vice President of Sacred Heart University in Puerto Rico. He was Project Director in Latin America on research and social justice programs with the Ford Foundation, the International Development Research Centre of Canada, and UNICEF. During the time of this research in Cabbagetown, he was an assistant professor of anthropology at Georgia State University.

Duncan Hart has awards from the National Endowment for the Humanities, National Endowment for the Arts, the National Science Foundation, the Ford Foundation, and the Fulbright Scholar Program among others. He has been an invited lecturer internationally from the University of the Andes in Colombia to Xinjiang University (Urumqi, China), Neustadt Lecturer (Oklahoma City University), the National Labor Relations Board of the United States, George Mason University, and Tulane University among others.

He is the author of *Crafts, Capitalism and Women* and *The Ceramics of Raquira: Gender, Work and Economic Change* (Both University Press of Florida). He is co-author/editor of the award-winning book *Fractured Faiths: Spanish Judaism, the Inquisition and New World Identities* (New Mexico History Museum and Fresco Books). He has authored other titles in the Monographs on Religion and Tolerance series of the Institute for Tolerance Studies.

He has appeared in PBS documentaries on the role of the Spanish Inquisition and its legacy of hidden Jews in the American Southwest. He is a documentary filmmaker with dozens of films on the Jewish Learning Channel and a series of anthropological films in the permanent collections of the Luis Angel Arango Library (the National Library of Colombia) and the *Fundación Patrimonio Fílmico Colombiano* (Foundation for Colombian Film Patrimony) in Bogotá, Colombia.

ACKNOWLEDGMENTS

WITH PROFESSOR DAVID BIDNEY of Indiana University I learned important theoretical constructs in the anthropology of religion and developed analytical skills to study that area of behavior. His intellectual challenges throughout a decade of seminars, student assistantships, Shabbat dinners, and research guidance gave me an indelible model of the humanist scholar and an understanding of the linkages between religion and culture. He encouraged me to study the impact of religious behavior on intolerance on society.

Anthropologists Paul Doughty and Solon Kimball guided me to understand community studies, which gave me background for this research on the urban mill village. Before them were the philosopher Gregory Pritchard, who challenged me in critical thinking and the English professor Hazel Presson, who expanded my understanding of literature and writing.

Dr. Martin Luther King, Jr. gave me words of inspiration and guidance to me as a young anthropologist in Atlanta to focus on the roots of racism in the American South. I thank Dean Glenn G. Thomas of the College of Arts and Sciences at Georgia State University for his confidence and unfailing support during the research period and initial analysis of these materials. The support and guidance of Dr. Charles Tauber was invaluable as I processed my experiences in Cabbagetown.

I give special appreciation to anthropologists Nina S. de Friedemann, Alma Gottlieb, and Tim Knowlton, historian Harry Feldman, and my research partner and wife, Gloria Abella Ballen for reading and analyzing early drafts of this text. Each made detailed, critical corrections and suggestions to bring this writing into its current form. This book would not exist without their insights and thoughts.

Historian Clifford Kuhn helped me to understand the relationship between Fulton Cotton Mill and its workers. I appreciate folklorist John Burrison for inspiration to explore the unique folklore of Georgia related to this work. The suggestions of anthropologist James Peacock guided me to explore the symbolism of stories and music in the lives of people in Cabbagetown. The ethnomusicologist Vanessa Paloma Elbaz helped me understand the cultural role of music and its behavioral impact on people.

In seminars at the University of Oxford Professors Robert Chazan, Jeremy Cohen, and Anna Sapir Abulafia introduced me to early Church history and the creation of the Christian sense of exclusivity and divine right, which led to the Othering of Jews and other non-Christians. Working with historians Stanley Hordes and Roger L. Martínez-Dávila has expanded my understanding of religious intolerance in Spain and the persecution of hidden Jews living in Spanish lands.

204

The National Endowment for the Humanities and the National Science Foundation provided funding at various stages that have helped make this book possible. Support from Georgia State University was valuable during the years of this research, including released time to complete the project.

In my career I had experience in a private religious university that helped me put the Christian belief systems that I recorded in Cabbagetown into perspective. I thank the families who shared their lives with me and trusted me with their beliefs. My goals in this writing has been to represent their information accurately, protect their privacy, and describe their beliefs and social perceptions that have become part of shaping the contemporary political landscape in the United States.

May this look into the day-to-day lives of evangelical people in this Georgia community facilitate the understanding of their grievances and the roots of Christian nationalism and the MAGA movement.

Ron Duncan Hart
Santa Fe, New Mexico

APPENDIX ONE
Cabbagetown after Fulton Cotton Mill

The Fulton Cotton Mill closed in stages during the 1970s. During the 1974 recession production was reduced significantly, leading to layoffs and the loss of jobs. In 1978 most operations were terminated although one small department continued to function until 1981. When I returned in 1979, I had access to information about the history of the mill, extensive detailed records preserved over the decades by the Elsas family and later archived at the Georgia Institute of Technology.

The closing of the mill ended the century of life as mill workers in this urban village. As the older people passed away and their children moved, I gradually lost contact with those I had known. New people were moving into the neighborhood in the 1980s and 1990s, and the old mill village was evolving into its gentrified avatar of today with only the memory of its mill village history.

The renaissance of re-culturized communities like Cabbagetown reflects the revitalization of communities that had lost their original economic base and have taken on a new identity as gentrified cultural centers. Anthropologist James Peacock[19] point out that we can only understand these events in the American South as they are impacted by shifts in the economics and politics of the larger world. The American South became the Global South, and low-skilled manufacturing lost the dominance it once had. With the success of the rights movements and the end of the Jim Crow way of life, the vestiges of the Confederacy began to drift to the background.

After the Hart-Geller Immigration Act of 1965 opened the door for increased immigration into the United States, Atlanta became a more international city. In 1950 there were only 4,000 foreign born people in Atlanta.[20] The demand for labor that had driven Atlanta's economy for 150 years was growing, and that attracted immigrants to the city. By 1995 the foreign-born population was 266,000, and by 2020 that number had risen to over 775,000.

Today, Atlanta is a cosmopolitan city. Fifty years ago, there were no restaurants in Cabbagetown, and the only bar was the country music haven Kwitcherbellyakin Tavern. Today, you can walk the streets where chic cafes and taverns, from the Carroll Street Cafe to the Cabbagetown Arms, offer menus from Southern foods to international cuisine. The area features restaurants that offer French, Chinese and Asian fusion, and Latin American as well as Southern food.

In 1975 U.S. congressman Andrew Young of Georgia filed a request for the mill village to be named to the National Register of Historic Places, and it was approved in 1976. The old mill village had everything within walking distance, and not everyone had a car. Little's Store had good ham hock and pinto beans, and some neighbor or friend would always be there to talk and exchange gossip. Just down the street was a church. The liquor store was not too far away. Uncles, aunts, cousins, and grandparents lived just around the corner. The closing of the mill in 1981 was a turning point, as happened with mill closings across the South. Writing about the closing of mills in small town Georgia, Billie Coleman[21] describes the interest in the charm of the old mill villages and people recreating the sense of community that once existed in them.

I have followed the evolution of Cabbagetown from the mill village that I knew to its new gentrified manifestation, as the mill was turned into a museum, then upscale apartments. In the 1980s photographer Raymond Herbert opened a studio gallery on Carroll Street. Rents were still relatively low, and some people envisioned this neighborhood becoming an art gallery district. That dream was not fully realized, but in the 1990s gentrification was beginning.

A Revitalization and Future Trust was established in 1988 to renovate houses in Cabbagetown and build new ones. After the announcement of the 1996 Olympics in Atlanta, Joyce Brookshire, a singer/songwriter known as the Duchess, wrote a song entitled, "What Will We Do With the Homeless?" to call attention to the problem of affordable housing as Atlanta was making its multi-million-dollar buildup to the Olympics.[22]

In 1995, the mill was sold for conversion into lofts, and Aderhold Properties began the conversion of the old mill into The Lofts, a complex that is prime real estate today, as are the renovated houses of Cabbagetown. What was the noisy mill is now a quiet gated community of architecturally creative lofts carved out of this unique example of Atlanta's earliest industrial architecture. Once unpainted mill village houses where I sat on the porches talking to mill workers are now painted to match their new standing in the world, and they sell for hundreds of thousands of dollars. The average income in the neighborhood now is over $100,000, a far reach from the salaries of the workers who once lived there.

Cabbagetown became a place of interest for artists, and as Atlanta grew, it became prime real estate located near the downtown. Younger people with different cultural interests moved in, and the rustic mill village houses were transformed into upscale housing. Today, Cabbagetown is an artsy enclave in a new hip Atlanta. The streets are as busy today as they have ever been, and this is still a walking neighborhood much as it has been since the first houses were built in the 1880s.

Helping to close the circle of this history, Jacob Elsas, the great-great grandson of the founder of Fulton Bag and Cotton Mill, lives in the neighborhood, and he and his wife Nina run The Patch Works Art and History Center which has the mission of preserving the mill village history and identity through community-based programming.[23]

Appendix Two

The People of this Study

Six community organizations were operative during the time I was in Cabbagetown, including the Neighborhood House or "mission", the Sing, the clinic, the tie-making cooperative, and the grocery buying cooperative. Each of these organizations was taken over by one of the family networks in the village. There was a Citizens Mutual Club which attempted to address broader social issues in the village, but like the other local organizations, it seemed to be largely ineffective.[24]

Many of the people had an Appalachian background,[25] and they had limited formal education, with the average person having completed only the seventh grade in school.[26] After the mill sold its houses, the private investors who bought them rented their houses to anyone. Although most of families still had a connection with the mill, it was no longer exclusively a neighborhood of mill workers.[27] Working at the mill was often a long-term affair. When I asked non-mill workers about other recent jobs, half of them mentioned that they had worked in the mill previously.

Most of my research was with members of the "White family", a four generational extended family. It included the grandmother Corey and her two daughters, Effie and Ruthie who had fifteen children between them. I came to know Effie's family best, including her husband, their three children and grandchildren, sixteen people in that family. Ruthie's husband had passed away, but her twelve children and their husbands, wives, and children numbered another sixty people. Then the cousins, neighbors, and in-laws expanded that group to more than 100 people. I observed and interacted with perhaps half of that group, hearing family stories that sometimes overlapped with each other. I also had contacts with others involved in the community center and people I met in corner stores, churches, community sings, school, front porches, or in the street. I had some degree of personal contact with more than 20 percent of the estimated 1,200 people living in the neighborhood at the time.

I made a demographic survey to establish a base of information about the overall village. The survey included 60 of 350 households, some 17 percent of the population. The average household size was 3.3 persons for an estimated population of approximately 1,200 people in the village. Before doing the survey, I told key people in the village that I would be doing it, and that it was a part of my work at the university. I assured people that the survey was completely anonymous and no names would be recorded, and almost all agreed to answer the questions. I did the house-to-house interviews personally, so most people knew who I was. I chose the families to be interviewed in each block, based systematically on house numbers, and I covered every block in Cabbagetown. I did the survey during the late afternoon and early evening hours after work in the summer of 1970, during months that people would frequently be on their front porch after eating supper. That made approaching them to ask questions fit into the regular routine of their lives.

One-third of the residents were immigrants from the Appalachian regions of northern Georgia, South Carolina, and North Carolina, and another forty percent were born locally of immigrant parents from the same areas. Forty-two percent had six years or less of formal education, and, among those, thirteen percent had been to school three years or less, including a few among the older people who had never attended school. I registered no high school graduates, although I did identify three graduates from Cabbagetown through other contacts. In comparison, 51 percent of Whites in the United States in 1964 were high school graduates.[28]

The median residence was twenty years, and some families had lived there forty and even sixty years. Three-fourths (45) of the families were renting their houses, with one-quarter (15) owning them. As can be expected, the house owners were more stable, rarely moving. Ten had owned their property from five to twenty years, probably representing those who could buy their houses after the mill began selling them in the 1950s. Five families had owned their houses for more than twenty years, and they tended to be larger houses more distant from the mill.

One-third of the inhabitants of Cabbagetown were non-mill workers, who recently moved there and were not members of one of the extended families. The non-mill residents tended to be less stable, and forty percent of that group had moved in the last year. The neighborhood was almost equally divided between households of people over 50 years old, and those under 50. The older husband and wife households or a widowed survivor living alone were 46 percent of the community, and they were mostly mill families. The younger nuclear and composite families averaged almost five persons per household, and they were 54 percent of the households. About half of these younger households did not have a connection with the mill and were young renters who had moved into the village.

Appendix Three
Strike Statement, 1897

"1,400 MILL WORKERS ON A STRIKE. WOULD NOT WORK WITH NEGROES."
The Atlanta Constitution, August 5, 1897.

Women [in Cabbagetown] Refuse to Work with Negro Women and Go on a Strike.

OTHER OPERATIVES HAVE JOINED THE STRIKES

Textile Workers Will Conduct the Strike and Announce That They Are Determined to Push the Fight Through—A Lively Mass Meeting of Strikers Yesterday.

Because twenty negro women were put to work [at the mill] yesterday morning, over 1,400 [White] men, women and children employed in the mill quit their machines and walked out.

The strike was started by the white women employed at the mill, who refused to work with negro women. The women and children struck at 8 o'clock in the morning and the men walked out at noon. The mills were promptly closed and it may be weeks before they are operated again.

The strikers after quitting work lost no time in organizing. A meeting was held at 3:30 o'clock in the Federation of Trades Hall. Committees were appointed and the strike was given a good shove off by the other trade unions.

The big strike was entirely unexpected by the operators of the bag and cotton mills. Yesterday morning at the regular hour for beginning work, the entire force of nearly 1,500 hands were at the factory and nothing unusual could be noticed. The women had been told on the previous evening that the negro women would be put to work in the folding department yesterday morning, and it seems that some of them had already discussed the matter before going to the factory.

When the hands congregated around the factory at 6 o'clock they were told that the twenty negro women had already gone upstairs to begin work. This seemed to enrage the girls who work in the folding department. One of them, a young woman named Brooks, waited until Mr. Jacob Elsas, one of the proprietors, arrived, and then the trouble began. Miss Brooks walked up to Mr. Elsas and said she wanted to know if he intended to put a crowd of negroes in with her and the other girls.

Mr. Elsas informed her that he was running the business and that it was not a matter to inquire about.

Miss Brooks was warm on that particular subject, and she told the proprietor that the girls were running that part of the business and that trouble would ensure if the negroes were put to work.

As Mr. Elsas walked away, she told him that they would not go to work if the negro women were allowed to remain.

Mr. Elsas disregarded this threat, and the negroes were set to work. The 200 girls employed in the folding department refused to even enter the factory, but after lingering for a while around the gate, went quietly to their homes. The strikers claim that three employees named Rachel Hughes, Oscar Todd and Mrs. Bailey remained in the folding department and taught the negroes how to work.

Endnotes

1   Southern Education Foundation. N.D.
2   McLaughlin, et.al. 1995
3   https://www.pewresearch.org/religion/2022
4   PRRI, 2022
5   Smith, Rotolo and Tevington 2022
6   Shimron 2023
7   https://www.pewresearch.org/religion/2022
8   Smith, Rotolo and Tevington 2022
9   Thurow 2013:147
10 https://www.pewresearch.org/short-reads/2016/02/23/u-s-reli
gious-groups-and-their-political-leanings/
11 https://crcc.usc.edu/report/the-varieties-of-american-evangelicalism/
12 Kilgore 2023
13 Graham and Homans 2024
14 Oliphant, James and Nathan Layne. 2023. Young 2015. Mooney 2012
15 Fahmy 2019
16 Smith, Gregory A. 202
17 Bender 2024
18 https://truthsocial.com/group/make-america-great-again.
May 14, 2024
19 Peacock 2010, Bone 2018
20 Dameron and Murphy 1997:50
21 Coleman 2017:8
22 Snodderly 1994:14-15
23 https://thepatchworks.org/about/
24 I made a demographic survey to establish a base of information
about the overall village. The survey included 60 of 300 households, approximately 20 percent of the population.
25 One-third of the residents were immigrants from the Appalachia regions
of northern Georgia, South Carolina and North Carolina, and another 40 percent
were born locally of immigrant parents from the same areas.
26 Forty-two percent had six years or less of formal education, and,
among those, thirteen percent had been to school three years or less, including
a few among the older people who had never attended school.
27 This was a stable community with a median residence of 20 years.
28 Pew Research Center on Demographic trends and economic
well-being. https://www.pewresearch.org/social-trends/2016/06/27/1
-demographic-trends-and-economic-well-being/

Glossary of Terms

Christian nationalism — This is the belief that "Christian" principles should be used as governing policy and laws in the United States. The term "Christian" as used in this phrase commonly refers to "evangelical Christianity". Some people refer to "biblical" principles, which might not appear in the Bible, but are references to something they culturally oppose, such as feminism, abortion, same sex marriage, interracial marriage, integration, and LGBTQ recognition among other issues.

Christian superiority — This is the belief that Evangelical Christianity is the only correct path to connect to the God in which they believe. Other forms of Christianity and non-Christian religions are seen as erroneous and not valid.

Evangelical Christianity — Evangelical Christianity refers to practice of Protestantism that emphasizes having a life changing conversion experience, belief in the inerrancy of the Bible, and actively proselytizing non-Evangelicals. Approximately 25 percent of Americans are considered to be evangelical, the largest religious grouping in the country.

Evangelical exceptionalism — This is related to the belief in Christian superiority, and it means that Evangelicals are exceptional because they have the true teachings of God, making them unique. Belief in their exceptionalism means they deserve special attention.

Fundamentalism — Within evangelical circles there is a subgroup called fundamentalists who believe in the inerrancy of the Bible and believe that they are the only ones to practice the fundamental or original truths of the teachings of Jesus. Beliefs should be absolute with no nuance.

Grievance — Grievance is a protest against real or imagined wrongs or other causes for complaint. Grievance appeals to those who feel they are disenfranchised and are victims of public policy.

Pentecostal — Pentecostal Holiness churches are the mystical branch of evangelical Christianity in which people believe in miraculous faith healing, being possessed by the spirit of God in an alternate state of reality, glossolalia or speaking in unknown tongues as the voice of God. It emphasizes a close, direct personal connection with God, absent of human intervention.

Proselytize — Evangelical churches are known for aggressively recruiting new members based on promises of a new life. This is the largest Christian movement world-wide today.

214

Mainstream Christianity — Historically this term has referred to older, established Protestant denominations, such as Episcopalians, Lutherans, Presbyterians that emphasize ritual more that evangelization.

Make America Great — This phrase has been used in conjunction with Christianity and refers to the belief that only Christian practice can make America a great nation. This is a belief that the United States has been chosen by God for special blessings because it is a Christian nation. That is used to explain its political and military power in the world today, as well as its wealth.

ARCHIVES

Fulton Bag and Cotton Mills Digital Collection. Archives & Records Management, Library and Information Center, Georgia Institute of Technology. Atlanta, Georgia.

BIBLIOGRAPHY

Alinsky, Saul. 1971. *Rules for Radicals*. New York: Random House. Page xx.

Anderson, Carol. 2016. *White Rage: The Unspoken Truth of Our Racial Divide*. Bloomsbury: Bloomsbury Publishing.

Adorno, Rolena. 2014. *The Polemics of Possession in Spanish American Narrative*. New Haven: Yale University Press.

Alberta, Tim. 2023. *The Kingdom, the Power, and the Glory: American Evangelicals in an Age of Extremism*. New York: HarperCollins Publishers.

Alexander, Jeffrey C, Ron Eyerman, Bernhard Giesen, Meil J. Smelser, Piotr Sztompka. 2004. *Cultural Trauma and Collective Identity*. Berkeley: University of California Press.

Alexander, Jeffrey C. 2004. "Toward a Theory of Cultural Trauma," in *Cultural Trauma and Collective Identity*, edited by Jeffrey C. Alexander, et.al. Berkeley: University of California Press. Pages 1-30.

Arsenault, Kerri. 2020. *Mill Town: Reckoning with What Remains*. New York: St. Martin's Press.

Andrews, Gerald Bruce. 2019. *A Mill Village Story: A Southern Boyhood Joyfully Remembered*. Montgomery, Alabama: New South Books.

"Atlanta Area Study on the Churches' Response to Violence." Unpublished mimeographed manuscript. March, 1969. Georgia State University Library.

Austin-Broos, Diane. 2003. "The Anthropology of Conversion: An Introduction," in *The Anthropology of Religious Conversion*, edited by Andrew Buckser and Stephen D. Glazier. Lanham, MD: Rowman & Littlefield Publishers, Inc. Pages 1-12.

Bailey, Kenneth. 1968. *Southern White Protestantism in the Twentieth Century*. Gloucester, MA: Peter Smith.

Balmer, Randall. 1989. *Mine Eyes Have Seen the Glory*. Reprinted by Oxford University Press, 2006, 4th edition.

Batson, C. Daniel. 2013. "Individual Religion, Tolerance, and Universal Compassion," in in *Religion, Intolerance, and Conflict: A Scientific and Conceptual Investigation*. Edited by Steve Clarke, Russell Powell, Julian Savulescu. Oxford: Oxford University Press. Pages 88-106.

Bender, Michael C. 2024. "The Church of Trump: How He is Infusing Christianity into his Movement," in *The New York Times*. https://www.nytimes.com/2024/04/01/us/politics/trump-2024-religion.html?smid=em-share.

Beaver, Patricia. 1976. "Symbols and Social Organization in an Appalachian Mountain Community." Ph.D. dissertation. Durham: Duke University.

Beckerman, Gal. 2022. *The Quiet Before: On the Unexpected Origins of Radical Ideas*. New York: Crown.

Belew, Kathleen. 2018. *Bring the War Home: The White Power Movement and Paramilitary in America*. Cambridge: Harvard University Press.

Belew, Kathleen and Ramon A Gutierrez, editors. 2021. *A Field Guide to White Supremacy*. Oakland: University of California Press.

Bevington, Rickey. 2015. "The Many Myths of Cabbagetown", in *Atlanta Considered*. GPB. NPR. September 18, 2015. https://www.gpb.org/blogs/atlanta-considered/2015/09/18/the-many-myths-of-cabbagetown.

Bialecki, Jon. 2017. "Eschatology, Ethics, and Ethnos: Ressentiment and Christian Nationalism in the Anthropology of Christianity," in *Religion and Society*. Vol. 8. Annual 2017.

Bidney, David.
• 1967. *Theoretical Anthropology*. Second Augmented edition. New York: Shocken Books.
• 1963. *The Concept of Freedom in Anthropology*. The Hague & Mouton & Co.

Blank, Rebecca M., James M. Sallee and Kerwin Kofi Charles. 2007. "Do State Laws Affect the Age of Marriage? A Cautionary Tale about Avoidance Behavior." NBER Working Paper Series. Working Paper 13667. Cambridge, MA: National Bureau of Economic Research. http://www.nber.org/papers/w13667.

Blee, Kathleen M. 2008. *Women of the Klan: Racism and Gender in the 1920s*. Berkeley: University of California Press.

Bone, Martyn. 2018. *Where the New World Is: Literature about the U.S. South at Global Scales*. Athens: University of Georgia Press.

Booker, Lauren. 2019. "How a Mill Settlement in Atlanta Evolved into Modern-Day Cabbagetown," in *All Things Considered*. Marketplace. WABE. https://www.wabe.org/how-a-mill-settlement-in-atlanta-evolved-into-modern-day-cabbagetown/

Brookshire, Joyce. No date. Interview by George Stoney and Judith Helfand. L1995-13_AV0738, The Uprising of '34 Collection, Special Collections and Archives, Georgia State University. Atlanta.

Buck, Pem Davidson. 2001. *Worked to the Bone: Race, Class, Power, and Privilege in Kentucky*. New York: Monthly Review Press.

Buckser, Andrew and Stephen D. Glazier, editors. 2003. *The Anthropology of Religious Conversion*. Lanham, MD: Rowman & Littlefield Publishing Company.

Bullock III, Charles S, Susan A. MacManus, Jeremy D. Mayer and Mark J. Rozell.
- 2019a. *The South and the Transformation of U.S. Politics*. Oxford: Oxford University Press.
- 2019b. "The Rise of the Christian Right in the South and Its Impact on National Politics," in *The South and the Transformation of U.S. Politics*. Oxford: Oxford University Press.

Burrison, John
- 2012. *Roots of a Region: Southern Folk Culture*. Oxford: University Press of Mississippi.
- 2000. *Shaping Traditions: Folk Arts in a Changing South*. Athens: University of Georgia Press.
- 1991. *Storytellers, Folktales and Legends from the South*. Editor. Athens: University of Georgia Press.

Butler, Rhonda and Pam Durban Porter. 1976. *Cabbagetown Families, Cabbagetown Food*. Atlanta: Patch Publications.

Cameron, Rebecca J. and Arthur D. Murphy. 1997. "An International City Too Busy to Hate? Social and Cultural Change in Atlanta: 1970:1995," in *Urban Anthropology and Studies of Cultural Systems and World Economic Development*. Vol. 26, No. 1. Pages 43-69.

Campbell, John C. 1921. *The Southern Highlander and his Homeland*. New York: The Russell Sage Foundation. Reprinted 1969 by The University Press of Kentucky.

Cannell, Fenella. 2005. "The Christianity of Anthropology," in *Journal of Royal Anthropological Institute*. Vol. 11, Issue 2. June 2005. Pages 335-356.

217

Cannell, Fenella, editor. 2006. *The Anthropology of Christianity*. Durham: Duke University Press.

Carden, Allen. 1986. "Religious Schism as a Prelude to the American Civil War: Methodists, Baptists, and Slavery," in *Andrews University Seminary Studies*, Spring 1986. Vol. 24, No. 1. Pages 13-29.

Carlile, Alexandra, Quinn Galbraith, Ben White. 2020. "Religion as a Source of Tolerance and Intolerance: Exploring the Dichotomy," in *The International Journal of Religion and Spirituality in Society*. Vol. 10, Issue 2. Pages 89-104.

Carter, Dan T. 1995. *The Politics of Rage: George Wallace, the Origins of the New Conservatism, and the Transformation of American Politics*. New York: Simon & Schuster.

Catanzaro, Christine de. No date. "History of the Fulton Bag and Cotton Mills". Fulton Bag and Cotton Mills Digital Collection. Archives & Records Management, Library and Information Center, Georgia Institute of Technology. Atlanta, Georgia.

Catledge, Oraien E. 1985. *Cabbagetown Photographs*. Austin: University of Texas Press.

Caudill, Harry M. 1963. *Night Comes to the Cumberlands: A Biography of a Depressed Area*. Boston: Little, Brown and Company.

Clarke, Steve, Russell Powell, Julian Savulescu, editors. 2013. *Religion, Intolerance, and Conflict: A Scientific and Conceptual Investigation*. Oxford: Oxford University Press.

Cochran, J. Otis. N.D. "Report on Cabbage Town." Atlanta: Community Relations Commission.

Coleman, Billie. 2017. *Central Georgia Textile Mills*. Charleston, SC: Arcadia Publishing.

Coleman, Simon. 2003. "Continuous Conversion? The Rhetoric, Practice, and Rhetorical Practice of Charismatic Protestant Conversion," in *The Anthropology of Religious Conversion*, edited by Andrew Buckser and Stephen D. Glazier. Lanham, MD: Rowman & Littlefield Publishers, Inc. Pages 15-27.

Corrigan, John. 2020. *Religious Intolerance, America, and the World: A History of Forgetting and Remembering*. Chicago: The University of Chicago Press.

Corrigan, John and Lynn S. Neal. 2010. *Religious Intolerance in America: A Documentary History*. Second Edition. Chapel Hill: The University of North Carolina Press.

Cors, Alexander. 2021. "Cabbagetown: An Atlanta Neighborhood in the 1920s: Exploring a Bustling Mill Town and its Residents in the Tumultuous Twenties." Emory Center for Digital Scholarship. https://storymaps.arcgis.com/stories/ee518f7717304be08af934b2dcdae022.

Cox Richardson, Heather.

- 2023. *Democracy Awakening: Notes on the State of America*. New York: Viking.
- 2020. *How the South Won the Civil War: Oligarchy, Democracy, and the Continuing Fight for the Soul of America*. Oxford: Oxford University Press.
- 2007. *West from Appomattox: The Reconstruction of America after the Civil War*. New Haven: Yale University Press.

Curtis, Jesse. 2021. *The Myth of Colorblind Christians: Evangelicals and White Supremacy in the Civil Rights Era*. New York: New York University Press.

Davis, Ennis. 2020. "Urban Revitalization: Atlanta's Cabbagetown" in *Atlanta: The Jaxson Magazine*. https://www.the jaxsonmag.com

DeLoach, Doug. 2010. *Peg-legged Salon: An Abbreviated History of Cabbagetown*. Macon: Georgia Music Foundation.

Dennerstein, Leonard.

- 1994. *Antisemitism in America*. Oxford: Oxford University Press.
- 1987. *The Leo Frank Case*. Athens: University of Georgia Press.

De Tocqueville, Alexis. 2002. *Democracy in America*. A Penn State Electronic Series Publication. State College: The Pennsylvania State University.

Duncan Hart, Ron.

- 2020a. *Jews and the Arab World: Intertwined Legacies*. Santa Fe: Institute for Tolerance Studies. Best Book Award. New Mexico/Arizona Book Awards.
- 2020b. *Crypto-Jews: The Long Journey*. Santa Fe: Institute for Tolerance Studies.
- 2016. *Fractured Faiths: Spanish Judaism, Inquisition, and New World Identities*. Author/Editor with Josef Diaz and Roger Martinez-Davila. Santa Fe: The New Mexico History Museum and Fresco Books.
- 2011. *Islam and Muslims: Religion, History and Ethnicity*. Santa Fe: Institute for Tolerance Studies.
- 2007. *A Phoenix Rising: Resurgence of the Middle East and Asia as World Powers*. Santa Fe: Gaon Books.

- 2003. "Women's Folk Art in La Chamba, Colombia" in *Crafting Gender: Women and Folk Art in Latin America and the Caribbean*. Edited by Eli Bartra. Durham: Duke University Press. Pages 126 to 154.
- 2002. "St. Vicente Ferrer and the Anti-Semitism of Fifteen Century Spain" in *Halapid*, Vol. IX, No. 2. Spring. Pages 1ff.
- 2000. *Crafts, Capitalism, and Women: The Potters of La Chamba, Colombia*. Gainesville: University Press of Florida. Ermine Wheeler-Voegelin Prize in Ethnohistory Nominee.
- 1998. *The Ceramics of Ráquira, Colombia: Gender, Work, and Economic Change*. Gainesville: University Press of Florida.
- 1993. *El Arte Del Chamanismo, La Salud Y La Vida* (The Art of Shamanism, Health, and Life). Co-author with Jaime Bernal and Ignacio Briceño. Bogotá: Instituto Colombiano de Cultura Hispánica.
- 1981. *Social Research in Puerto Rico*. Editor. San Juan: InterAmerican University Press.
- 1971. "Living in Urban Cabbagetown" in *The Not So Solid South*. J. Kenneth Morland, editor. Southern Anthropological Society Proceedings, No. 4. Athens: University of Georgia Press.
- 1969. "One Poor White," in *New South*. Vol. 24, No. 4. Pages 49-59.

Dunbar, R.I.M. 2013. "The Origin of Religion as a Small-Scale Phenomenon," in *Religion, Intolerance, and Conflict: A Scientific and Conceptual Investigation*. Edited by Steve Clarke, Russell Powell, Julian Savulescu. Oxford: Oxford University Press. Pages 48-66.

Elbaz, Vanessa Paloma.
- 2021. "Jewish Music in Northern Morocco and the Building of Sonic Identity boundaries" *Journal for North African Studies* (2021) https://doi.org/10.1080/13629387.2021.1884855
- 2016. "De tu boca a los cielos: Jewish women's songs in Northern Morocco as Oracles of Communal Holiness" *Hesperis-Tamuda,* Vol. LI-Fascicule 3 (2016) 239-261.

Eyerman, Ron. 2019. *Memory, Trauma, and Identity*. London: Palgrave Macmillan.

Fahmy, Dalia. 2019. "7 Facts about Southern Baptists." Pew Research Center. https://www.pewresearch.org/short-reads/2019/06/07/7-facts-about-southern-baptists/

Fink, Gary. 1993. *The Fulton Bag and Cotton Mills Strike of 1914-1915, Espionage, Labor Conflict, and New South Industrial Relations*. Ithaca: ILR Press Cornell University.

Flinders, Matthew & Hinterleitner, Markus. 2022. Party Politics vs. Grievance Politics: Competing Modes of Representative Democracy. Society. 10.1007/s12115-022-00686-z. https://www.researchgate.net/publication/359167903_Party_Politics_vs_Grievance_Politics_Competing_Modes_of_Representative_Democracy

Fox, Aaron. 2004. *Real Country: Music and Language in Working-Class Culture*. Durham: Duke University Press.

Fox News. "Bill Clinton suggests Trump slogan racist – but he used the same one". September 9, 2016.

Galbraith, Quinn, Alexandra Carlile, Ben White. 2020. "Religion as a Source of Tolerance and Intolerance: Exploring the Dichotomy," in *The International Journal of Religion and Spirituality in Society*. Vol. 10, Issue 2. Pages 89 to 104.

Garrett, Franklin M. 1969. *Atlanta and Environs: A Chronicle of Its People and Events*. Reprinted from 1954. 4 volumes. Athens: University of Georgia Press.

Gary, Rodney and Tami Linn West. *Cabbagetown Historic District Design Guidelines*. Atlanta: The Commission.

Goodson, Steve. 2007. *Highbrows, Hillbillies and Hellfire: Public Entertainment in Atlanta, 1880-1930*. Athens: University of Georgia Press.

Gorski, Philip S. and Samuel L. Perry. 2022. *The Flag + The Cross: White Christian Nationalism and the Threat to American Democracy*. New York: Oxford University Press.

Grable, Stephen W. 1982. "The Others Side of the Tracks: Cabbagetown – A Working-class Neighborhood in Transition During the Early Twentieth Century." *Atlanta History Journal*. Vol 26. No. 2-3.

Graeber, David and David Wengrow. 2021. *The Dawn of Everything: A New History of Humanity*. New York: Farrar, Straus and Giroux.

Graham, Ruth and Charles Homans. 2024. "Trump is Connecting With a Different Type of Evangelical Voter," in *The New York Times*. Jan. 8, 2024. https://www.nytimes.com/2024/01/08/us/politics/donald-trump-evangelicals-iowa.html

Grem, Darren. "Southern Baptists." New Georgia Encyclopedia, last modified Sep 10, 2013. https://www.georgiaencyclopedia.org/articles/arts-culture/southern-baptists/

221

Grigsby Coffey, Michele and Jodi Skipper, editors. 2020. *Navigating Souths: Transdisciplinary Explorations of a U.S. Region*. Athens: University of Georgia Press.

Gutiérrez, Ramón A. 2021. "A Recent History of White Supremacy," in Kathleen Belew and Ramón A. Gutiérrez, editors. *A Field Guide to White Supremacy*. Oakland: University of California Press. Pages 251-264.

Hall, Will. 2009. "Analysis: What Do Numbers Mean — Is the SBC in Decline? Part I Membership & Baptisms," in *Baptist Press*. June 10, 2009. https://www.baptistpress.com/resource-library/news/analysis-what-do-the-numbers-mean-is-the-sbc-in-declinepart-1-membership-baptisms/

Hanke, Lewis. 1974. *All Mankind is One: A Study of the Disputation Between Bartolomé de Las Casas and Juan Ginés de Sepúlveda in 1550 on the Intellectual and Religious Capacity of the American Indian*. Dekalb: Northern Illinois University Press.

Harari, Yuval Noah. 2015. *Sapiens: The Birth of Humankind*. New York: Vintage.

Harding, Susan. 2000. *The Book of Jerry Falwell: Fundamentalist Language and Politics*. Princeton: Princeton University Press.

Harte, Tiffany. 2022. "A Tale of 3 Strikes: The Fulton Bag and Cotton Company and the Labor Movement in Atlanta", Atlanta History Center. https://www.atlantahistorycenter.com/blog/a-tale-of-3-strikes.

Hartigan, J. 1997. "Establishing the Fact of Whiteness," in *American Anthropologist*. 99 (3). Pages 495-505.

Harvey, Paul. 2019. *Southern Religion in the World Three Stories*. Athens: The University of Georgia Press.

Hein, Virginia H. 1972. "The Image of 'A City Too Busy to Hate':Atlanta in the 1960s," in *Phylon*. The Atlanta University Review of Race and Culture. Vol. XXXIII, No 3, Pages 205-221.

Hernandez, Bonar Ludwig. 2021. "The Las Casas-Sepulveda Controversy: 1550-1551." In *Ex Post Facto*. Vol 10. Pages 95-104. San Francisco: San Francisco State University.

Hill, Carole E.
- 1998. "Contemporary Issues in Anthropological studies of the American South," in *Cultural Diversity in the U.S. South: Anthropological Contributions to a Region in Transition*. Carole E. Hill and Patricia D. Beaver, editors. Southern Anthropological Society Proceedings, No. 31. Athens: University of Georgia Press. Pages 12-33.

- 1979a. "Toward Internationalism: Urban Continuity and Change in a Southern City," in *Cities in a Larger Context*. Edited by Thomas W. Collins. Athens: University of Georgia Press.
- 1979b. "Ethnicity as a Factor in Urban Social Change," in *Journal of Urban Studies*. Vol. 3. Pages 197-121.
- 1977. "Anthropological Studies in the American South: Review and Directions," in *Current Anthropology*, 18 (2). Pages 309-336.
- 1975. *Symbols and Society*. Editor. Southern Anthropological Society Proceedings No. 9. Athens: University of Georgia Press.

Hill, Carole E. and Patricia D. Beaver, editors. 1998. *Cultural Diversity in the U.S. South: Anthropological Contributions to a Region in Transition*. Southern Anthropological Society Proceedings, No. 31. Athens: University of Georgia Press.

Hill, Jane H. 2008. *The Everyday Language of White Racism*. Chichester: Wiley-Blackwell.

Hoffman, Bruce and Jacob Ware. 2024. *God, Guns, and Sedition: Far Right Terrorism in America*. New York: Columbian University Press.

Holloway, Gary. 1989. *Saints, Demons, and Asses: Southern Preacher Anecdotes*. Bloomington: Indiana University Press.

Hoverd, W.J. and C.G. Sibley. 2013. "Religion, Deprivation and Subjective Wellbeing: Testing a Religious Buffering Hypothesis," in *International Journal of Wellbeing*. Vol. 2 (2). Pages 182-196. https://doi.org/10.552/ijw.v3i2.5

Huber, Patrick. 2004. "A Hillbilly Barnum: Fiddlin' John Carson and the Modern Origins of His Old-Time Music in Atlanta," in *Atlanta History*. Vol. 46. No. 1, Pages 25-53.

Israel, Jonathan. 2017. *The Expanding Blaze: How the American Revolution Ignited the World, 1775-1848*. Princeton: Princeton University Press.

Jeansonne, Glen. 1971. "Southern Baptists Attitudes Toward Slavery, 1845-1861" in *The Georgia Historical Review*. Vol 55, No. 4.

Jikeli, Günther, editor. 2020. *The Return of Religious Antisemitism?* Basel: MDPI.

Johnson, Luke. 1989. "The New Testament's Anti-Jewish Slander and the Conventions of Ancient Polemic Author(s)," in *Journal of Biblical Literature*. Vol 108, No. 3 (Autumn, 1989). Pages 419-441.

Jones, Robert P. 2021. *White too Long: The Legacy of White Supremacy in American Christianity*. New York: Simon & Schuster.

223

Joshi, Khyati Y. 2020. *White Christian Privilege: The Illusion of Religious Equality in America.* New York: New York University Press.

Kerby, Lauren R. 2021. "The Dispossessed? Lived History and White Christian Nationalism". *Berkley Forum.* Berkley Center for Religion, Peace & World Affairs. Georgetown University.

Kilgore, Ed.
- 2023. "Do Evangelicals Think Trump is Jesus? in *New York Magazine* (Intelligencer section). May 8, 2023. https://nymag.com/intelligencer/2023/05/do-white-Evangelicals-think-trump-is-jesus.html
- 2022. "Mixing Christianity With Nationalism Is a Recipe for Fascism," *New York Magazine* (Intelligencer section) Sept. 18, 2022. https://nymag.com/intelligencer/2022/09/mixing-christianity-with-nationalism-is-a-recipe-for-fascism.html

Kirk, John A. 2011. "Not Quite Black and White: School Desegregation in Arkansas, 1954-1966," in *The Arkansas Historical Quarterly*, Vol. 70, No.3 (Autumn 2011). Pages 225-257. https://www.jstor.org/stable/23193404

Kolavalli, Chaya. 2023. *Well-Intentioned Whiteness: Green Urban Development and Black Resistance in Kansas City.* Athens: University of Georgia Press.

Kuhn, Clifford Matthew.
- 2005. *Living Atlanta: An Oral History of the City, 1914-1918.* Atlanta and Athens: Atlanta History Center and University of Georgia Press.
- 2001. *Contesting the New South Order: The 1914-1915 Strike at Atlanta's Fulton Mills.* Chapel Hill: University of North Carolina Press.
- 1993. "A Full History of the Strike as I Saw It: Atlanta's Fulton Bag and Cotton Mills Workers and Their Representations Through the 1914-1915 Strike." Ph.D. Dissertation, University of North Carolina, Chapel Hill. Ann Arbor: University Microfilms International.

Labarre, Weston. 1962. *They Shall Take Up Serpents.* Minneapolis: University of Minnesota Press.

Lawless, Elaine J.
- 1988. *God's Peculiar People: Women's Voices and Folk Tradition in a Pentecostal Church.* Lexington: The University Press of Kentucky.
- 1989. *Handmaidens of the Lord: Pentecostal Women Preachers and Traditional Religion.* Philadelphia: University of Pennsylvania Press.

Lefever, Harry. 1970. "The Church and Poor Whites," in *New South.* Vol. 25, No. 2, Spring. Pages 20-32.

Luhrman, T.M.
- 2022. *How God Becomes Real: Kindling the Presence of Invisible Others.* Princeton: Princeton University Press.
- 2012. *When God Talks Back: Understanding the American Evangelical Relationship with God.* New York: Vintage Books.

Lehmann, Chris. 2021. "We All Live in the John Birch Society's World Now", *The New Republic.* November 23.

MacLean, Nancy. 1991. "The Leo Frank Case Reconsidered: Gender and Sexual Politics in the Making of Reactionary Populism," in *Journal of American History.* Vol. 78, Issue 3, December 1991, Pages 917-948.

Malinowski, Bronislaw. 1967. *A Diary in the Strict sense of the Term.* New York; Harcourt, Brace & World.

Martinez-Davila, Roger, Josef Diaz, Ron Duncan Hart, editors. 2016. *Fractured Faiths: Spanish Judaism, the Inquisition, and New World Identities.* Santa Fe: The New Mexico History Museum and Fresco Books.

McDermott, Monica. 2006. *Working-Class White: The Making and Unmaking of Race Relations.* Berkeley: University of California Press.

McDermott, Monica and Annie Ferguson. 2022. "Sociology of Whiteness," in *Annual Review of Sociology.* No. 48. Pages 257-276.

McLaughlin, Don, Catherine O'Donnell, Lynn Ries. 1995. "Private Schools in the United States: A Statistical Profile, 1990-1991." Washington, D.C. National Center for Educational Statistics. Statistical Analysis Report. U.S. Department of Education.

McMath, Jr., Robert C. 1989. "History by a Graveyard: The Fulton Bag and Cotton Mills Records", in *Labor's Heritage.* Pages 4-9. Also collected in Fulton Bag and Cotton Mills Digital Collection. Archives & Records Management, Library and Information Center, Georgia Institute of Technology. Atlanta, Georgia. N.D.

Merlan, Anna. 2019. *Republic of Lies: American Conspiracy Theorists and Their Surprising Rise to Power.* New York: Metropolitan Books Henry Holt and Company.

Miller, Donald. 1999. *Reinventing American Protestantism: Christianity in the New Mellennium.* Berkeley: University of California Press.

Miller, Edward H. 2021. *A Conspiratorial Life: Robert Welch, the John Birch Society, and the Revolution of American Conservatism.* Chicago: University of Chicago Press.

Miller, Steven P. 2014. *The Age of Evangelicalism: America's Born-Again Years*. Oxford: Oxford University Press.

Mitchell, Jerry. 2020. *Race Against Time: A Reporter Reopens the Unsolved Murder Cases of the Civil Rights Era*. New York: Simon and Schuster.

Mitchell, Margaret. 1936. *Gone with the Wind*. Reprint 1996. New York: Scribner.

Mooney, Michael J. 2019. "Trump's Apostle," in *Texas Monthly*. August. https://www.texasmonthly.com/news-politics/donald-trump-defender-dallas-pastor-robert-jeffress/

Moore, Gene-Gabriel. 1998. "An Urban Mill Town: Growing Up in Cabbagetown in the 1940s and 1950s" in *Atlanta Magazine*. November 1998. https://www.atlantamagazine.com/great-reads/an-urban-mill-town/.

Morgan, Henry. 1877. *Ancient Society*. Reprint 1985. Tucson: Univ. of Arizona Press.

Morland, J. Kenneth.
- 1971. Editor. *The Not So Solid South*. Southern Anthropological Society Proceedings, No. 4. Athens: University of Georgia Press.
- 1958. *Millways of Kent*. Chapel Hill: The University of North Carolina Press.

Monthly Labor Review. 1929. "Wages and Hours of Labor". Vol.28, No. 5 (May). Pages 179-197.

Neville, Gwen Kennedy. 1998. "Cultures and Communities in the New Old South: White Anglo-Saxon Protestants," in *Cultural Diversity in the U.S. South: Anthropological Contributions to a Region in Transition*. Edited by Carole E. Hill and Patricia D. Beaver. Southern Anthropological Society Proceedings, No. 31. Athens: University of Georgia Press. Pages 82-92.

Newman, Mark. 1997. "The Arkansas Baptist State Convention and Desegregation, 1954-1968," in *The Arkansas Historical Quarterly*. Vol 56, No. 3. Pages 294-313.

Oliphant, James and Nathan Layne. 2023. "Trump Keeps Edge among Evangelicals but There is an Opening for Challengers," Reuters. April 20, 2023. https://www.reuters.com/world/us/trump-keeps-edge-among-Evangelicals-there-is-an-opening-challengers-2023-04-20/

Österholm, Magnus. 2010. "The Ontology of Beliefs from a Cognitive Perspective." *ResearchGate*. https://www.researchgate.net/publication/267249344. Consulted 1-03-2023.

226

Peacock, James.
- 2010. *Grounded Globalism: How the U.S. South Embraces the World*. Athens: University of Georgia Press.
- 1998. "Anthropology in the South and the Southern Anthropological Society: Diversity, the South, Anthropology, and Culture," in *Cultural Diversity in the U.S. South: Anthropological Contributions to a Region in Transition*. Edited by Carole E. Hill and Patricia D. Beaver. Southern Anthropological Society Proceedings, No. 31. Athens: University of Georgia Press. Pages 190-199.
- 1975. "Weberian, Southern Baptist, and Indonesian Muslim: Conceptions of Belief and Action," in *Symbols and Society*. Carole E. Hill, editor. Southern Anthropological Society Proceedings No. 9. Athens: University of Georgia Press.
- 1971. "The Southern Protestant Ethic Disease," in *The Not So Solid South*, J. Kenneth Morland, editor. Southern Anthropological Society Proceedings, No. 4. Athens: University of Georgia Press.
- 1968. *Rites of Modernization: Symbolic and Social Aspects of Indonesian Proletarian Drama*. Chicago: University of Chicago Press.

Perry, John and Nigel Biggar. 2013. "Religion and Intolerance: A Critical Commentary," in *Religion, Intolerance, and Conflict: A Scientific and Conceptual Investigation*. Edited by Steve Clarke, Russell Powell, Julian Savulescu. Oxford: Oxford University Press. Pages 253-265.

Perry, Pamela. 2002. *Shades of White: White Kids and Racial Identities in High School*. Durham: Duke University Press.

Persson, Ingmar and Julian Savulescu. 2013. "The Limits of Religious Tolerance: A Secular View," in in *Religion, Intolerance, and Conflict: A Scientific and Conceptual Investigation*. Edited by Steve Clarke, Russell Powell, and Julian Savulescu. Oxford: University of Oxford Press. Pages 236-252.

Peterson, Richard S. and N.J. Demerath III. 1965. "Introduction" in *Mill hands and Preachers by Liston Pope*. New Haven: Yale University Press.

Pomerantz, Gary M. 1996. *Where Peachtree Meets Sweet Auburn: The Saga of Two Families and the Making of Atlanta*. New York: Charles Scribner's Sons.

Pope, Liston. 1965. *Mill hands and Preachers*. (Yale Studies in Religious Education). Reprint from 1942 edition. New Haven: Yale University Press.

Porter, Pam Durban, editor. 1976. *Cabbagetown Families, Cabbagetown Food*. Atlanta: Patch Publications.

Powell, Russell and Steve Clarke. 2013. "Religion, Tolerance, and Intolerance: Views from Across the Disciplines," in *Religion, Intolerance, and Conflict: A Scientific and Conceptual Investigation*. Edited by Steve Clarke, Russell Powell, and Julian Savulescu. Oxford: University of Oxford Press. Pages 1-12.

PRRI. 2022."Census of American Religion, Updates and Trends: White Christian Declines Slows, Unaffiliated Growth Levels Off." April 27, 2022. https://www.prri.org/spotlight/prri-2021-american-values-atlas-religious-affiliation-up-dates-and-trends-white-christian-decline-slows-unaffiliated-growth-levels-off/

Pruitt, Lisa R. 2022. "What Republicans Know (and Democrats Don't) About the White Working-class". *Politico*. https:politico.com/news/magazine/2022/06/24.

Rambo, Lewis R. 1993. *Understanding Religious Conversion*. New Haven: Yale University Press.

Rambo, Lewis R. and Charles E. Farhadian, editors. 2014. *The Oxford Handbook of Religious Conversion*. Oxford: University of Oxford Press.

Randall, Rebecca. 2017. "How Many Churches Does America Have? More Than Expected," in *Christianity Today*. https://www.christianitytoday.com/news/2017/september/how-many-churches-in-america-us-nones-non-denominational.html

Reagan, Ronald. 2004. "Speech Accepting the Republican Nomination for President". *Tear Down this Wall: The Reagan Revolution – a National Review History*. A&C Black.

Rhodes, Ron. 2015. *The Complete Guide to Christian Denominations: Understanding the History, Beliefs, and Differences*. Eugene, OR: Harvest House Publishers.

Rhyne, J.J. 1930. *Some Southern Cotton Mill Workers and Their Villages*. Chapel Hill: University of North Carolina Press.

Riccardi-Swartz, Sarah. 2021. "The Hybridity of Rural Fascism," *Hot Spots. Fieldsights*. April 15. https://culanthro.org/fieldsights/the-hybridity-of-rural-fascism.

Richardson, Miles. 1998. "Preface," in *Cultural Diversity in the U.S. South: Anthropological Contributions to a Region in Transition*. Edited by Carole E. Hill and Patricia D.Beaver. Southern Anthropological Society Proceedings, No. 31. Athens: University of Georgia Press.

Robinson, Roderick. "Cabbagetown: Once-dying Village Finds New Life among old Friends," in *The Atlanta Journal-Constitution*. https://digitalcollections.library.gsu.edu/digital/api/collection/PlanATL/id/7038/download.

Roel Reyes, Stefan. 2021. "'Christian Patriots': The Intersection Between Proto-fascism and Clerical Fascism in the Antebellum South," in *International Journal for History, Culture and Modernity*. Vol 9 (2021). Pages 82-110.

Rüpke, Jörg, Giuseppe Veltri, and Anne Sarah Matviyets, editors. 2023. *Tolerance and Intolerance in Religion and Beyond: Challenges from the Past and in the Present*. Oxford: Routledge.

Russell, Thomas Arthur. 2010. *Comparative Christianity: A Student's Guide to a Religion and Its Diverse Traditions*. Irvine, CA: Universal Publishers.

Schneider, Bill. 2023. "Grievance Politics, rather than Problem Solving, Now at the Heart of Republican Party," in *THE HILL*. 03/19/23. https://thehill.com/opinion/campaign/3907317-grievance-politics-rather-than-problem-solving-now-at-the-heart-of-republican-party/

Schweiger, Beth Barton and Donald G. Mathews, editors. 2004. *Religion in the American South: Protestants and Others in History and Culture*. Chapel Hill: University of North Carolina Press.

Schweiger, Gottfried. 2019. "Religion and Poverty," in *Palgrave Communications*. 2019:5:59. Pages 1-3. https://doi.org/10.1057/s41599-019-0272-3.

Sellers, Eddie William. 2018. *My Life in Stories: The Cabbagetown Years and the Dark Secrets of Child Abuse*. Self-published.

Sheff, David. 1988. "The Rolling Stone Survey: On Sex, Drugs and Rock & Roll," in *Rolling Stone*. May 5. https://www.rollingstone.com/culture/culture-news/the-rolling-stone-survey-on-sex-drugs-and-rock-roll-81616/

Shimron, Yonat. 2023. "Poll: A Third of Americans are Christian Nationalists and Most are White Evangelicals," in Religious New Service. February 8, 2023. https://religionnews.com/2023/02/08/a-third-of-americans-are-christian-nationalists-and-most-are-white-evangelicals/

Shurden, Walter B. 1993. *The Baptist Identity: Four Fragile Freedoms*. Macon, GA: Smyth & Helwys Publishing.

Smith, Gregory A. 2021. "More White Americans Adopted than Shed Evangelical Label during Trump Presidency, especially his Supporters". Pew Research Center. https://www.pewresearch.org/short-reads/2021/09/15/more-white-americans-adopted-than-shed-Evangelical-label-during-trump-presidency-especially-his-supporters/. September 15, 2021.

Smith, Gregory A, Michael Rotolo and Patricia Tevington. 2022. "45% of Americans Say U.S. Should Be a 'Christian Nation'". Pew Research Center. https://www.pewresearch.org/religion/2022/10/27/45-of-americans-say-u-s-should-be-a-christian-nation/

Smith, Sybil D. 2017. *Thank God for the Cotton: Memoir of a Mill Worker's Daughter.* Greenville, SC: Ambassador International.

Smith, Timothy. 2020. *Revivalism and Social Reform: American Protestantism on the Eve of the Civil War.* Republished from 1957 original. London: Barakaldo Books.

Snodderly, Ed. 1994. "What Will We do with the Homeless?" in *Southern Changes: The Journal of the Southern Regional Council,* 1978-2003. Vol. 16, No. 1. Pages 14-15.

Southern Education Foundtion. 2024. "The History of Private Schools and Race in the American South." https://southerneducation.org/publications/history-of-private-schools-and-race-in-the-american-south/

Spencer, Herbert. 1896. *A System of Synthetic Philosophy.* Reprinted 2011. Amsterdam: Obscure Press.

Stein, Stephen J. 1989. "An Ethnographic Cornucopia: Folklore and the Study of American Religions," in *Journal of Folklore Research.* Vol. 26, No. 3. Pages 249-258.

Telfair Sharpe, Tanya. 2000. "The Identity Christian Movement: Ideology of Domestic Terrorism," in *Journal of Black Studies.* Vol. 30, No. 4 (March 2000). Pages 604-623.

Teter, Magda. 2023. *Christian Supremacy: Reckoning with the Roots of Antisemitism and Racism.* Princeton: Princeton University Press.

The Atlanta Constitution. "1,400 Mill Workers on a Strike. Would Not Work with Negroes." August 5, 1897.

Thurow, Joshua. 2013. "Religion, 'Religion,' and Tolerance," in *Religion, Intolerance, and Conflict: A Scientific and Conceptual Investigation.* Edited by Steve Clarke, Russell Powell, and Julian Savulescu. Oxford: Oxford University Press. Pages 146-162.

Titon, Jeff Todd. 1988. *Powerhouse for God: Speech, Chant, and Song in an Appalachian Baptist Church.* Austin: University of Texas Press.

Tylor, Edward Burnett. 1871. *Primitive Culture.* Reprinted 2016. New York: Dover Publications.

Tyson, Ruel W., Jr., James L. Peacock, and Daniel W. Patterson, editors. 1988. *Diversities of Gifts: Field Studies in Southern Religion.* Urbana: University of Illinois Press.

Vance, J.D. 2016. *Hillbilly Elegy: A Memoir of a Family and Culture in Crisis.* New York: HarperCollins Publishers.

230

Warren, Donald I.,
- 1976. *The Radical Center: Middle Americans and the Politics of Alienation*. South Bend: University of Notre Dame Press.
- 1996. *Radio Priest: Charles Coughlin, the Father of Hate Radio*. New York: Free Press.

Weller, Jack. 1965. *Yesterday's People*. Lexington: University of Kentucky Press.

Whitehead, Andrew L. and Samuel Perry. 2020. *Taking Back America for God: Christian Nationalism in the United States*. New York: Oxford University Press.

Whitehouse, Harvey. 2013. "Religion, Cohesion, and Hostility," in *Religion, Intolerance, and Conflict: A Scientific and Conceptual Investigation*. Edited by Steve Clarke, Russell Powell, and Julian Savulescu. Oxford: Oxford University Press. Pages 36-47.

Williams, Joan C. 2017. *White Working-class: Overcoming ClassCluelessness in America*. Boston: Harvard Business Review Press.

Wolfe, Charles K. 2001. *Classic Country: Legends of Country Music*. Oxford: Routledge.

Wright, Gavin. 1974. "Cotton Competition and the Post-Bellum Recovery of the American South," in *The Journal of Economy History*. Vol. 34, No. 3 (Sept. 1974), Pages 610-635.

Young, Stephen. 2015. "Donald Trump Gets Touched by First Baptist Dallas' Robert Jeffress," in *Dallas Observer*. October 1. https://www.dallasobserver.com/news/donald-trump-gets-touched-by-first-baptist-dallas-robert-jeffress-7643576

Zainaldin, Jamil. 2017. "The Mill Industry and its Workers Created Modern Georgia," https://saportareport.com. Consulted 12/29/2022.

Index

234

238

WORKING MAN
Ron Duncan Hart

Gravels under feet and in shoes
Muffle screams of tired and beat,
P.M. sultry heat obliges who's
Lost to swallow cries of defeat,
Porch sitters TV watch life a way
Wishing to leave, having to stay.
And the seasons passed.
And Mill man's mettle cracks,
Working with hands and backs
That dimmed minds with age,
Mindless chores assuage.
The thump of the loom
Minds numbed in repetition
Begrudging in submission.
The same stories always told.
When the mill men get bold
In nights thick with drink,
Minds churned on the porch.
Emboldened dreams of power and torch.
Turned sour and clabbered on the morrow
With bitterness and wrenching sorrow
Minds churned in drunkenness.
Sometimes asking forgiveness
To the same good Lord
Who gave the drinking gourd
But was gone in the dewy morn.
And the television roared,
As gas fires soared,
Mightily conquering the seeping cold
That made Grandma feel so old.
And the factory whistle blew,
"To work, To work, To work."

Institute for Tolerance Studies
P.O. Box 23924
Santa Fe, NM 87502
www.tolerancestudies.org

Library of Congress Cataloging-in-Publication Data
Names: Duncan Hart, Ron, author.
Title: Evangelicals and MAGA: The Politics of Grievance a Half Century in the Making / Ron Duncan Hart.
Description: Santa Fe, NM : Institute for Tolerance Studies, 2024. | Series: Institute for Tolerance Studies monographs on tolerance | Includes bibliographical references and index. | Summary: "Cabbagetown is the former mill village of the Fulton Cotton Mill located near downtown Atlanta. This is a study made in that neighborhood of White mill workers with a focus on religious beliefs and practice in the late 1960s and early 1970s. People were protesting the integration of schools, civil rights, the ban on Bible reading and prayer in the schools, and women's rights in ERA and Roe v. Wade. It gives descriptions of Baptist and Holiness churches, faith healing, spirit possession, and conversion experiences. The role of racism, family organization, country music, and gender and masculinity are also discussed"-- Provided by publisher.
Identifiers: LCCN 2023047392 (print) | LCCN 2023047393 (ebook) | ISBN 9781935604907 (paperback) | ISBN 9781935604914 (kindle edition) Subjects: LCSH: Cabbagetown (Atlanta, Ga.)--Religion. | Cabbagetown (Atlanta, Ga.)--Race relations. | Race relations--Religious aspects--Christianity--History--20th century. | Race discrimination--Religious aspects--Christianity--History--20th century. Religion and politics--Georgia--History--20thcentury.
Classification: LCC BR560.C223 D86 2024 (print) | LCC BR560.C223 (ebook) | DDC 277.58/231--dc23/eng/20231120
LC record available at https://lccn.loc.gov/2023047392
LC ebook record available at https://lccn.loc.gov/2023047393

The Institute for Tolerance Studies, a 501-c-3 organization established in 2005 to provide a venue for research, publishing, and learning. It was organized with the purpose of promoting social justice, tolerance, respect, and acceptance between people of diverse backgrounds, addressing issues of antisemitism, intolerance, racism, hatred and bigotry.

The Monograph Series on Religion and Tolerance is one element in the Institute's goal to address issues of tolerance in religion. That is supplemented by its digital platform with expansive information on comparative religions.

www.tolerancestudies.org

Printed in the USA
CPSIA information can be obtained
at www.ICGtesting.com
LVHW091232210724
786027LV00001B/101